THE WORD ACCOUNT

BY KATHLEEN COFFEY

The Word Account

Trilogy Christian Publishers A Wholly Owned Subsidary of Trinity Broadcasting Network

2442 Michelle Drive Tustin, CA 92780

Cover design by: Sierra Deyoe with assets from Freepik

For information about special discounts for bulk purchases, please contact Trilogy Christian Publishing.

Manufactured in the United States of America

10 9 8 7 6 5 4 3 2 1

Library of Congress Cataloging-in-Publication Data is available.

ISBN: 979-8-89041-173-0

E-ISBN: 979-8-89041-174-7

TABLE OF CONTENTS

INTRODUCTION

The words you will see in the next 365 pages are words written with a pen on the pages of seven different notebooks. In November of 2018, I began opening my Bible every single morning and reading whatever the Lord put in front of me. I then would pick up my journal and write the words that He gave me about the passage that He gave me. This is not a study guide for Scripture; this is not a translation of His Word; this is an account of His Word. My account. My understanding of His living Word. The beautiful part of this is that if I read the same words tomorrow, He would give me something different to write. I pray that through His Word, and my words, you will find your words. Grab a pen, and listen to what He tells you—then write. This is the Word account, our word account.

JANUARY

January 1

Isaiah 43:19

As the new year begins, let's celebrate the future blessings as we look back on the blessings of the past. Our God does not just bless us for a moment; His blessings last. He is the God of the fresh start and the redeemer of the lost. He will fight to improve your life, no matter the cost. He doesn't require much of you, just everything you have to give. He doesn't want much from you, just every bit of life you have to live. He wants the next year of your life to be more blessed than the one before. He doesn't stop at "just enough," He is the God of exceedingly and abundantly more. He is the endless stream in the wasteland and the well of life-giving waters in the dessert. Creating you was His greatest accomplishment, and seeing you through is His pleasure. So do not allow the speed bumps of your year to take away from all of the mountains that you have climbed. The bad might have seemed bad, but now God has you good and primed. Our God is the epitome of restoration and the Father of the second chance. He doesn't just want to bless your present self; He will provide you with blessings in advance. Walk into this new year of life with a calm, trusting spirit, and breathe in His fresh air. He is not just going before you to do a mighty work; He is building you up with all the tools you will need to make sure that you are prepared.

Prompt: Where has He made a way for you in the wilderness in the past? What new thing do you want Him to do for you this year?

_____
_____
_____
_____
_____
_____
_____
_____
_____
_____
_____
_____

January 2

Jeremiah 3:19–20

Faith is our greatest strength, but faithlessness seems to be our custom. We serve a God who has given us the world, yet we often feel like we have nothing. I am not perfect, and you are not either, but we serve the God of perfection. Anytime we despise our situation, we ignore God's affection. Next time something goes wrong in your life, remember—the world is broken...not God. His perfection does not sway just because the world is flawed. When we succumb to doubt or faithlessness, it's not a description of who we are; it's an explanation of who we think God is *not*. We are quick to question the author if the narrative waivers from our expected plot. You have every right to feel the way you feel in times of grief or discomfort, but your feelings and your faith are not mutually exclusive. We are actually questioning God's goodness when we are doubting what He is doing. If I asked you this question: "Would you ever turn your back on God?" —what would your answer be? I know mine would be, "*Not me!*" But every time I dread the step out of my comfort zone or complain about His plan, I am turning my back on His presence. He desires us to be fully surrendered in genuine acceptance. God is gracious to give us endless redos, but I want to follow Him from the first take. I do not want to waste time not living out my calling because I am repenting for my mistakes. Do not let faith be a choice; it has to be the *only* option. Approach God's plan with gratitude and your expectations with caution.

Prompt: What have you expected God to do in the past that He did not do? How did that affect your view of Him? What are you expecting Him to do in the future? How will that affect your worship of Him?

_____

_____

_____

_____

_____

_____

_____

_____

_____

_____

January 3

Proverbs 11:4

Isn't it crazy that we spend our whole life chasing money, whether we think that we do or not? It's an instinctual habit to try and make more; it's not something you have to be taught. We are dependent upon money for the purchase of basic necessities and the finer things that are additional. It seems that when we do not have money, we are helpless, but when we do have it, we are invincible. Even those who are not obsessed with money still remain dependent upon its importance. It brings a sense of independency and assurance. But countless times, the Lord has spoken about the riches of the world and how it will lead you into ruin. He speaks of the importance of our focus and what it is that we are actually pursuing. Our true wealth is found in the richness of our spirit within. Our true worth can only be found in the Lord, not in the status of men. The riches of this world will pass away, but the Spirit of the Lord will remain eternally. Money and status do not mean anything in the long run because God deems you worthy. You will be richly blessed in heaven if you give God your full attention while you are here on Earth. The richness of the soul is the real establishment of worth. So let's do our best to ignore the distraction that money brings. You can get to heaven with a wealthy spirit but not with the purchase of things.

Prompt: If money were not an object, how would you spend your time? How can you make that part of your reality?

_____

_____

_____

_____

_____

_____

_____

_____

_____

_____

_____

_____

January 4

Luke 9:18–20

It's easy for me to read the Gospel accounts and question how anyone could doubt that Jesus was God's Son. But I have a book detailing His life, and they did not have one. So when I read these verses this morning, my heart exploded with respect. The disciples had faith that was simply predicated on things that He said. And that is what faith is, right? It's a firm belief without proof. It's the commitment to decision and the surrender of having the right to choose. It's the blind belief in truth, not because you uncovered it, but because God said it was so. It's about trusting the believing; it is trusting your "know." So when I read the Gospels from now on, I will read them with more empathy and honor. They trusted that Jesus was God's Messiah because they trusted their Father. And they did not just go to church and hear Him teach a few times; they left their known lives to follow Him. They accepted people's judgment and trusted their knowing from within. I want faith like that. I want faith that calls Jesus the Messiah when everyone else calls Him a prophet. I want faith that outweighs my knowledge. I want to walk this earth today in the same way that Peter did. Altering my life to match the way that Jesus calls me to live. Not because I have seen Him but because I trust His voice. Faith is a decision, and I have made the choice. Thank You, Lord, for loving me even when my doubt was greater than my faith. I want to have faith to believe in the resurrection before I see the empty grave.

Prompt: What is one decision you have made in life that was completely based on blind faith? What area of your life to you need to surrender to God in faith? How do you do that?

_____
_____
_____
_____
_____
_____
_____
_____
_____
_____
_____

January 5

Psalm 18:30–36

If God is calling you into something, you can be certain that He will give you all of the tools that you need. If you are following His path, you can be sure that you will ultimately succeed. Not because you are full of the right gifts but because He is giving you just the right portion of each gift. It's not your talent; it's your ability to handle His. You can trust that the Lord will give you the strength to summit if He has given you the green light to start the trek. He wants you to focus on the right now and allow Him to focus on what is next. If He has called you into a battle, trust that He will be your shield. If He has called you to sow a seed, trust that He will fertilize your field. If He has called you to run a race, trust that your feet will make it across the finish line. If He has brought you into play a game, trust that you will have all of the skills that you need to come off the sideline. Whatever you are facing today, trust that God will give you just the right portion to see you through to the other side. He does not want to keep you in a hard, unknown place; He just wants us to trust His time. I hope this brings you peace to know that God will always sustain you even when the road seems long and endless. He loves us, guides us, and defends us. You will never place your foot somewhere that God Himself has not walked first. Every moment of your life is first His before it is yours.

Prompt: What would you pursue if you knew you could not fail?

_____

_____

_____

_____

_____

_____

_____

_____

_____

_____

_____

January 6

Hosea 10:13–14

You cannot be surrendered and self-dependent; the two simply cannot cohabitate. You cannot conjoin two things that will not collaborate. You cannot be in full surrender to God if you have to have control over all situations. It's not a trusting commitment if you have to have planning consultations. I will be the first to admit that I am a "type A" control freak. I do not just want to know what is happening today; I want to know what is happening next week. Yet I pray the prayer of surrender and commitment to God daily, but maybe it's a prayer of self-convincing. Maybe I recite it so frequently because my spirit knows that I am resisting. I sing out, "I am all Yours, Lord! I will follow You where You lead!" But then, every time I hand Him the reins, I feel the need to intercede. God's plan is always better than ours, and He knows our dreams better than we do. He cannot exceed your expectations if you are always demanding to see an overview. Our desire for control will only lead to disappointment in our decisions and a never-ending climb to reach our dreams. My trust in God must be bigger than my self-esteem. I am good because God is good; my independence has no strength. Because when I do it alone, I either achieve with no fulfillment or make a million mistakes. So I am declaring today that I give up control because, God, I love You more than I love control. I do not want to hold back any more pieces of my heart and my soul.

Prompt: What are you scared to give up control over most? What would it feel like if you no longer controlled that thing or person?

_____

_____

_____

_____

_____

_____

_____

_____

_____

_____

_____

_____

JANUARY 7

James 1:16–18

God does not send us bad gifts; I know that seems logical, but in reality, we often get confused. We tend to heap the blame on God and use His judgment as an excuse. But God's judgment does not come in the form of overloading your life with bad circumstances. We have choices in life, and God respects our free will enough not to micro-manage. So when you participate in sin and face a poor consequence, do not attribute that to God. Certain things just happen when you do not obey His commands and laws. He does not sit on His heavenly throne with an "I told you so" attitude, ready to heap judgment onto us in the form of trials. But God will not interfere with sin's cycles. Those are a product of breaking God's law, but He is not reigning them down on you with condemnation. The "bad" happenings are just the end result of sin's manifestation. God gives us good and perfect gifts because that is what He is—good and perfect. He does not give them according to what you do; it's not some kind of repayment for your service. The portions that He gives and the times that He gives are mysterious but always recognizable. His gifts look like mountaintop moments; they do not look like trials. But the good news is that He can use a trial to deliver one of His gifts. But just because the timing aligns, it does not mean that the bad situation was also His. God loves you too much to send anything bad into your life. He does not start the battle, but He will always help you win the fight.

Prompt: What have you blamed God for in the past, or are currently blaming Him for in the present?

_____

_____

_____

_____

_____

_____

_____

_____

_____

_____

_____

_____

January 8

Proverbs 27:22

There is a lot of freedom that comes when you realize that you are not responsible for other people's actions. No matter how much you want to control a situation, it's not your to control what happens. And if you can get past the personal desire to control and realize that there is so much freedom to be found in letting go. You will realize that it's not your place to make sure that other people grow. In my time on this earth, I have learned quite a bit about people and their habits and behaviors. I have come to terms with the fact that I will never be anyone's savior. Can I help people? Certainly, but I am not going to change them. But I am going to hold them responsible without maliciously blaming them. It's not my job to save or change anyone; it's my job to introduce them to the only one that can. Their life is not under my control; it's in God's hands. And when you take that responsibility away, it leaves a lot more room for love. Instead of pointing people left and right, I will point them up above. People are not problems, people experience problems, and only God can solve them. So I am going to take a step back and be careful with what I get involved in. My job is to love people well and point them to Jesus; I am not the savior. I'll be a servant and a lover, but I don't need to be the change maker.

Prompt: Who do you need to set a boundary with? And what does that boundary need to be?

_____
_____
_____
_____
_____
_____
_____
_____
_____
_____
_____
_____
_____
_____

January 9

Mark 15:1–5

Have you ever been made to feel like the last choice or the leftovers? Like if there was a ranking of worth, somehow you would always be lower? I know that feeling well, but I think we all are familiar with it. We have all been in its self-deprecating grips. Even Jesus went through it right before He was crucified. The people had to choose between Him and a murderer, and they chose Jesus to die. They gathered around in a group and decided to pick Barabbas, the known murderer, over the Messiah. They unshackled the sinner and called Jesus a liar. I cannot imagine it, honestly. When I think about it for too long, my heart breaks. They killed the one who came to save. But on a scale of the human experience, this same type of scenario is what shatters my heart into a million pieces—when people are disregarded, and they are told that they are the reason. We have all been in that position to some extent, where we have been left as a last option, like an unbid-on item at an auction. But let me tell you, that is a lie from the pit of hell, and you are God's first selection. He does not see leftovers when He sees you or me; He sees absolute perfection. People may make you feel unwanted, but you are wanted by your creator. I know it's hard, but we cannot allow our worth to be dictated by other people's behavior. They chose Barabbas, and they might choose others, but that has more to do with them than it does with you. Do not let a lie steal your truth.

Prompt: What do you have to offer the world? What do you feel is missing about you?

_____

_____

_____

_____

_____

_____

_____

_____

_____

_____

_____

_____

_____

January 10

Acts 13:32–41

Have you ever thought about the fact that we stand on the promises of generations? Because of the prayers of ancestors and sacrifices of our Savior, do we get salvation? A blessing you might receive today could be the fulfillment of a promise that your grandparent prayed for. That is why we can't lose hope because we do not know what is in store. Think about the life and death of Jesus, which had been promised for centuries! Just because it did not happen within the lifetime of one generation did not make it a mystery. Do you trust that God's promises will come to pass? Even if it's not in your lifetime? Are you willing to pray prayers for the future of your family line? I love thinking about my ancestors and learning about my family lineage and accounts. I love knowing where they lived, what their names were, and what they were all about. But my hindsight stops at 300 years; I tend to forget about my ancestors at the beginning of time. We are all part of an intricate and long family line. And to think that my ancestors might have prayed for a blessing that I will reap today is overwhelming. Past prayers are always currently helping. What prayer will you pray today that is bigger than your lifetime? What blessing are you working on that your grandchildren will find? Do not lose hope in the tomorrows because we have foundations formed from generations past. The promises anointed by God will always last.

Prompt: What prayer will you pray today that extends past your lifetime?

January 11

Luke 14:25–35

What is worthwhile in life is often not easy, but it is the work that makes the reward so much sweeter. It is always more satisfying to succeed based on effort, not to succeed because you are a cheater. Discipleship is no different, and it requires a great cost in order to receive the great reward. It will cost you everything you have while simultaneously being something you could never afford. Jesus tells us to take up our cross and follow Him into the unknown and the uncomfortable. We must be willing to endure a lifetime of crucifixion so that we may receive an eternity of wonderful. If your walk with the Lord is easy, check the trail markers to make sure that you are on the right path. If you are doing the true work of God, you should be receiving Satan's wrath. We get too wrapped up in our "calling" and forget about why we were created. We were not made for gaining personal accolades; we were made for Christ's life to be demonstrated. Being loved by God is simple, but being a disciple of God is the most difficult thing you will ever do. We are not required to hang on a cross with nail-pierced hands, but our hearts should be so bought in that we would of God asked us to.

Prompt: What is the hardest thing that you have ever done? What reward came from doing that hard thing?

January 12

Ecclesiastes 1:1–12

Our life is so fleeting even God likens it to a vapor, here and then gone. Do not bet on your life because time is not something you can count on. I heard this recently: "How you spend your hours is how you spend your day, and how you spend your days is how you spend your life." Once our day is written, it is impossible to rewrite. So if your days are not spent seeking God, how will God be your life's purpose? If He is not worth fifteen minutes of your day, then how do you show God that He is worth it? You are living your life right now, the life that God created you to live. Are you going to live devoted or die distracted? We have each been given a finite opportunity to walk on Earth and spread the love of Christ. Is the way you fill your days worthy of Jesus' sacrifice? Are you living in surrender or living for society? Are you living devoted or living defiantly? You have twenty-four hours today to live for Christ, can you at least give Him half of one? I promise you can give up your social media scrolling if He could give up His Son. Heaven is our promised paradise for eternity if we will surrender to God daily. God deserves our steady, not our shaky. What is one thing you can alter today that will remove a distraction that is keeping you from God? In what way could you commit to improving that bond? Today is one of the days He died for; He is worth fifteen minutes of your time. We will ultimately be judged on our life full of the days that we design.

Prompt: What things distract you? What are three things you could start or stop doing that would allow you to gain a greater sense of focus?

_____

_____

_____

_____

_____

_____

_____

_____

_____

_____

_____

_____

January 13

Psalm 65:5–8

The God of all creation hears every word that you pray. The same God that formed the galaxies hears the words that you say. The God of Abraham, Isaac, and Jacob is the same God of you, you, and me. The God that is right next to me is the same God who split the Red Sea. I know we mutter, "God is good," but even that feels like a disservice. How can we ever explain our gratitude with our flawed hearts to a God who is perfect? Do you ever sit in this place and allow God's majesty to overtake you completely? Do you ever truly allow yourself to feel His power deeply? One thing I have learned recently is that we, as humans, need meaning. If we can understand something, then we have no problem believing. But God is not meant to be understood, and we can not make meaning out of His mercy. So we either surrender and accept, or start to feel doubtful and unworthy. I think that I am coming to terms with the never-ending capacity of God's supremacy. That His power, authority, and love have so much intensity. That He moves mountains and wipes my tears away at the same time. The He is in control of the universe, but for me, He still finds time. That my daily comfort is just as important to Him as the sunrise and the sunset. I will never get His seconds; I only get His best. And I just want to sit in that; I just want to be enveloped by the magnitude of my reality. I want to bask in His grandeur and His beauty.

Prompt: When and where do you feel God most intensely? How can you spend more time in that place?

_____
_____
_____
_____
_____
_____
_____
_____
_____
_____
_____
_____

January 14

Luke 12:8–10

We have all heard the saying that actions speak louder than words, but words still hold weight. They have the power to destroy and the power to cultivate. On average, a human speaks around 13,000 words a day—that's 13,000 opportunities to lead people to Christ! How many of your 13,000 words are giving life? We are born again when we surrender, but our renewing of faith lies in our testimony. We have the freedom of speech, but do we have the restraint to make our talk holy? Think about this...if you had to take away every word yesterday that was not about God, how many words would you have to count? Would it be a majority or a small amount? How many words would you speak if you could only speak words regarding God today? Would you fill the air with profession or have little to none to say? This does not mean that, as Christians, we are called to talk non-stop, but when we do speak, it should be uplifting. We were sent to lead the lost to the one they are missing. That does not mean that you have to be an evangelist; it might just mean that you need to be empathetic. Instead of firing the bullets, be the medic. If God is the true devotion of our hearts, we will not be able to stop ourselves from talking about Him because our words are just a reflection of our spirit within. Try and speak one more word about God today than you did yesterday. Allow your surrender to overflow into the words that you say.

Prompt: If you could have one sentence that described you, what would you want that sentence to be? Or what is one compliment you still think about today?

_____

_____

_____

_____

_____

_____

_____

_____

_____

_____

_____

_____

January 15

Jeremiah 3:12–13

How unnerving is it to think that our pride could lead us to our greatest humility? That the more we preach our own power, the more we realize that we lack ability. Earth pride will bring your earthly praise but eternal emptiness. What good is all of the money in the world if, when you die, you are penniless? God does not want your riches; He wants your repentance. He does not want you to be perfect; He wants you to humbly accept forgiveness. You could spend your whole life building up a reputation of stature, but you will spend eternity in surrender. Do not spend your life gaining the admission cost when heaven is free to enter. The gospel, at its core, is simple—Jesus gave His life for you, and you must surrender your life to Him. But it's scary to think that we could stop ourselves from getting in. Pride is gripping; it's a controlling mechanism of our flesh. We can never give God the glory if we are convinced that we are the best. It's hard to admit that we are not right or the best because our society tells us to be in love with our self. Too much self-righteous love will actually destroy your spiritual health. You are only good because God is good; take pride in Him—not you. You are good because of what He has done, not because of anything that you do. Trade your self-absorption for Christ's adoration, and trade your pride for humility. Spend less time boasting about your righteousness and more time confessing your inabilities.

Prompt: What are you best at in this life? How can you use those gifts to honor God instead of yourself?

_____

_____

_____

_____

_____

_____

_____

_____

_____

_____

_____

January 16

Matthew 20:29–34

Your desires are important to God, and I think we often forget that. God does not ask us to give up our desires; He just asks that we change the format. That we would desire Him with all of our heart and seek Him before earthly pleasures. That we would want a relationship with Him more than we want any earthly treasure. I love the stories in Scripture about Jesus healing the blind because He always asked them: "What do you want Me to do for you?" As if it was not *extremely* obvious what they wanted Him to do! Jesus could have healed everyone without question, but He wanted to make sure that it was what *they* wanted because the last thing God wants is to leave you disappointed. This is not to say that He will provide us with all of our desires, especially because some of them are indecent. He wants to bless us with perseverance and courage, not just with desires that are convenient. If you are desperately desiring something and blaming God for not giving it to you or allowing it to happen, let me stop you for a moment and say—have you actually asked Him? Have you actually told God your desires, or do you expect Him just to know them? I can assure you that He knows your thoughts, but if you really desire something, He wants you to show it. Do not sulk because you are still blind; tell Him that you want vision! He might just be waiting in your desperation to make His decision. If we desire God's will, He will bless our desires of desperation. Your outcry might just be His activation!

Prompt: If you could ask God to give you one thing, knowing that the answer would be "Yes," what would it be? Why do you want that? Share it with Him.

_____

_____

_____

_____

_____

_____

_____

_____

_____

_____

_____

January 17

1 Corinthians 9:1–18

If someone has to force you to do right, then should you really receive praise for doing right at all? Would you consider a child's first steps to be those that were assisted when, without stabilization, they would fall? Or do you wait and reward the child when they have independently walked on their own? Should the reward come at the point of action or when the information is known? Growth requires action and the willingness to push past the point of comfort. It is about understanding that the best moments come after the moments that you suffer. It is about willingly serving because you desire to give, not because you are told. It is about learning to be humble while simultaneously learning to be bold. If you are a Christian because your parents "say that you are," then you are just like a child that has not taken their first steps. Being an apostle of Christ is rewarding but far more difficult than one may expect. It requires personal commitment, hard work, humility, and the desire to make the Lord's name shine. It requires giving your 110 percent, 100 percent of the time. You will not be rewarded for what you were forced to do or what you did because you knew that you "should." Servanthood is not born out of forced labor; it is born out of the desire to do good.

Prompt: Are you currently serving somewhere or someone with unrighteous motives? For instance, are you serving at church but grumbling about it while getting ready, or doing a favor for someone and rolling your eyes that they asked? Think deeply about one thing you need to give up doing or how to start doing it with righteous motives.

_____
_____
_____
_____
_____
_____
_____
_____
_____
_____
_____
_____
_____

JANUARY 18

Ezekiel 6:11–14

Every knee will bow, and every tongue will confess that God is the Almighty one, even those who deny Him. The day of judgment will come for all of us because we all sin. Remember back to a time when you had done something wrong, and your parents pulled you aside. Suddenly nerves and regret replaced your self-assured pride. How humbling was it to be reprimanded for your decisions and all of your wrong behavior? How much more humbling will it be to admit your sin to your Savior? That is why salvation and surrender are so important because mercy will be provided to those who have committed. Your sin will be forgiven as long as you have submitted. But what about those who deny Christ's love and refuse to acknowledge His existence? Unfortunately, it will be too late to receive eternal repentance. Does that not break your heart into a million little pieces? That someone could spend eternity in hell, and us staying silent about God could be the reason. You can be uncertain about everything in life but do not let your salvation be an uncertainty. How can you call God fictitious when He calls you worthy? If you want to spend eternity with God, you should want to spend your life with Him, also. When the day of judgment comes, don't you want to be sure of where you are going to go? It's not either now or never; it's now for forever. Do you really want to give up eternal paradise for earthly pleasures?

Prompt: What is one thing that you do on a daily basis that you would be embarrassed if God saw you doing it? Why is there a narrative of shame surrounding that thing?

_____
_____
_____
_____
_____
_____
_____
_____
_____
_____
_____
_____
_____

January 19

Proverbs 19:11

People are destined to mistreat you, disappoint you, and harm your heart in some way. It could be an isolated incident or repetitive words that they say. Other's offenses are not the factor that we can control, but they should be an expectation. The real test of character is whether you will love them back without limitations. Is your love for others circumstantial? Or is it steadfast in its pursuit? Are you willing to exchange love with those who persecute? If you really think about true love, it has nothing to do with self and everything to do with the beloved. And the example of true love was sent to us from above. God showed us how to love when He sent His Son to die in our place. And He reminds us of the love daily, as He allows us to seek His face. He does not love us when we love Him; He loves us without conditions. True love does not waiver in the face of opposition. So the bad news is that all of the people in your life will break your heart, but the good news is—you do not have to stop loving them. Let's stop hating and start hugging them. We cannot control what others do, but we can control our heart's response. We cannot control who people will be, but we can control who we are and are not. So who will you be? The sum of others' actions or a reflection of your Savior? Love would be so much richer if we chose to be like our creator.

Prompt: What is the most hurtful thing that you can remember someone saying to you? Have you forgiven them for it?

_____

_____

_____

_____

_____

_____

_____

_____

_____

_____

_____

_____

January 20

Mark 7:1–23

It is truly remarkable how bound we can be to human traditions without even realizing our allegiance. We become so accustomed to the expectation of how things have always gone that we fail to even think twice about the reasons. We are quick to speak our minds when a tradition is at risk of being altered or forgotten. Yet we keep our mouth shut even when slander of our God's commands are common. Take a moment and examine the traditions that your heart deems important enough to form an emotional connection to. Be honest with yourself—have you given it too much—maybe even spiritual value? Have you put more effort into traditions than you have in reading your Bible? Do you really yearn for more of His spirit, or are you attempting to plan an organized "yearly" revival? We, as humans, are used to living with restrictions, but the spirit of God will not. You may be used to buying a heartfelt moment, but God's Spirit cannot be bought. Our religious traditions do not please the Lord, but our open and willing hearts do. He cares more about your availability to be flexible than He does about your consistent commitment to what you are used to. We must let go of the situations that control us and surrender that trust to Him. Would you rather live the same year repeatedly or experience true unending change within?

Prompt: Where/when do you feel closest to God? Where/when do you feel furthest from God?

_____

_____

_____

_____

_____

_____

_____

_____

_____

_____

_____

_____

January 21

John 11:17–27

Our God is a healer, although His healing will not always come in the way that we expect. Just because we do not receive our request, it does not mean that we are being treated with neglect. Take the story of Lazarus as an example; Martha and Mary had prayed for Jesus' arrival and divine healing for their brother. But Jesus did not arrive "on time," so they closed their brother's eyes and pulled up the cover. Then Jesus shows up, and they are understandably inconsolable. They are questioning Jesus' love got Lazarus when his death was controllable. They are mourning the "no" of their request and questioning the love of Jesus. And on paper, they have every reason. That is until Jesus begins to talk to Mary and Martha about His plan of resurrection. He lovingly talks to them about how their map did not align with His direction. That the plan they prayed for was not the right avenue for Lazarus' healing to take place. That if they trusted Jesus, they would see Lazarus again face to face. And you know what? He raised Lazarus from the dead; He did indeed heal His friend. So just because we turn the page and see blank space, it does not mean it is the end. It just might not be the "yes" that we were expecting, but it does not mean that it is a "no." The rain always comes before the rainbow.

Prompt: What has God said "no" to in the past that ended up being a blessing in your life?

_____

_____

_____

_____

_____

_____

_____

_____

_____

_____

_____

_____

January 22

Psalm 73:1–12

It's hard to see the proud and arrogant be successful and question your own posture of humility. It's frustrating to work hard and be outperformed by someone with natural ability. It's easy to feel slighted and question how God could show favor to those who oppose Him. How could He possibly give someone a greater portion who repeatedly chooses not to glorify Him? All the while, I feel as if I am serving God with a humble heart and willingly bowing in reverence. But my posture still is not gaining me any "worldly" preference. And you know what? It's not supposed to; it's not going to look like the world's preference does. A successful life on Earth is measured in different ways than a successful life serving the Son. My second place on Earth does not translate to second place in heaven. Comparing myself to others will only lead to questions. If the arrogant gain more ground, then I can confidently know that God did not want me to gain that ground. I find hope in knowing that He will exalt the humble and humble the proud. And that does not mean it will happen on Earth, so just because you do not see it does not mean it's not true. Other people's success is not stealing any favor from you. When you are faced with a tough road, don't compare, don't envy, and run your path knowing that it will give you more strength. I would rather have eternal glory than earthly glory that is fake.

Prompt: Who are you envious of? What do they have that you want? What do you have that they don't?

_____
_____
_____
_____
_____
_____
_____
_____
_____
_____
_____

JANUARY 23

Colossians 3:15–17

If we are called to glorify God in all that we do, shouldn't we intrinsically be peaceful people? There should be no piece of our life's puzzle that involves evil. I know that we are human, and therefore we sin and repent. But sinning should not be the default for the way that we live. So if we really think about God's command to glorify Him in everything, our life should be a steady stream of praise. Every moment of our day should aim to bring God fame. That means the moments when you talk to a friend and the moments when you meet someone new. That means the moments when you are stuck in traffic and looking in your rear view. That means the grocery store interactions and the way you should up at a meeting with your co-workers. That means the way you interact with service workers and how you tip your servers. That means how you cook a meal for your family and how you prioritize your baby's health. That means how you treat and talk to yourself. You see, it's about every moment, every detail of your life, and shifting the aim to glory. It's about making God the main character of your life's story. And in doing so, you will find a life of peace, not because everything will be perfect, but because you are welcoming God into the imperfection. Life becomes much more purposeful when we focus on God's affection.

Prompt: Name five things that make you angry. How do you react when each thing is done? How could you avoid these situations or react differently?

_____

_____

_____

_____

_____

_____

_____

_____

_____

_____

_____

_____

January 24

Acts 20:22–23

You do not always have to have a plan of action to take action. You can act before you are certain what will happen. It's the root of faith and the uncomfortable nature of giving up control. It's the true test of trusting the Lord with all of your soul. If you are compelled by the Spirit to do something—then do it. Do not wait for it to make sense or until you have the blueprint. You know when it's the Spirit calling you; there is no explanation for that sense of urgency. Even if it is met with an immense amount of uncertainty. I am urging you today while simultaneously encouraging myself to trust the Spirit's guidance without hesitation or question. I want to be a daughter who does not second-guess my Father's directions. Because when we walk where God is calling us to walk, good things will follow. But it does not mean that everything in life will be instantaneously good by tomorrow. I guess I could say more accurately that it might not look or feel good, but it will feel right. Even if your circumstances seem dismal with your human sight. If it's the call of God, it will be worth it, and you will be ready to face the challenges that lie ahead. Not with a sense of fear, nervousness, or dread, but instead with a sense of courage and confidence, knowing that you are walking behind the Almighty Savior. He would never lead you into or leave you in any danger.

Prompt: What is one fear that you have that you wish you did not have? How is that one thing holding you back in life?

January 25

Mark 4:21–25

Why do we sometimes feel the need to conceal our faith to protect the feelings of others? Shouldn't our faith make us feel more appealing to our sisters and brothers? But we cover it up in certain situations to make other people feel more comfortable and accepted. But acceptance is not only shown when our faith is neglected. We have been given a light in this dark world, so why would we dim it down and conceal its brightness? Why would we not appreciate in full the illumination that God has provided us? Because the truth is people may be uncomfortable around your light because it causes them to see things that they have never seen. They might not be upset with the light; they might just be upset when they realize they need to be washed clean. And if you choose not to shine in certain situations, you never know who might miss out on their revelation. Their introduction to Jesus might just hinge on your illumination. I am not writing this to convince you to turn up your light so bright that it's blinding, but I am encouraging you to keep it on. A room should look noticeably different when you are there versus when you are gone. Dimming won't make people more comfortable; it will only make you feel convicted. People feel Jesus when your light is emitted.

Prompt: When do you feel most confident? Why do you feel most confident then?

_____

_____

_____

_____

_____

_____

_____

_____

_____

_____

_____

January 26

Jeremiah 6:10–11

Have you ever been so excited about something that you literally could not contain it? The words started pouring out before you could actually explain it, like a shaken-up soda bottle with a popped top. There is no containing it, even if you wanted it to stop. I can think about many instances when that was the case in my life, but only a few revolve around the Lord as the sole topic. Most of the moments have been based around people, experiences, or objects. I could talk forever about places I've traveled, races I've run, and people that I've met along the way. But none of those topics would transform your life; they might just fill a portion of your day. But Jesus can change people's lives and bring a sense of excitement to the ordinary. So the fact that I'm not spewing with zeal is honestly embarrassing and scary. God deserves my uncontainable joy, so why is it not always there? Why are my focus and excitement often elsewhere? I want to spew with God's love and radiate His mercy; I do not want it to be contained. When I walk into a room, I want that room to change. I love the Lord, I trust the Lord, and now I just have to give Him my attention. He deserves my awards, not just my honorable mention. I want to be like a shaken-up soda bottle that is spewing from every seam. We should not be able to contain a love so extreme.

Prompt: Name one experience that you had recently that excited you. How can you see God as a part of that experience?

_____

_____

_____

_____

_____

_____

_____

_____

_____

_____

_____

_____

January 27

Luke 6:39–40

It's our command to lead other people to Jesus, right? I think we can all agree on that truth. But how are we supposed to encourage other people to follow Jesus if we are not even in pursuit? The *only* thing more dangerous than not leading people to Jesus is leading them in the wrong direction and claiming it's God's way. You are not just blatantly disregarding your command; you are messing with people's fate. Because if you claim to be a representative of Jesus but act nothing like Jesus, you could actually hinder their understanding. Do not claim to be on His firm foundation if you know it's crumbling where you are standing. I know it sounds intense, but that is because it is intense and it crucially important. We cannot bring other people along on the wrong path if our directions are distorted. The only way to ensure we are walking the right way is if we see Jesus a few steps in front of us. If you do not have Him in your sights, then it is time to readjust. Praying, reading God's Word, and worshipping Him are all ways to align your GPS to His true North. Do not alter people's compass until you have confirmed yours. It's a privilege to lead others to Christ, but it's dangerous to lead others astray. If we are off by even one degree, we might be leading them away. Seek God, seek His direction, and trust the Spirit's guidance. Don't encourage others to follow in your footsteps if you know that you are out of alignment.

Prompt: What do you do on a daily basis to be sure that you are following God's path? How do you know if you are on His path?

_____

_____

_____

_____

_____

_____

_____

_____

_____

_____

_____

_____

January 28

Amos 2:6–8

It's important to understand that tradition does not always equate to righteousness, and neither does popular opinion. That is why we must consult God before we make any and all decisions. We serve a God of mercy and justice who forgives our mistakes without hesitation. But we will fall into a quicksand of sin if we look to the world for confirmation. Think about our world today; what does society deem as righteous? The unfortunate truth is—everything that opposes God's likeness. So if you frame your life around societal standards, you will surely be far from God's standard. Tradition or trend will never be the answer. The answer is always God, and His Word is our guide. Your decisions will always be unsteady if you allow the world to decide. God hated sin so much that He sacrificed Himself in order to see its demise. In return, shouldn't we praise Him instead of patronizing Him? Why would I ever think that my way or the world's way would be greater than the way of God, who created us all? Our traditions and standards, when in opposition to God's commands, are our greatest downfall. Why would we want to please the world but spend our life repenting when we could just follow God with obedience? It's our responsibility to choose discipline over deviance. Do not conform to the sins of the world; popularity does not make them any less of a sin. Do not forfeit your place in heaven because you are trying to fit in.

Prompt: Name three people who you want to please. Why do you want to please them? What will happen if you don't?

_____

_____

_____

_____

_____

_____

_____

_____

_____

_____

_____

_____

January 29

Luke 8:19–21

We are all believers under the precious blood of Christ, and we are all called children of the king. But we must learn to accept that being His children means that we are family and not just some unrelated offspring. We all come from different backgrounds, cultures, and traditions, but that does not change the fact that we are all His. We are so eager to focus on the people that are similar to us that we are not even aware of all of the blessings that we miss. "Family" is most often described by blood relation, but are we not all related under the blood of Jesus Christ? We all became citizens of a heavenly nation the moment that He made the sacrifice. So why are we so quick to avoid relationships with people that look or behave in a different way? They may not share your same last name, but that does not give you the right to treat them like a castaway. We were created to interact, intermingle, and immigrate past our comfort zones. We must love until our description becomes "us" and not "they" or "those." God grant is the vision to see our peers as our siblings and love them with a familial love. We are all scattered and integrated here below and furiously loved by the one above.

Prompt: What privileges do I have that others do not?

_____

_____

_____

_____

_____

_____

_____

_____

_____

_____

_____

January 30

Genesis 15:1-21

We all have desires and dreams that we want to come to fruition here on this earth, but only God truly knows our hearts. We might go to Him on our knees about one thing, and then, at the end of our prayer, we feel as if we do not even know where to start. Our dreams and our goals may be big—but I am here to tell you that God's plans are *bigger*. They are far more wonderful than our plans and far more intricate than anything we could configure. Take Abraham, for example—he prayed for a child but settled for his servant to be his heir. But God does not always deliver what we ask for; He delivers more than we even know is there. He did not just give Abraham a child—He gave him two and made him the father of nations! It is amazing what God will do in our life if we allow Him to make almighty alterations. So as you take your dreams to the Lord, hand them over to Him and trust in His plan. He will give you more than you could ever imagine because He does not operate within the confines of man. If God does not grant you your desires—be patient because something better is coming. He is the God of abundantly more, not the God of nothing. Allow God to take your plans and form them into something even greater. Remember, He is the Almighty *creator*.

Prompt: What would your perfect day look like? What is stopping you from living it?

_____

_____

_____

_____

_____

_____

_____

_____

_____

_____

_____

_____

January 31

Psalm 88:3–9

It took me years to realize that it was okay to pray truthfully to God and that my prayers did not have to be wrapped up nicely in a bow. I do not have to sugarcoat my feelings because they are something that God already knows. When my heart is in anguish or overflowing with anger, I can cry out to the Lord in honesty. Not because He desires my sorrow but because He desires all of me. So many people refuse to talk to God because they are scared that they will not know what to say. They try and improve their vocabulary before they open their mouths to pray, not realizing that God already knows their true desires in the deepest depths of their hearts. The best way to pray is simply to start. I am so encouraged when I read scriptures of anguish and desperate cries of questions. It's nice to read that others grow frustrated as well when God does not do what they expected. You can speak your heart to God because He knows the truth behind your feelings. Think of it as something you are expressing, not something that you are revealing. God loves you for who you are, not who you pretend to be. Your prayers may be eloquent, but they are void if they lack honesty. Do not avoid communication with the Father because you are fearful of expressing how you feel. God does not want your polished words; He wants prayers that are real.

Prompt: What is one thing that you feel that you are too scared to tell anyone about? Give it to Jesus.

_____

_____

_____

_____

_____

_____

_____

_____

_____

_____

_____

_____

FEBRUARY

FEBRUARY 1

Matthew 26:31–35

Have you ever done the thing that you said you would *never* do? Have you ever woken up from a bad dream and then realized that the nightmare was true? Have you ever drawn a line of boundary and then crossed it? Have you ever cherished something and then flippantly lost it? The answer is yes; unfortunately, we all have allowed sin to override our judgment. We have all traded in our discipline for a moment of indulgence. What comes after that mistake? Most of the time, it's shame, regret, and self-deprecation. We feel that if we punish ourselves enough, it will fix the situation. Peter followed Jesus for a handful of years and saw the miracles of God with his own eyes. Yet in the moment of question, he chose to compromise. Was Jesus appalled at this decision? No, He knew it would happen even before He asked Peter to follow. What I am trying to explain is that God's love does not change based on how you behave tomorrow. You might have denied Jesus three times yesterday, but if you repent, then you are forgiven. God does not need you to punish yourself; He needs you to start living! Your mistake is never bigger than God's mercy. No matter how many times you mess up, God will still call you worthy. Look at all of the work Peter did after he denied Jesus! His mistakes were not his worth; they were just a moment of weakness. We all mess up and fall short of righteousness, but our past does not dictate our future. We might have been lost, but we are not losers.

Prompt: What is something you have asked God to forgive you for but *you* have not forgiven yourself for? Free yourself from that shame now.

_____
_____
_____
_____
_____
_____
_____
_____
_____
_____
_____
_____
_____

February 2

Psalm 111:10

I believe that there is a misconception about "fearing God," especially in our generation today. We have grabbed a hold so tightly of the miracle of grace and relationship that we forget that there was a price that was paid. We often leave our fear in the Old Testament and view God as our new covenant companion. Yes—the wrathful nature of God was satisfied at the cross, but it is much deeper than our shallow-minded understanding. We must fear God out of reverence and submission. Our fear must not be based on timidity but on recognizing our inferior position. We must fear Him when we sin and fear Him when we are operating close to righteousness. Not because we are at risk of His wrath but because we are eternally blessed. God is closer to us than any friend, but that does not make him *a* friend. We are separated from that perfect bond because of our sins. We must grab hold of grace and cherish our relationship with our creator. All with the understanding that He is not our "buddy;" He is our *Savior*. May our hearts be so in tune with His night ones that we tremble at the mention of His name. We must stop our view of a "casual relationship" and fix our hearts on the fact that He eternally reigns.

Prompt: Who do you respect most in your life, and how did they earn your respect? Who do you expect respect from, and why should they respect you?

_____

_____

_____

_____

_____

_____

_____

_____

_____

_____

_____

_____

_____

_____

February 3

Mark 5:21–24

I am so glad that Jesus spoke with action and not just words. Some of the loudest statements that we make are those that cannot be heard. Jesus did not just speak encouragement and healing—He actually encouraged and healed. His authority was not just His title; His authority was revealed. I want to have a lot more action behind my words, especially my words of courage. Because speaking brings thoughts to life, but acting gives them purpose. When Jairus came and fell at the feet of Jesus, Jesus did not ask for more information. Because Jairus' question was important, but his action showed desperation. Jesus immediately left His place among admirers to go heal Jairus' daughter, who was dying. Jesus did not need any more details or clarifying. I want to heal, not just talk about how glorious healing would be. I don't want to stand in wonder at a locked door; I want to unlock it with my key. I don't want to talk about how good God's Word is; I actually want to consume it. I want my words to be met with movement. Because being where you are is a gift, but taking a step forward makes that your present. Think of every act of courage as one step closer to heaven. Let's move, let's do, and let's put some action behind our voice. Doing produces results; speaking produces noise. Let's heal, pray, read, and encourage, and *go*. That is one powerful combo. Jesus did not tell us to talk about His journey; He tells us to follow Him. Instead of being the ones who talk about the problems, let's be the ones who mend them.

Prompt: What is one thing you have always wanted to do? What is stopping you from doing it? What actions can you take to make it happen?

_____

_____

_____

_____

_____

_____

_____

_____

_____

_____

_____

_____

FEBRUARY 4

Proverbs 30:1

Have you ever been so exhausted that breathing felt like running a race? The expansion of your chest with each breath felt like lifting a weight. The depths of despair are isolating, but they are also void of hope. That is why people use a million different things to cope. I have been there; I have felt the weight of my own breath and seen the world grow dim. I have pushed God away in those moments instead of letting Him in. I have muttered words of hopelessness because, at the time, they felt true. But as I look back now, I see that despair was clouding my view. So, as I write this now, I am here to encourage you from the advice of my own experience. I hope that a piece of your heart will allow your body to hear it. "I am weary, God, but I can prevail." I will cling to heaven when I am going through hell. I will keep breathing, in and out, and in and out, even when it gets heavy. I will not maximize my problems; I will look forward to my blessing. Because the truth is—you will prevail because God is on your side. He is with you every step along this wild ride. I know the depths seem too deep to get out of, but God is a miracle worker. He brings clarity from the ruins of disorder. Keep going—keep putting one foot in front of the other and matching an inhale with an exhale. This pit will not be your ending; it will be part of a testimony that you tell.

Prompt: What makes your heart feel heavy? What sets your heart on fire?

_____

_____

_____

_____

_____

_____

_____

_____

_____

_____

_____

_____

_____

_____

February 5

Hebrews 10:36–38

I remember hearing a sermon about how you are either growing closer to God or you are drifting away. On the highway of righteousness, there is no middle lane. You cannot be stagnant or lukewarm; you are either hot or cold. He either has all or no part of your soul. It makes sense on paper, and it sure sounded good in the pastor's sermon that Sunday. But it feels a little different being reality and not just words that you say. I do not know about you, but I have had many moments in my faith walk where I have felt "paused." I was not charging forward, but I also was not lost. It felt like I was sitting down on the side of the path, watching and waiting for directions. Or like I paused a conversation on the phone because I had a poor connection. The pause felt comfortable; it felt like a deserved rest after a long commute. But when I was sitting, I was in *no* position to be moved. And when you are complacent with being sedentary, movement becomes a dread. It becomes more enticing to follow your feelings instead of going where you are led. The "pause" is the equivalent of taking steps back because God keeps moving forward. If we choose to sit with ourselves, then we are choosing not to walk with the Lord. Don't pause your walk; keep chasing after God, even if your pace slows. We should be steps closer today and even closer tomorrow. God delights in our pursuit, and it breaks His heart when we stop moving. There is no "might be" —we either are or are not pursuing.

Prompt: When was the last time you did something that made you uncomfortable? What was it, and why did you do it?

_____
_____
_____
_____
_____
_____
_____
_____
_____
_____
_____
_____
_____

FEBRUARY 6

Proverbs 28:27–28

Being kind to other people is not optional as a Christian. It's not a personality trait; it's our life mission. We are created to love other people as we love ourselves, and not just because it sounds good. It does not need to just be heard; it needs to be understood. Love is the root of thriving, and that is what we are called to walk into. It's not always easy, but it is certainly simple to do. I do not believe in karma, but I do believe that all of our choices have consequences. If we refuse to pay the kindness tax, we will rack up a lot of expenses. When we choose to overlook a needy soul and avoid an opportunity to help, don't you see that it has implications that far exceed being concerned with ourselves? Because we are a representative of Christ, and He is the creator of kindness and care. Which means that we must carry kindness everywhere! If we bring kindness into a room of destruction, the light will drown out the darkness. One act of kindness speaks louder than any act of harshness. And if you dish out harshness, you will reap the consequences of that action. We cannot control what and when, but we can influence the chances of what will happen. I don't know anyone who wakes up in the morning and says, "I want to make this world a worse place." So if that's true for you, then be aware of what you bring into your surrounding space. Put kindness out, and reap the benefits of that genuine extension of empathy and mercy. No matter what *your* opinion may be, *He* says that everyone is worthy.

Prompt: What is the kindest thing that anyone has ever said to you or done for you? What do you think the kindest thing is that you have ever done for or said to someone else?

FEBRUARY 7

Psalm 78:32–39

You **will** sin, but you are not *a* sinner. At least, this is true if you are born again. Because salvation pulls us toward righteousness, but our flesh pulls us toward sin. And that is the difficult balance that we must face as Christians. How do we lean more on the side of righteous behavior? The only answer I have found to be true is just to focus on the Savior. It's easy to make sin a regular part of your routine because it feeds the flesh's desire. But one spark of sin can ignite an untamable fire. God knows that we will sin, but it does not mean that He condones it. He is incredibly merciful, but He is not a sin proponent. Sinning is a choice—always...although, at times, it might not feel like it is. But we are responsible for the life that we live. If we sin 107 times today, God will forgive us 108 times. But He is meant to be our friend—not our "mess up" hotline. You make sinful choices, but it is not who you are. God made sure of that with the cross, the nails, and the scars. Let's start today; let's choose our Savior over our flesh's desire for sin. I don't know about you, but I am tired of letting my flesh win. God deserves our commitment, and our commitment is equal to our choice. I would rather not have to repent when I could rejoice. My sin is not who I am, and I refuse to claim it as a part of my identity. It is actions of mistakes, but it is not what's within me. I am a child of God—born again and saved. I won't allow my sin to keep me in the grave.

Prompt: What sin do you feel has a grip on you more so than others? What makes this sin so enticing to you? How can God help?

_____

_____

_____

_____

_____

_____

_____

_____

_____

_____

_____

_____

_____

FEBRUARY 8

Isaiah 51:6

Where are your roots planted? Do not just read this, but really think about it. You do not have to confess it out loud, but it should be something that you can privately admit. Maybe you say they are rooted in Jesus, but really, they are rooted in your new boyfriend. Maybe you say they are rooted in the Word of God, but all of your actions are displaying that they are rooted in sin. This is not made to be a letter of condemnation; I pray that it is a priority check. That you take a moment to prune your branches to see what is left. You do not have to proclaim your heart to others; you can just start by admitting your allegiance has been fractured. Do not reprimand yourself for chasing the meaningless; just start today by focusing on what matters. People, jobs, finances, pets, and all other aspects of life are important, but they do not make good roots. You would not plant a banana peel and expect to harvest fruit! So why plant flesh and expect to reap the supernatural harvest that God has promised? Maybe you are not in a healthy spiritual place because you are not being honest. The people, the ways, and the things of this world will pass away. So if you remove all of the finite material, what would remain? Plant roots of relationship with Jesus and watch how your harvest of earthly treasures multiplies. He cannot deliver if you constantly deny.

Prompt: Name your top five priorities in honest order. How could you reorder them to potentially create a healthier life for yourself?

_____

_____

_____

_____

_____

_____

_____

_____

_____

_____

_____

_____

FEBRUARY 9

1 Timothy 6:6–10

If you woke up tomorrow and your life was perfect, how would it look different from today? What are those little (or big) requests that are included every time you pray? What aspects of your life would be different, and which people would be involved? If suddenly, the complicated puzzle of life was solved. It's a loaded question that narrows in on the temptation of ultimate contentment. But what is stopping you from living in it? What is missing from your life today, and what will happen if you find it? Would you actually be content even if God supplied it? I find myself praying for contentment often, not because I'm not happy but because I want more. It's my greedy flesh that always wants to know what's behind the next door. It's the "grass is always greener" mentality when I already have more than enough to eat. I get what I want, and then I want what I see. It's cyclical...so if you woke up to a perfect life tomorrow, in a week, it would just be normal. It's a never-ending pattern that goes in a repeating circle. Contentment is not "when;" contentment is "now." Instead of asking God "for," let's ask Him "how?" How can we be content with out today and be grateful for the prayers that we prayed yesterday? Instead of wondering and wandering—what would happen if we stayed? There will be imperfections in your life, but life will never be perfect on this side of heaven. Contentment is rooted in present gratitude, not idealized perfection.

Prompt: If you woke up to a perfect life tomorrow, what aspects of your life today would be included? What is missing from your current life?

_____
_____
_____
_____
_____
_____
_____
_____
_____
_____
_____
_____
_____

FEBRUARY 10

John 11:11–16

I think often times our unanswered prayers are actually just misinterpretations of God's real answer to us. What we think is neglect is actually real love. I feel that it's a more realistic thought to have that I may be the one at fault and not God. After all, He is perfect, and I am flawed. When was the last time that you doubted God because you said "amen" and heard no response? When was the last time you questioned Him when things went wrong? I have been in situations where I have walked through the door He led me to and not liked what awaited me on the other side. I have been patient and still questioned if He was on time. I have prayed prayers I was sure He would answer and then never received the words I expected. I have been at the point of feeling hopeless and neglected. But I realize now that it's only because my expectations were pre-determined, and I was not open to interpretation. God never was the one who had the wrong information. I misunderstood, misinterpreted, and expected answers that were not useful for my growth. So instead of questioning if God heard me correctly, I will just accept His "yes" and "no." You might pray for one area of your life but then receive something else entirely. Trust that His ways are always right and they are always timely. He does not speak wrongly; we might just hear Him incorrectly. He will answer prayers, but not always directly.

Prompt: When was the last time you did not get what you wanted, but instead, you got what you needed?

_____
_____
_____
_____
_____
_____
_____
_____
_____
_____
_____
_____
_____

FEBRUARY 11

Matthew 8:14–17

Fasting is a practice that oftentimes gets overlooked or ignored. It is something that we all know of but very rarely gets explored. Too often, fasting is equated to "hunger" when it should be equated to discipline. It is less about lamenting and more about listening. Jesus knew the power of fasting, and He withheld it from His disciples while He was among them. He knew that it would magnify their awareness of their sin. So instead of fasting in His presence, the disciples were constantly being taught. Jesus did not need them to give up eating the fish; He needed to show them how they were caught. But what about now? Where do we fall into the mix of prayer and fasting? Fasting should be done to re-coordinate the heart to operate in the things of life that are lasting. It does not require a big display or a lot of time; it only requires a willing heart. How can you know that you will not receive anything from a fast if you are not willing to start? Fasting is proven to have power as it forces us into an awareness of our spirit. It brings the volume of distractions down so that when God speaks, you may hear it. It is not made to be displayed or expressed as an applauded practice. It was designed to be implemented as a habit. If you feel led to fast, do not try and "figure it out" —just do it. And if you think you will not last, allow God to prove it.

Prompt: What is one thing that you could give up for a day? A week? A month? A year? How would that benefit your body, mind, and spirit?

_____

_____

_____

_____

_____

_____

_____

_____

_____

_____

_____

_____

FEBRUARY 12

Jonah 3:1–5

You can ignore your calling, but you cannot avoid it. You may refuse God 1,000 times, but God will never quit. We are either working with God or against God; there is no other way. His mercies are new every morning, and your commitment must be established every day. I love the story of Jonah because his stubbornness led him straight into the belly of a whale. He did not just "happen" to fall off of a boat. He actually ignored God's commanded details. God did not strike him down with wrath; He made him spend three nights in a rather uncomfortable situation. Jonah became fish food because of his lack of cooperation. Do you know what happened on the third day? The whale spat him out, and Jonah went straight to Nineveh as God had commanded. He could not avoid it because God had planned it. If he had just obeyed God, there would still be the same outcome, just not the three-night stay under the sea. I don't know about you, but when I read about Jonah, I see me. I see all of the moments in my life when I ignored God's plan and made my life *way* more difficult in the process. I see all of the times that I chose what I thought was good and ignored God's best. And you know what? He still led me to Nineveh and said, "I told you there is work to do." Jonah is me, and if I had to guess, Jonah is you. You can run away from God, but His plan will come to pass. His patience abounds your restraint. His plan will come to pass whether you commit or complain.

Prompt: Is it more important for you to be right or to do right? How is this shown in your life?

_____

_____

_____

_____

_____

_____

_____

_____

_____

_____

_____

_____

FEBRUARY 13

Micah 7:5–7

It is important to remember that only God can truly satisfy your soul. We look for other broken pieces in this world to try and patch ourselves up, but only God can make us whole. We pour our whole hearts into relationships that leave only scraps behind for the Lord. And then, when we experience heartbreak, we run to God to be restored. This is not about discouraging relationships; it's about building them on a spiritual foundation. It's about strengthening your relationship with the Lord first so that you will be better equipped for other relations. Too often, we compare our relationships on Earth with our heavenly birthright. We are hurt by people on this earth and allow that to cloud our heavenly sight. We put our trust in broken people, and because of our hurt, we fail to extend our trust to the Savior. We blindly equate the love of God to a past lover's behavior. All of these scenarios are born out of placing God in second place. God needs to be your one desire, not your "just in case." Your relationship with God will falter if you expect Him to operate like your earthly relationships. He is waiting with open arms and perfect love with no judgment or risk. He will provide you with everything you need and love you with a love that is greater than love itself. But we must understand that all relationships must be built on His foundation because they will crumble if they are built on anyone else.

Prompt: Who are you dependent upon? Do you rely on them more than you rely on the Lord? What does balance look like in relationships?

_____

_____

_____

_____

_____

_____

_____

_____

_____

_____

_____

_____

FEBRUARY 14

John 13:31–38

If you ever feel like you have pushed God past His point of mercy, I encourage you to read the Bible. In every story, you will be reminded that God is an ally—not a rival. Take, for instance, the story of Peter's denial of Jesus. He walked alongside Jesus for years and years and still allowed Satan to attack his weakness. Imagine looking into the eyes of someone you love and telling them that they will betray you. Knowing that they would deny you three times and the pain that you would be put through. Now take that feeling of raw emotion and anger and bow before that person and wash their feet. Oh, and while you are at it, tell them that you are entrusting them to make your life's work complete. As a broken human, I can honestly say that my pride and anger would get in the way. It would take *a lot* of Jesus for me to even find nice words to say. But this is our God...the merciful forgiver and the provider of eternal grace. He does not hold us to our past denials, and He forgives us for our mistakes. He does not see problems; He sees our potential and the willingness of our souls. He knows that it is a daily battle to give Him all control. Your mistakes of the past have stayed in the past, but He needs you to work diligently every day and every minute of this ticking clock. If you do not believe me when I say you are forgiven...God turned Peter into the church's rock.

Prompt: What do you feel is holding you back from reaching your potential?

_____

_____

_____

_____

_____

_____

_____

_____

_____

_____

_____

_____

_____

_____

FEBRUARY 15

1 Corinthians 7:17

I love the saying, "The Lord does not call the qualified; He qualifies the called." He does not need you to change anything because everything will change when the Spirit has been installed. I look back on my life five to ten years ago, and I do not even know who that person is. Not because I lost myself, only because I realized that I was His. I want you to know today that God wants you as you are; you do not have to change yourself to gain His love. He sees your faults and still says that you are more than enough. He does not need you to take any prerequisites; He just needs you to love Him with your entire heart. In order to be closer to God, He does not need you to pick yourself apart. He tells us to "come as we are," not "come when you are the best version of yourself." Because the truth is that, in order to become better at anything, we need His help. Do not wait to come to God when you have it all figured out; He will help you figure it out. Do not wait to find proof for faith; faith just needs a slight absence of doubt. Think about everyone He used in the Bible; none of them were qualified by the world's standards. He does not need our solutions; He just needs us to know that He is the answer. You do not have to change anything about yourself; He will make you a new creation without your efforts or pursuits. You being 100 percent authentic is when you are at His best use.

Prompt: What parts of you are you most proud of? When do you show up as your most authentic self?

_____

_____

_____

_____

_____

_____

_____

_____

_____

_____

_____

_____

FEBRUARY 16

Matthew 16:5–12

How do you know when someone is actually telling you the truth? What aspects of their words give you proof? Is it the words themselves, or is it your relationship with the person? How do you decipher that what they are telling you is the real version? This is not to urge you into cynicism; if anything, it's to push you closer to authenticity. It's good to evaluate the information you receive and think about it deliberately. Jesus was adamant with His disciples about not trusting the words of the Sadducees and Pharisees. Just because someone has a title does not mean they have expertise. That is why we must know the Word of God like the back of our hand. So when people speak false truths, we immediately recognize and understand. It's not about telling other people that they are wrong; it's about knowing the truth for yourself. False teachings should be as potent as rotten food—they should smell. Guard your ears to false information, do not just trust someone because they claim that it is true. If it goes against the Word of God, that is your number one clue. God gave us the Holy Spirit for many reasons, and one of those is discernment. It's a gift that allows us to hear things, and the Spirit will either deny or confirm it. Listen to the Spirit, read the Word of God, and test all of the words that you hear. Do not follow someone's "truth" if that "truth" is unclear.

Prompt: What sources do you go to for information? Why do you put your trust in those sources?

_____

_____

_____

_____

_____

_____

_____

_____

_____

_____

_____

_____

FEBRUARY 17

Amos 3:3–7

Part of faith is believing that everything happens for a reason and trusting that it is all part of God's plan. Even the parts of life that seem incredibly difficult to understand. Have you ever had something happen in your life, and then years down the road, it makes sense? You realize that it was never a part of your plan, but it was a part of His. It's easy for me to write these words down on paper, but it's much more difficult for me to actually believe it every minute. Many times I have reached my "faith" limit. But time and time again, He has proved to me that He has a reason for every single thing that occupies our day. Because long before we walked it, He cut our pathway. Even the turns we make that are in opposition to Him, He knew we were going to take them. He knew which promises we would keep and when we would break them. We cannot surprise Him; therefore, His plan involves all of our choices. He loves us way too much to let any of them destroy us. I have faith in God's timing, His plan, and His decisions because, time after time, He has never let me down. Instead of leaning on doubt, I will lean on the one who wears the crown. The author and perfecter of our story has written a good book. Even if every instance is not quite how you thought it would look. Whatever seems confusing right now will one day be an "Aha!" moment of God's grace. But in the in-between... have faith.

Prompt: If you had to give your life a title up until this point, what would it be? Are you happy with that title, or do you wish it was something else?

_____

_____

_____

_____

_____

_____

_____

_____

_____

_____

_____

_____

_____

FEBRUARY 18

1 Samuel 1:21–28

The proper fuel for surrender is humility, but often times we use the fuel of desperation instead. We will submit to His plan, but only when our plans are dead. It takes trust, love, and desire to fully surrender yourself and the one's that you love. It takes massive amounts of humility to admit that what you have been given is only because of God above. It always touches my heart to hear mothers and fathers say that their children are God's gift to them, but they are rightly His. It's encouraging to see parents release control of what they feel for what actually is. I do not have children, but I do have more gifts and loved ones than I could possibly describe on paper. Even on my best days, I have to remind myself that it is only because of my Savior. None of what I own is mine; even my body is out on loan. Every harvest that I have reaped is just the result of a seed He has sown. I do not want to just acknowledge this truth when times get tough and I have no other options. I want to know, act, and believe that He is the gift giver and He is sovereign. I want to be found on my knees in humility, not with my arms wrapped protectively around my possessions. They are mine because He deemed them so, not because of my protection. So I will give Him praise for it all, and I want to be found doing so on my knees in a humble posture. Everything I have is an inheritance because I am the king's daughter.

Prompt: What is something that you have yet to surrender to God? What is holding you back?

_____

_____

_____

_____

_____

_____

_____

_____

_____

_____

_____

_____

_____

_____

FEBRUARY 19

Luke 9:51–56

It's easy to place vengeful thoughts on those that cause you grief. Sometimes seeing others suffer brings us a form of relief. I do not think it stems from hatred; I think it stems from wanting empathy. Knowing that if others experience grief, they might have a deeper outpouring of sympathy. It's human nature to want to be understood and treated well, but it's not necessary for spiritual care. As Christians, we must be deeply and genuinely empathetic regardless of whether or not we have been treated fair. We cannot wish harm on others just because they harm us; our love is resolute, not reciprocal. We must be selflessly caring and not emotionally critical. Is it fair when others mistreat you? Of course not, but neither was the cross. We have gained eternal salvation, so it's okay if we experience some mistreatment or loss. Think about all of the times that people mocked Jesus, yet He still treated them with love and respect. He absorbed their hatred, but He did not reciprocate their neglect. Why? Because what good can come from two wrongs? Why fight hate with hostility? Revenge does not produce relief; it produces bigotry. How do we fight our human nature to become more empathetic and less vengeful? The answer is simultaneously complex and incredibly simple. The answer is: seek Jesus and aim to become more like Him and less like the flesh. You can still show love even if you are not treated the best. It's called mercy, and we receive an endless amount from God, so it's time we give some away. Your sympathy is not dependent on what other people do or say.

Prompt: What is a grudge that you still hold onto today? What hurt is hidden under the anger and resentment?

_____

_____

_____

_____

_____

_____

_____

_____

_____

_____

_____

_____

February 20

Hebrews 10:32–35

Do you remember when you were first saved? Think back to the time of your salvation. When you first accepted the most kind and gracious invitation. Do you remember that stirring in your Spirit and the feeling of delight and levity? When your Spirit was soaring even though the world was heavy? That is the feeling I am talking about, the intensity of your independent desires to become a heavenly member. I remember that day and the days following when all my focus was on how I could be a better servant. I was focused on diving deeper into His love, maybe even trying to earn it. My soul was on fire, and I was zealous and full of embers. But it's funny how the fire gets less fierce the longer I have walked in surrender. It's not because I love God less; it's just that I have grown used to stoking the flames. The radical transformation no longer felt like such a radical change. I want it back. I want the zealous, heart on fire, raging spirit to be present. I want to be freshly anointed every day until I get to heaven. I do not want a stale faith that burns like smothered ash in brimstone. I want the flames to burn like dry would upon dry stone. Fierce, intense, and bright—every day I am here on this earth, I want to burn *bright*. I want every day to feel like the day I gave my life.

Prompt: When were you first saved? Recount the feelings, environment, and surroundings of the moment you surrendered your heart to Christ.

_____

_____

_____

_____

_____

_____

_____

_____

_____

_____

_____

_____

_____

_____

FEBRUARY 21

Matthew 23:27–28

Anytime I read any portion of Scripture about the Pharisees, I feel like I am witnessing a bully get put in their place. Jesus often told them that they were wrong, and He said it straight to their face. I find myself reading these scriptures with a smirk on my face and an arrogant mind. Until I realized this morning that when I disobey Jesus, I am one of their kind. Talk about a gut punch... ouch, it's quite the wake-up call. I do not ever want to be associated with white-washed walls. I do not ever want to be arrogant and self-righteous in my actions, especially when I am speaking about my Savior. I want my behavior to represent my beliefs and my beliefs to influence my behavior. I do not just want to "look" like a Christian but spew misinformation like a Pharisee. I do not want to be clouded by self-righteousness; I want spiritual clarity. But I can think of times in my life when I reacted more like a Pharisee than Jesus. Instead of being a servant, I felt like a genius. That's Pharisee behavior, and I do not want to behave in that way ever again. I want to become more like Jesus every day; I do not want to just point out other people's sins. I want my inside to be so full of Jesus that I exude His love everywhere that I go. I am here to serve Jesus and others, not tell other people "yes" and "no." I want to read this scripture and not feel the conviction of the Pharisees. I do not want others to see a white-washed tomb when they see me.

Prompt: Is your opinion the truth? Do you think others see you as judgmental or accepting?

_____

_____

_____

_____

_____

_____

_____

_____

_____

_____

_____

_____

February 22

Proverbs 1:10–19

We all have gut feelings, right? Where you can sense something before it actually happens. As Christians, we know that it is the Holy Spirit, not some kind of premonitory magic. The miracle is not having the feeling; the miracle is actually listening to that discernment. Are you going to listen to the voice of truth or be persuaded by the serpent? The formative years of middle school to high school are packed with people warning you about peer pressure. It seems that every adult during that time is a professional at giving ethical lectures. "Do not give in to peer pressure," "You do not need to drink or smoke," and "Do not do something just because everyone else is." I could rattle off an endless amount of warnings from the "say no to peer pressure" list. But what happens when you are forty-five and you do not have a guidance counselor setting your boundaries? How do you know how to say "no" when the peer pressure is mounting? You listen to the voice of God and do what He tells you to do. You avoid the trends and chase what is true. Will you be mocked? Probably. Will you be left out? There's a good chance. But if they avoid you when you are chasing God, then they probably were never going to help your faith advance. "Trust your gut" or, more accurately, the discernment of the Holy Spirit. You will always feel it even if you do not hear it. Take the path less traveled; it will be quiet but intimate and rewarding. We are called to keep renewing, not keep conforming.

Prompt: When was the last time that you gave in to peer pressure and did something that you did not want to do? Why did you do it? How could you have stood up for what you believed was right?

_____

_____

_____

_____

_____

_____

_____

_____

_____

_____

_____

_____

February 23

1 Timothy 5:21–22

Being zealous is not bad unless the zeal is not attached to the love of God. Zeal is beneficial when it's attached to admiration, not when it's attached to applause. How can we channel our energy into the right avenue of use? How can our zeal be abundant but not abused? Make God your main priority, give Him your focus, and be patient in His process. Seeking God might dim your zeal a bit, but only because you will rid yourself of the excess. What I hear God saying is: "Seek Me first, wait on My command, and you will experience abundant zeal." This newly established boost of vigor will be cemented upon feelings that are real. You will not have to clamor about your willingness to serve; you will just serve willingly. You will not have to convince others with your actions; you will prove that with your authenticity. It's great to be on fire for God as long as the fire is sustainable. It's better to be small and never-ending than it is to be short-lived and uncontainable. Speak the truth of God; do not spew it. Live the Word of God; don't act it. Make zeal an attribute by making following God a habit. I am not discouraging Christians from being bold or active, but I am discouraging uncontrollable zeal. Instead of laying hands on everyone that you meet, maybe first take time alone with God and kneel. God wants us to be full of vigor, but He would rather us be full of Him. Your authentic actions will follow your authentic Spirit within.

Prompt: What is one thing that you do more talking about instead of doing?

_____

_____

_____

_____

_____

_____

_____

_____

_____

_____

_____

_____

February 24

Matthew 4:1–11

I love this passage of Scripture about Jesus being tempted in the wilderness; it reminds me that I have control over my body; it does not control me. I do not have to follow its path, especially if my spirit disagrees. Jesus was out in the wilderness fasting for forty days and forty nights. Every atom in His body was urging Him to take a sip or a bite. Even Satan appeared to Him and tempted Him with bread. But He simply chose not to break His fast instead. This might not be the story of your circumstance, but we all have desires of our flesh. Far too often, we trust that our flesh knows best. But maybe, just maybe, we should take a moment and think about our desires before we just fulfill them. Because in that moment of temptation, Satan's bread would not have satisfied Jesus; it would have killed Him. Can you think of a situation in your life where your answered desires led to destruction instead of satisfaction? An instance where what your desires expected is not what actually happened. Then what comes next? Repentance, regret, and shame. All because you allowed your flesh to run the game. It's a feeling of freedom when you realize that your body can sit in the passenger seat; it does not have to drive. With spiritual discernment, you get to choose what keeps you alive. Because God will never leave you, forsake you, or take you into a battle that you will not win. But your desires will lead you headfirst into sin. So, let your flesh inform you, but do not let it give instruction. It can be a really great guide at times, but it cannot always be trusted.

Prompt: What feeling do you give too much power to? How could you allow it to sit in the passenger seat instead of driving?

_____
_____
_____
_____
_____
_____
_____
_____
_____
_____
_____

February 25

Hosea 4:4–5

How many times have you heard the words "Don't be a tattle tale?" It seems like second nature for us to point out all of the ways in which people fail. But what good does that do? How does that solve anyone's problems? Sometimes, we feel that we could live someone's life better than they do if given the option. We have all done it, right? Someone slips up, and we call them out immediately. Not with humility but conceitedly. It makes us feel good at the moment, to be "right" and make the other person feel wrong. Because for whatever reason, when others show a moment of weakness, we feel strong. It's not our job to be the judge, and it's not our job to be the jury, either. We are all on equal levels as fellow believers. We can hold each other accountable, but accountability does not look like a pointed finger. Accusations do not resemble our Savior. If you want to hold someone accountable, that is done by having a conversation with them privately. It is not shouted from the rooftops; it is done quietly. I repent right now for all of the times that I have tattled and accused. It was not my place to speak, and it was not my job to do. I want to do a lot less finger-pointing and a lot more hand-holding. I want my reaction to include more listening and less scolding. Let's stop accusing other people, even if we know that we are right and they have made a mistake. Instead of sharing our opinion, let's share how Jesus saves.

Prompt: When was the last time you gossiped about someone behind their back? What good did it accomplish?

_____

_____

_____

_____

_____

_____

_____

_____

_____

_____

_____

_____

FEBRUARY 26

Psalm 53

Where dread is present—God is ignored. God is the ever-present life-saver, but He can not save you if you continue to jump overboard. Our world is full of negativity, disdain, and "realistic" approaches that are actually just pessimistic beliefs. Many seek joy or a break from the struggles, but they fail to find any relief. We live in a world that is desperate for joy and unity but rolls its eyes at a belief of a creator. They are seeking to be saved from the agony of this broken world, but they refuse to bow before their Savior. So they are left dreading life instead of finding joy in the midst of less-than-ideal situations. Instead of stepping into the unknown with willingness, they complain when something fails to meet their expectations. We all have bad days, but examine your life and determine if joy or dread is more common. When your expectations are not met, how will you respond? Will the joy of the Lord reign in your heart even in the midst of trial? Will you cling to your desired outcomes and expectations or God's promises for survival? Where dread grows—faith shrinks, and where complaining sounds—praises cease. The joy of the Lord produces eternal blessings, while dread focuses on constant decrease.

Prompt: What is one part of your day or week that you dread? Is it necessary, or how could you alleviate it?

_____

_____

_____

_____

_____

_____

_____

_____

_____

_____

_____

_____

_____

FEBRUARY 27

Matthew 18:6–9

It is easy to play the blame game in life and place the accusation on the shoulders of others, but how often do we take the blame? When given the opportunity to plead our case, how often do we testify against our own name? Pride is quick to point out the faults of others but slow to examine one's own effects. Yes, someone might have led you into temptation, but *you* took the steps. We must claim responsibility for our sins and unrighteous habits. The earthly jury and judge have no power to declare your eternal status. So instead of participating in bad habits and then explaining to God all of the reasons you are forced into this behavior. Hit your knees, humble yourself, and take responsibility at the feet of your Savior. Instead of wasting your breath on blaming others, accept the charge of your own sin. Then instead of closing off and hiding from God, welcome His conviction. Instead of explaining to God "why," ask God "how" to stop your sinful habits. His mercy and forgiveness will fill your heart and help you find balance. So whatever it is that you find yourself struggling with today, swallow your pride and claim the blame. Our Savior died on the cross so that when we come to Him with wreckage, we can leave forever changed. Satan may use others as a tool of temptation, but ultimately you determine your steps. So will accusation or confession fill the words of your breath?

Prompt: What is one thing that you make excuses for that is actually just laziness in disguise?

_____

_____

_____

_____

_____

_____

_____

_____

_____

_____

_____

_____

_____

FEBRUARY 28

Luke 12:13–21

I heard this preached in church yesterday, and I want you to think about it... "We have blessed ourselves into misery." We have made means more attainable in abundance for significantly less energy. We have the world's knowledge at the tip of our fingers and the ability to speak to someone at any time. We do not grow our food anymore; now, we order it to our house so we can skip the line. We have the most knowledge of any generation and the most advancement than we have ever had before. So shouldn't we technically be happier because we have everything and more? But look at the rates of depression, anxiety, and suicide—it's evident that we are not living in harmony. We might be shiny on the outside, but we as a society are rotting internally. Because an accumulation of "stuff" does not translate to an abundance of contentment. Throwing "things" at a broken heart will not mend it. The newest iPhone or trendy shoes will not bring you joy that lasts. It will be like a flickering light that burns fast. Our true contentment can only be found in Jesus, and if we keep looking to the world, we will grow further from finding Him. We must stop looking to external goods to make us happy and find peace from the Holy Spirit within. I promise that the world will never be able to provide you peace and authentic, lasting satisfaction. Our joy is rooted; it's not a response or reaction.

Prompt: What brings you joy? Is your joy dependent upon external circumstances or inner peace?

_____

_____

_____

_____

_____

_____

_____

_____

_____

_____

_____

_____

MARCH

MARCH 1

Proverbs 20:15

Have you ever been around someone who exudes wisdom and knowledge with ease? They speak significant words that hit deep like it's a breeze. I bet you valued your time with them, and I bet you seek out their company as often as you can. In our world, wisdom is in high demand. It's a gift from God, and it's one of the spiritual gifts that God freely gives to everyone who asks for a portion. In other words...we have the right to claim our fortune. Think about that wise role model in your life once again; now, what if that was you? What if someone else needed greater knowledge, and you were who they turned to? As a Christian, this idea of being a wise person should not be a far-fetched idea because it's our inheritance. We should be boasting in our God-given wisdom from a place of gratitude, not arrogance. God wants us to seek wisdom, which is why He has provided us with the ability to receive it in abundance. Instead of seeking society's intellect, let's seek God's spiritual substance. Wisdom is a rare gift these days, but it's in very high demand. It's just another avenue to extend a helping hand. Would you rather be popular and trendy or steadfast and wise? We each have the opportunity to be truth-givers in a world full of lies. Let's be deep wells in a world full of shallow springs. Let's focus less on wants and more on needs. Let's ask God for more wisdom, and let's speak that knowledge to all who will hear. Here is the thing about true wisdom...it will find hungry ears.

Prompt: Who is your role model, and what have they done to earn that privilege? Who do you think you are a role model for, and why?

_____

_____

_____

_____

_____

_____

_____

_____

_____

_____

_____

_____

MARCH 2

Hebrews 10:26–31

It is true that God's mercy is endless, but what happens when your sin is endless also? You can say that you have surrendered, but how can you be a follower if you do not follow? I think this is where the mercy of God gets abused, and the judgment of God is forgotten. God will forgive you of your sin, but He cannot continue to replant new seeds around fruit that is rotten. Salvation is not a free pass to sin; it's an invitation of conviction. It's not living a life of pleasurable freedom; it's willingly and joyfully living with restrictions. It does not mean that you will not mess up, but it does mean you should be actively working towards making less of a mess. Christ did not die on the cross so that you could freely and habitually transgress. We will all fall short and sin every day, but we should not be a slave to our sins. Pay attention to the areas you are asking for forgiveness in again and again. If your heart is bound to God, then the habits of the flesh will slowly fade away. It does not mean that you will be perfect; it just means that you should not commit the same sin again every day. Habits are not mistakes, and routines are not slip-ups; they are established and deliberate. And if it's gone past the point of being a decision, then ask for deliverance. Sin is not ever "just the way that you are" or "something you will always deal with," Jesus died so that you would be free! Every time you choose sin over righteousness, you are nailing Him to that tree.

Prompt: What is a sin that you repeatedly commit every day? What is holding you back from freedom from that sin?

_____

_____

_____

_____

_____

_____

_____

_____

_____

_____

_____

_____

MARCH 3

Matthew 26:14–16

I find it interesting that Judas asked the chief priests, "What are you willing to give me?" When he was in the act of betrayal. Reading those words this morning was absolutely painful. Why? Because those are the exact words that we speak in the moments that we choose to sin. You might not voice them out loud, but they are being spoken from within. Think about it; you would not sin if it was not going to provide you with some form of treasure. So we ask the question and weigh the odds between righteousness and pleasure. If you change the lens of sin from a mistake to a betrayal, how does that affect your demeanor? What if you thought about the fact that your sin was equated to handing over the redeemer? With God, we never have to question what He will provide us in return for our commitment; the cross answered that question. So if you are inquiring about an action's worth, chances are it's a transgression. Not only did Judas intend to betray, but he went to the Last Supper knowing what he had done. He decided to act like nothing had happened even though the betrayal had begun. Jesus knew his actions and still chose to wash his feet. God does the same thing for you and for me. If you are questioning an action's worth, run to the answer instead. He has already proved that He loves you by breaking His body, just drink the wine and eat the bread.

Prompt: Name a time that you felt betrayed and how that made you feel. How has the relationship with the person who betrayed you played out? Has there been amends or forgiveness?

_____
_____
_____
_____
_____
_____
_____
_____
_____
_____
_____
_____
_____
_____

MARCH 4

2 Timothy 4:1–2

We were not created to live for self; we were created to live for service. Our life is not meant to be full of pleasure; it is meant to be full of purpose. We lose sight of God's call on our life when we separate His will from our wants. When we live for ourselves instead of living for the Son. Your relationship with God is not routine; it should be deeper than Sunday morning. It's a constant relationship that should be growing and forming. You must be in love with Him in every season, not just in times of convenience. You must welcome the spirit of conviction and live a life of obedience. You were created for a purpose, I cannot tell you the details, but I can assure you that it is for more than self-fulfillment. How will other people come to know God if you keep your relationship in concealment? How do you testify the good news on a daily basis? Do you openly share? Or keep it reserved for safe places? Are you in love with God enough to lose the love of others that do not agree with your alignment? Or would you choose accommodating others over your God-given assignment? Our purpose can easily be lost in routine and self-pursuit. We were made for community, not made for solitude. How are you spreading the love of God and walking out your purpose? How is your life resembling a life of service? If you are unsure, pray for conviction and direction. Your life should resemble God's reflection.

Prompt: Who is someone that you know *of* but want to get to *actually* know? How can you make plans to get to know them on a deeper level? What is stopping you from doing so?

_____

_____

_____

_____

_____

_____

_____

_____

_____

_____

_____

_____

MARCH 5

Luke 10:38–42

Have you ever thought about the fact that the Lord called us to work hard, but He never called us to be busy? Our efforts of hard work will be rewarded, but unnecessary busyness can be risky. I am not implying that your to-do list is a waste of time and should therefore be thrown away. I am simply stating that we must be more mindful of how we spend our day. Are we working hard for the Lord, or are we too busy focusing our minds on filler? Have we become so focused on living this life to the "fullest" that we have ignored the life-giver? Do we disguise our work as servanthood only to avoid spending time with our Father? Are you aware of God's plan in your life, or are you too busy trying to be your own author? It is a shame how many blessings we miss because we are too busy to realize that they are there. It is like we are communally so focused on our own lives that we are caught in an incessant stare. God loves diligent servants, but He requires our hearts to be set on Him. We must trust the ways of this world will always fail to satisfy the Spirit that is within. If Jesus came up to you today...be honest...would you have time to talk with Him in your schedule? Every day, we choose something that is useless over something that is special. Work hard for the Lord, but do not become so busy that you miss the blessings that you do not have planned. God is trying to give you a gift, but He cannot give it to you when you have full hands.

Prompt: What is one thing you could give up to have more time for meditation and reflection? What would happen if you gave that up?

_____

_____

_____

_____

_____

_____

_____

_____

_____

_____

_____

_____

_____

MARCH 6

Matthew 26:57–63

We were not created to be "worst care scenario" kind of people or pessimistic thinkers. Finding fault in everything is not part of God's nature. But in a broken world, it's easy to get caught up in negativity and the predictability of catastrophe. It's hard to trust in goodwill when all you see is tragedy. If you look for fault or darkness, you will find it; that is why you have to change your lens. We must highlight the goodness of humanity instead of broadcasting only sin. Even the most righteous, giving person can be painted as the enemy. Jesus Himself was killed for His supposed sin when, in fact, He was the remedy. What good will come from focusing on the bad in other people? Proving that another has failed will not cause anyone to heal. God instructed us to keep our minds fixed on things that are pure, good, lovely, honorable, and true. Do not focus on the broken; focus on the possibility of a broken piece being made new. What do you have to lose besides the weight of negativity? What virtue are you overlooking while searching for pessimistic validity? If you spend more time accusing than you do loving, how will you ever resemble Jesus? Spend more time fixing and less time showcasing other's broken pieces. If you fill your mind with the bad, your heart and soul will follow. You were made to be full of hope, not drenched in sorrow.

Prompt: What media outlets uplift you? What media outlets drain you? How much time do you give to each? How could you spend that time instead?

_____

_____

_____

_____

_____

_____

_____

_____

_____

_____

_____

_____

MARCH 7

Acts 18:9–11

God will never lead you past the point of His protection. If He encourages you to go one way, you can trust in His direction. We come in contact with trials and pushbacks because of the free will of man—not the plan of our Father. His plans were not made for us to struggle; they were established so that we would prosper. That is why it is so important to live our lives according to God's will and not through the lens of our own discretion. We see through the distorted lens of this broken world that is set on our desires and obsessions. God's plan has everything to do with your success, but it has nothing to do with your understanding. We must humble ourselves to view God's plan as compassionate, not demanding. He is not a ruler that points His finger in a direction and demands that His servants begin to walk. He points His finger, grabs your hand, and matches your step while listening to you talk. He senses our hesitations and reassures our souls in the midst of uncertainty. When we feel lost, hopeless, or insignificant—He reminds us that we are worthy. He is not impatient, He is not in a rush, and He does not put more on you than He knows you can handle. All He needs is your surrender and for you to follow Christ's example. He will never call you in the direction of misfortune because His plan for your life was designed for good. We must follow without a doubt even when the plan is not understood.

Prompt: What would happen if you took action toward the one goal that scares you the most?

_____
_____
_____
_____
_____
_____
_____
_____
_____
_____
_____
_____
_____
_____

MARCH 8

Isaiah 42:10–17

If you are a born-again Christian, I want you to take a moment and think back on your life previously. It is easy to pinpoint when you were saved because the change happened immediately. You may look back on your life and not even recognize the person of the past. When God begins to move in your life, change happens—and it happens fast. Although all of our previous lifestyles differ, I think we all can agree that being born again ignores a flame in all of us that is inextinguishable. Our flame burns on the fuel of His grace instead of the sustenance of trouble. Words that once filled our mouths now have no place in our minds, let alone a place in our vocabulary. The fear and worry that once defined us is now just a tool of the adversary. The dark days fade away, and a new light becomes visible as it radiates every situation. You trade worry and gossip for prayer and meditation. Not because you are trying to "become a new creation" —you simply are, in fact, a new creation. You depend on God's purpose and plan, not the world's standards and limitations. All of this is to say being born again is the beginning of a lifestyle of outcry. It is impossible to remain silent or accept living on standby. Do not be ashamed of your new-found freedom or of your past ways. Be proud of the creation He has formed you into—the broken vessel of the past was a phase.

Prompt: What parts of you still feel broken? What parts of you do you wish God would "fix"? Ask Him to help restore those things.

_____

_____

_____

_____

_____

_____

_____

_____

_____

_____

_____

_____

_____

MARCH 9

Isaiah 51:12–16

Did you know that, as a child of God, fear does not have to be part of your experience? You do not have to walk through life anxious or drenched in weariness. It's easy to believe on a good day, but what about on a day when your world seems to be collapsing? What do you do when the good thoughts are fleeting, and the negative thoughts are lasting? On the good days, toss an anchor out and allow it to latch on tight to the "good day" ground. Then on the days when the storms pick up, you will know where stability is found. Anchor onto a Bible verse, a worship song, or a word from the Lord. Recite it, declare it, scream it if you need to! Whatever helps you move forward. We were made to withstand the storm, so when one comes, greet it like an expected houseguest. It's not an opportunity for you to be at your worst; it's an opportunity for God to show you His best. You are allowed to feel anxious, scared, or overwhelmed, but do not allow it to become your identity. You are not intended for stress; you are intended for serenity. You were not created to bow to the storm; you were created to walk with the Father on the waves. This world might destroy, but our God saves. What are your anchors in times of fear? What realigns your soul to peace? Remember, in order to allow an anchor to take hold, you have to first release.

Prompt: What makes you feel calm in the midst of fear? Why?

_____

_____

_____

_____

_____

_____

_____

_____

_____

_____

_____

_____

_____

MARCH 10

Proverbs 27:10

Friendships are a gift from God, and to me, they are a representation of divine intervention. Family was given by birthright, but friends come into your life with God's purpose and intention. Some friendships are unending, and some are seasonal, but all have a purpose in the grand scheme of your story. But we often do not cherish a commodity when we have an abundance of inventory. Think about your friends of the present and your friends of the past. Think about the years that have gone by and the memories that last. Why did God bring that friend into your life? And why was that other friend there for a season? I will boldly state that I believe every friend is there for a reason. I have been through a few friendship heartbreaks, but I do not regret the friendship that was cultivated. I learned that love is simple, but people are complicated. I've unfortunately not cherished some friends, and I've given some friends too much weight. But I will not overlook the fact that each friendship brought something into my life that was or still is great. To all of my friends, I want to say I'm grateful for you and for your companionship and love. Each of you has uniquely modeled a piece of heaven above. I am honored to have people in my life that love me by choice, not just because of blood relation. Every friendship has been part of my current formation. Call one or two of your friends today, and express your gratitude for their affection. It is not by happenstance that God formed these connections.

Prompt: Who is a friend that you are most grateful for today, and why? What friend do you miss most from your past, and what is stopping your friendship from continuing?

_____

_____

_____

_____

_____

_____

_____

_____

_____

_____

MARCH 11

Luke 17:1–3

We will sin. I think there is no arguing that it is not "if" but "when." We are imperfect humans living on a flawed planet, attempting to serve a perfect creator. We do have to take responsibility for our behavior. It's okay to mess up every now and then, but Jesus explained how causing others to sin is a massive mistake. It is sinful of us to mess with someone else's fate. We must be aware of our own sin but hyper-aware of how our sin might be causing another person to stumble. God gives us grace when we make mistakes, but we do not need to drag anyone else into our trouble. The example that is coming to my mind right this moment is bringing someone else into a lie. You give them an ultimatum that in order to be your friend, they must not tell the truth but deny it. That is not being a friend; that is dragging another person into a burning building with you. Shame on us for ever making someone else's life hard to go through. Same goes for drinking alcohol; do not peer pressure a person, even if it is a "lighthearted" gesture. Why would we drag people down when we have the opportunity to make them better? We have a duty to serve Jesus and serve others well. That service means leading them toward heaven, not hell. I take full responsibility for my sin, and I do not ever want to be the cause of someone else having to ask for forgiveness. Let's be friends who influence righteousness, not instigate the need for repentance.

Prompt: How might your sin impact others? Do you feel like you are an influential person? Why or why not?

_____
_____
_____
_____
_____
_____
_____
_____
_____
_____
_____
_____
_____

MARCH 12

Psalm 119:158–160

It's easy to look upon unbelievers with disbelief when you are a believer…does that make sense? It's hard to see others "think" that they have it good when they don't even know what good is. But that is a slippery slope of judgment and an even more slippery slope to pushing them away. Why would someone want to listen to what a judgmental person has to say? I have been in situations before where an unbeliever was asking me for advice, and the only advice I could give them was Jesus. They wanted the puzzle pieced back together, but they did not even have the pieces. It can be frustrating, annoying, and at times even maddening. When they could have the cure to the problem that is happening. But that is not our place to judge, and it's not our place to inflict our opinions upon them. Trying to tell people they are lost won't necessarily help them win. And if you find pleasure in watching others lose, then that is a personal problem that you need to address with God. Remember… we are all broken and flawed. Do not be amazed when an unbeliever comes to you with problems that seem pointless. Life is overwhelming when you are the master of your own choices. Love them well, be there for them, and lead them to Christ by example. Do not roll your eyes and make them feel like their life is too difficult to handle.

Prompt: Who is someone in your life that doesn't know Jesus, and how could you point them toward Him today?

_____
_____
_____
_____
_____
_____
_____
_____
_____
_____
_____
_____
_____
_____

MARCH 13

Psalm 32:6-7

It's okay to lack self-confidence, but we must try and have God-confidence. We must be certain of His goodness in the hidden and the obvious. It's okay to take the pressure off of your shoulders and hand the pressure to Him. It's way easier to put faith in who God is than in who you have been. If you face the world on the basis of your daily portion of confidence, you will be left with inconsistency because your inner dialogue of self-worth and expectations change minutely. There is no place in the Bible that talks about the importance of self-belief. The fruits of the Spirit say nothing about having self-esteem. That is all from the world, and it adds a layer of complication to our lives and minds. It leads us on an endless search for something we were never meant to find. But if your confidence is in God, there will never be a reason to worry or doubt. He will give you what you need and take away what you need to be without. If God is your refuge and hiding place, then you cannot take refuge in yourself too. If you have confidence and faith in God, then you do not need to have faith in yourself. I promise that you will crack under pressure because you were not built to carry the heaviness. Too much of you and not enough God leads to a big mess. If your world revolves around your abilities, take inventory of your confidence. Your worth is found in Christ Jesus, not in your perceived amount of competence.

Prompt: What is the biggest weight on your shoulders right now? How would it feel to get rid of it? Ask God to help lift the burden.

_____
_____
_____
_____
_____
_____
_____
_____
_____
_____
_____
_____

MARCH 14

Acts 4:32–37

The world has taught us that we work hard for our possessions, and by doing so, we "earn" them as if each thing in life was something that we have to win. This mentality of working for "things" is dangerous because it places the result on the work itself. It shifts our minds from diligence to dominance and from hard work to wealth. We earn so that we can take claim of certain things, which leads to a false sense of authority. Instead of having mutual respect for all of mankind, we begin ranking based on seniority. We accumulate stuff only to desire what we do not have at the moment. Suddenly our peers begin to persecute us because our colleagues are now seen as our opponents. All for what reason...a promotion, a bonus, or an award or recognition? Our world has normalized slander in order to gain a higher-ranking position. So we work our way up the ladder of life for more titles and more possessions. But by filling our heads with selfish ambition, we fail to recognize the Lord's lessons. Nothing we could ever earn in this lifetime is our own because our life itself is our Father's. We can either get caught up in the waves of wealth or wait humbly for the promises that God has to offer. You did not "earn" that high-paying job or promotion; you received a blessing of God's favor. You cannot take credit for the good in life, but in the bad, admit you need a Savior. The things of this world will pass away; it is time that we focus on the eternal reward. It's about praising God for His everlasting blessings—not about what we can or cannot afford.

Prompt: If you had all of the money in the world, what would change about your life? What would you want to stay the same?

_____

_____

_____

_____

_____

_____

_____

_____

_____

_____

_____

MARCH 15

Proverbs 12:10

If you are kind in your core, then you will be kind to your community. If kindness is your custom, it will be expressed at every opportunity. The closer your steps align with Jesus, the more kind your heart will become. It will not be something that you actively pursue; it will just be done. You will not have to fake it or grit your teeth behind a smile because the joy will be sincere. Not because you will overlook human flaws but because you will see it clearly. True kindness springs up from the well of joy which is given to those who accept salvation. It's easy to show others love when you are living a life of adoration. If you want to know the status of someone's soul, see how they treat all living things in their environment. Do they have a spirit of humility or a spirit of entitlement? And by "they," I mean "you" because we should focus on our hearts, not the shortcomings of another's. So ask yourself this question: am I more of an adversary or a lover? Am I kind to my community, to the animals, people, and environment? Am I naturally caring or quick to be violent? Am I short-tempered or patient with everyday life situations? Do I showcase sensitivity or just aggravation? The status of our soul is showcased in our day-to-day lives. Your reactions are just your faith on display in disguise. If you cannot be kind to a stranger, then I doubt your natural posture is compassion. Your soul is on display with every word, every response, and every reaction.

Prompt: Do you more often treat others the way you *want* to be treated or treat others the way that they *treat* you? How does it feel to treat someone well when they treat you poorly?

_____

_____

_____

_____

_____

_____

_____

_____

_____

_____

_____

_____

MARCH 16

Romans 1:8–10

It's easy to thank God for what He does in your life, but how often do you thank Him for what others do? We tend to get so caught up in the pursuit of God that we forget that we are being pursued. If I asked you: Do you think God uses you? I am sure that your answer would be yes. So if you are included in the works, why wouldn't others be included in the process? I think too often we wait for our blessings to come straight from heaven or our answers to be spoken from the mouth of God. We want a direct connection because we fear that anything less is a fraud. But if you avoid the words of another, you might just be missing the audible voice of the Almighty. It might not come the way you expected it but do not discount it if it's timely. We are the body of Christ, dependent on the Lord but working together in unison. Teamwork is not just necessary; it's lucrative. If you are a servant of God, and I am a servant of God, what do we have in common besides our title? Isn't it our job to build the kingdom and spread the good news of the Bible? Allow the craftsmanship of the body of Christ to soak into your soul. Allow the comprehension to sink in that you are a piece, not the whole. As you thank God for His mercy today, also thank Him for the way He uses other people on a daily basis. If you choose to recognize God's work, you will begin to see His love on other people's faces.

Prompt: If you had to create a team of eight people, who would those people be? Why?

_____

_____

_____

_____

_____

_____

_____

_____

_____

_____

_____

_____

MARCH 17

Luke 3:21–23

Society likes to convince us that we are all late to the party, and if we don't have life figured out by the time we are twenty-five, then it's too late. I think the expectation of college and career has accelerated this need to know your fate. I am currently twenty-seven years old, and I have spent the last five years trying to figure my life out. I have walked through many doors with hope and come back through the same doors with doubt. I have believed the lie that I am "too late to start something new" because all of my friends have found their careers. But recently, I found freedom from that comparison by allowing God to affirm my journey instead of my peers. Jesus did not even begin His ministry until He was thirty years old, and then He was crucified when He was thirty-three. If God only needed Jesus for three years, I trust that He knows what is best for me. It does not matter how old or young you are; God has a plan that often does not align with society's status quo. Your time will come but don't discount all of the time you spent learning to grow. We give way too much weight to careers. Jesus was a carpenter way longer than He spent walking in His ministry. God's plans unfold a little differently. God designed you to be unique, and that extends into the way that He uses you during your time on this earth. Our timeline is none of the world's concern.

Prompt: Is there anything that you want to do in life but feel like you are too late to start? What would happen if you did it?

_____

_____

_____

_____

_____

_____

_____

_____

_____

_____

_____

_____

MARCH 18

1 Corinthians 15:33–34

Do not allow naive thinking to override your convictions. Whether we think so or not, our environment impacts our decisions. I do not care how confident you are or how self-disciplined you attempt to be. We still are influenced by our surroundings and replicate what we see. Paul writes to the church of Corinth that "bad company corrupts good character." He did not explicitly state participation; he just referred to negative influences being there. We already know how actively sinning will produce negative personal results, but have you ever thought about the sins around you? Have you ever thought about your own morality being shaped by what others do? The truth is that even though you might not be doing it, seeing it be done normalizes the negative behavior. The normalization of sin is the slippery slope into danger. Because if others do it around you, it begins to numb your moral senses. Soon enough, the offenses become a lot less offensive. Just because something is routine does not make it righteous. Your association is where you develop your likeness. So, be careful about what you say and do, but also about who you surround yourself with. Your environment plays a major role in the life that you live. Surround yourself with a good crowd that is seeking morality and righteousness. Do not sit back and let negative influences take control, choose your circle and where you spend your time with mindfulness.

Prompt: They say that we become a combination of the five people that we spend the most time with. Who are your five people? Are you happy with being a combination of these people? Why or why not, and who would you add instead?

MARCH 19

Malachi 3:13–15

Arrogance comes to life in many different forms, but it is always loud. It cannot hide away like a timid thought because it is far too proud. It's easy to spot the arrogance in other people because it usually rubs us the wrong way. Their actions seem aggressive, and so do the words that they say. But what about the arrogance within our own spirit? Are we aware of its existence? Do we acknowledge it with regard or with resistance? I am not just talking about societal arrogance and our outward appearance to cultural norms. Arrogance is not rooted in whether or not you conform. It's rooted in your spirit and radiates in every action of your day. It is opposing surrender because you want to do it your own way. In what ways is your spirit arrogant? In what ways are you patting yourself on the back for your excellence? How are you treating other people? And what lens do you see them through? In what ways has your arrogance clouded that view? I know these are a lot of questions, but only you have the answer to them. God's kingdom will never grow if you are only concerned with whether or not you win. Arrogance is sneaky, it's cruel, and it's dangerous. It advances your self-confidence and inhibits your ability to be gracious. Because why would you need to surrender if you could do it better alone? Instead of being a know-it-all, what if you just allowed yourself to be known?

Prompt: What inflates your ego? Why?

_____

_____

_____

_____

_____

_____

_____

_____

_____

_____

_____

_____

MARCH 20

Romans 13:11–14

If you knew for a fact that Jesus was coming back today at noon, how would you choose to live your day? Would you spend time with your family, worship, and praise, or simply meditate and pray? I could ask 500 people for their answers, and all 500 would be unique to their own hearts. Whether praising God for their final moments on Earth or eager for their heavenly start. Out of all the ways our moments would be spent differently, there is one equalizing factor that would be common, and that is righteous behavior. We all would make sure that our last moments would be glorifying to our Savior. We do not know the day or hour of our Lord's return, but we are living in the end times, so we must be ready. In the turbulent waters of the decaying world, we must hold steady. We must expect Him at every moment and fill our seconds with work that is pleasing to Him. If Jesus knocked on your door unexpectedly, would you be too embarrassed to let Him in? We are broken, imperfect beings, but we need to stop using our imperfections as an excuse for unrighteousness. Do not blame it on confusion when it was just a lack of compliance. Practice evaluating how you spend your time, and if it is not glorifying the Lord, then stop and give your attention to something else. We must learn to commit our minds to higher callings and regulate ourselves. Set alarms throughout your day at times when you may be tempted to give in to meaningless behavior. So that, at the moment that He returns, we are proud to meet our Savior.

Prompt: If you knew today was your last day, how would you live it? Be detailed in your description.

_____

_____

_____

_____

_____

_____

_____

_____

_____

_____

_____

MARCH 21

Daniel 7:15–16

When you have negative thoughts, do you ever ask God why you are having them? Too often, we accept them as "normal," and by doing so, we allow them to win. Maybe it's negative self-talk or even a scary bad dream that haunts our night. Do you ask God for revelation, or do you just accept the fright? I am guilty of giving way too much credit to Satan and allowing him the privilege of claiming those thoughts. I attribute them to him, as if doing so allows him to be caught. I have a bad dream and blame him for the haunting night of distress. Instead of asking God for healing, I just accept that I lost rest. The same goes for negative self-talk or thoughts about other people that are hateful or ill-informed. Instead of asking God why I had them, I just accept them as part of the world's broken norm. I think I need to ask God for more interpretations instead of just accepting thoughts that are intrusive. I want my mind to be a place of righteousness, not a residency for thoughts that are abusive. We do not have to settle for negative thoughts or scary dreams; God has called us into so much more than that. Our default should be peace and joy, not hateful, scared, and sad. Satan does not have power over your life, not even a single thought of your day, so do not let him have it. Intrusive, scary thoughts are not meant to be something that we just allow to happen. Get curious, and get protective over your mind because it is sacred. It's a house of righteousness, not a residency of fear and hatred.

Prompt: What is one thing you wish you could change about yourself? What is one thing that you would *never* change about yourself?

_____

_____

_____

_____

_____

_____

_____

_____

_____

_____

_____

March 22

1 Corinthians 14:18–19

Spiritual gifts are a blessing given to us in a supernatural way by God Himself. They are not given to elevate our status; they are given to help. Tongues are the one gift that God gives freely to everyone if they ask to receive them with the right heart. It's easy for your spiritual ego to be inflated when the spiritual gifts start. Speaking in tongues does not make you more "spiritual" than another, and if it is causing pride to rise up, then it's better to stop. If it's only making you feel better, then it's best not to. I remember praying for the gift of tongues for the sole reason that I felt less holy than my peers. God did not give me the gift of tongues until my "why" changed, and that took years. We all want a little bit more from God, but ask yourself this question— "What am I doing with what He has already given me?" Are you properly utilizing the gifts that you have received? Are you using the gift to better serve Him, or is the gift only serving yourself? When you speak in tongues, is it edifying the church, or is it providing any help? Is prophesying inflating your ego, or is it elevating the name of Jesus Christ? Are the gifts that God has given you being used to impact more than just your life? I am grateful for the gifts I have been given, but I will be the first to admit that I do not use them to their full potential. They shouldn't be self-promoting; they should be influential. They should bring you closer to God, not make you feel above others. Your gift is not just about you; it's about impacting your sisters and brothers.

Prompt: What is something that you are naturally good at that others are not? How do you use this gift?

_____

_____

_____

_____

_____

_____

_____

_____

_____

_____

_____

MARCH 23

John 21:15–19

God is not interested in leaving us behind and allowing us to reside in our place of mistake. His interest is in making us new and allowing us to be saved. So when we sin and fail, He is not content until we overcome that sin. He is not at peace until the restoration process begins. Take this scripture as an example, Jesus reinstated Simon Peter. He went from being the betrayer to the church leader. Jesus asked him a question three times just to ensure that Peter's mistake was washed clean. Jesus fought for Peter and wanted him on His team. In what ways has Jesus fought for you? How has He restored your life and washed you clean? What has been your version of "Peter...will you feed My sheep?" Can you think about a time when Jesus relentlessly pursued your restoration? When He fought for your salvation? I can, and my prayer is that you can too. I hope that, at the very least, you are reminded that Jesus does not want you to lose. He wants your redemption; He wants you to be following in His footsteps. He hates when you are walking on the path of self-pursuit and missing what is best. But He is patient with us, and He has no expiration date on His forgiveness. We can spend a lifetime making mistakes, and He will forgive us in minutes. We can be at our lowest and trust that He will be there to lift us back up. His judgment is far overshadowed by His love.

Prompt: Recount a battle that God helped you fight. How did it feel to have His help?

_____

_____

_____

_____

_____

_____

_____

_____

_____

_____

_____

_____

_____

MARCH 24

Psalm 47

When was the last time that you sang praises to the Lord out loud? Was it last Sunday when the worship team was singing, and you were in the crowd? Or was it yesterday evening on your drive home from work or as you were showering for the day? I am talking about vocalizing worship, not the prayers that you pray. God does not need a perfect tune, just the genuine outpouring of your heart. If you do not know where to begin, opening your mouth is a great place to start. The psalms of David and the hymns of your time were all created with cries. They never would have been known if they were not vocalized. I do not think that we are all called to vocational worship, but I do think that we are all called to sing. That can be home alone or in your car; it does not have to be on a stage or as a part of a worship team. God gave you a voice, and He is pleased when you use it to glorify Him. Praising is an outpouring so that you can welcome more of God in. At some point today, open your mouth to heaven and vocalize your praise. A great place to start is by blessing God's name. Sing out loud to worship music or harmonize alone. It can be something remembered or something unknown. Try and make it a habit or a natural part of your daily rhythms. It's not an added task, just an alternate addition. Give God **five** minutes of your time that you otherwise would have given to a TV, podcast, book, or radio. If you do it once, I promise that the five minutes a day will multiply and grow.

Prompt: How often do you sing out loud? What is your favorite song to sing?

_____
_____
_____
_____
_____
_____
_____
_____
_____
_____
_____
_____

March 25

1 Timothy 4:6–10

It's really easy to mistake old sayings for Scripture. And put your trust in things that sound moral or familiar. But just because it's been said for centuries does not make it biblical. Something is not righteous just because it's traditional. That is where discernment and discipline become crucial in the establishment of right and wrong. It's easy to flip through the pages of Scripture and see what does reign true and where we have been wrong all along. We cannot be people who fall willingly into wrong beliefs or unbiblical teaching. Our understanding of Scripture must be deeper than just accepting what the pastor is preaching. Just like these journal entries that I write every day, they are inspired by the Word of God, but they are not written in red. Don't believe things because they sound good; believe what He has said. Do not fall into the trap of unbelief because you were quick to believe everything. Old sayings and Scriptures are not the same. The best way to know the truth is to know the Word of God and compare all that you hear to Scripture. Let's be people that examine, study, and consider. We have access to the written Word of God and to the creator directly. There is no excuse for us to claim truth incorrectly. We must be scholars of Scripture and inspectors of counterfeit truths. If it isn't biblical, do not believe it; the Scripture provides the proof.

Prompt: What is one thing you believed as a kid that you realized is actually not true? How did realizing this impact your life?

_____
_____
_____
_____
_____
_____
_____
_____
_____
_____
_____
_____
_____
_____

MARCH 26

Hebrews 12:7–11

Discipline truly is the greatest form of love, although it might not seem like it all of the time. That's because the sentiment is usually hidden under an opposing emotion that is difficult or impossible to find. But the motivation for discipline is always love, safety, or just all-around improvement. There is always intention behind a discipline; it's never solely for amusement. Think about your childhood and some of the moments that you were reprimanded. It was only in the moments that you had not practiced what they had commanded. God is the same way, except infinitely more loving and always seeking your benefit. His sternly expressed commandments are actually drenched in sentiment. Why does He convict you for your sinful behavior even though it makes you feel bad at the moment? Because that sin is destructive, and He knows it. He does not slap your hand to embarrass you; He slaps it to keep you from touching the fire. He does not want to change you; just change your desires. Same goes for self-discipline; it's an act of self-care. Setting parameters for yourself even if no one else knows that they are there. Do not run away from discipline; if anything, run towards it and embrace it. Problematic behavior will not disappear unless you face it. Thank God for strict guidelines and boundaries that keep you safe. Instead of cursing God for moving you, thank Him for not letting you stay in the same place.

Prompt: What rules did you hate as a kid? What rules do you hate today? Is there any correlation between the two?

_____

_____

_____

_____

_____

_____

_____

_____

_____

_____

_____

_____

MARCH 27

James 4:11–12

What good is accomplished when bad is spoken? What can possibly be mended by being more broken? Speaking slander of others might feel good at the moment, but what outcomes does it produce? We should never find pleasure in words of abuse. The reality is people *will* disappoint us, make us angry, and cause us to lose our patience. But it's our responsibility not to allow their behavior to influence how we behave. Two wrongs do not make a right, and slandering another for their actions does not fix anything. Gossip and "venting" are dangerous forms of self-medicating. How do we stop our habit of slander? How do we keep quiet about others' mistakes or sins? The answer is—instead of letting words out, let God in. Before you open your mouth in emotion, open your heart to Jesus. Instead of labeling people as "wrong," just remind yourself that they have a weakness. Instead of unloading your frustrations about another to another, first, ask God why you are so emotional about this. God does not want people's mistakes to become your responsibility; He wants them to become His. So, next time you are about to open your mouth to emotional accusations, take them to God first. Slander will never make a bad person better; it will only make good people worse.

Prompt: What do you regret saying the most? Who did you say it to? What do you wish you would have said instead?

_____

_____

_____

_____

_____

_____

_____

_____

_____

_____

_____

_____

_____

MARCH 28

Exodus 20:4–6

If someone were to ask you plainly: "Do you put anything before your God?" I would guess that your answer would be "No!" We have to examine what we give our attention to because what we focus on grows. It is easy to proclaim your allegiance to God, but take a moment and examine your praises. Are they fully engulfed by God, or do you lift certain things higher depending on life's phases? For instance, when you get a new job or a promotion at work, do you speak more about your work environment than you do about the Spirit? Is your relationship with the Lord constant, or do you only sing Him praises when others can hear them? Do you wake up each day and thank the Lord for opening your eyes or praise your cup of coffee for the energy? The line is often blurred between praising something and being complimentary. You might think it's silly to compare a relationship with God to the dependency on a cup of coffee, but what is your first thought in the morning? And it does not have to be coffee; it could be Facebook—this is simply just a subtle warning. Do you put other things before God? The answer is yes; unfortunately, we all do. But we must be extremely careful of what and who we sing our praises to. God commanded us not to make an image that we bow down to, and that does not just mean a golden idol. Let's be sure to live in a way where we are truly only dependent on God for survival.

Prompt: Name five things that you could not live without and why you could not live without them. What would happen if they were taken away?

_____

_____

_____

_____

_____

_____

_____

_____

_____

_____

_____

MARCH 29

John 6:25–59

It is important to work hard, but do not work so hard for the world that you forget the real work you were called to do. We were not created to see the same way the world sees; there is a different lens that we are called to look through. That is why we need to stop comparing ourselves to the world's standards and start measuring ourselves against God's Word. We need to be diligent about studying God's commandments, not just operating based on information that we have heard. What good is working for bread today if you will just be hungry again tomorrow? You can't take ownership of something that you are only allowed to borrow. That is why our nourishment must come from the bread of life, not the stale bread of *this* life. We can either live in the fullness of our salvation or live in the overwhelming atmosphere of strife. It is important that we choose our nourishment carefully because what we put in, you will get out. This life is an endurance race of obstacles, and if you do not fuel properly, you will fail to complete the workout. So would you rather eat day to day and spend your time praying for your nourishment needs to be met? Or would you rather eat once from the bread of life and eternally be set? Would you rather work for the day or work towards eternity? I don't know about you...but I am trading my crumbs for certainty.

Prompt: What do you want your legacy to be? What are you doing today to impact that legacy?

_____

_____

_____

_____

_____

_____

_____

_____

_____

_____

_____

_____

MARCH 30

Matthew 10:16–20

It's easy to read the Gospels and cast judgment onto the disciples for their mistakes and hesitation. It's easy to read about their doubt now and judge their dedication. But we are on this side of the cross, with years of teaching and a Bible that resembles a blueprint. We read about their life, but it was actually the life that they lived. And Jesus did not sugarcoat His commands to them; He actually was extremely blunt. Telling them openly that they would be greatly persecuted up front. Telling them to be sheep among wolves and to be calm in the face of persecution. And you know what...they did it, even though they were riddled with confusion. If they did it then, how much more should we be willing to do it now? They were instructed to "do," and we are instructed "how." Are we willing to be sheep among wolves, or would we rather blend in for the sake of personal comfort? Do our priorities in life, or His, come first? I would like to think that I would have been a committed disciple, but I sometimes struggle with my dedication, even in this day in age. And I have read every account of Scripture and gotten instruction page by page. My goal is to check my actions and see if I am behaving like a sheep. I want to live like a believer, no matter what backlash I receive. The disciples were essential for the work of Jesus, as well as for our faith. I want to walk the talk and live what I claim.

Prompt: If you could ask God one question today and receive an immediate answer, what would you ask Him?

_____

_____

_____

_____

_____

_____

_____

_____

_____

_____

_____

MARCH 31

Proverbs 2:12–15

With age comes wisdom, but that wisdom is formed out of learned experiences. Most often, we gain wisdom from living it—not hearing it. We love to "see for ourselves" and write our own narrative of understanding. It's easier to make decisions based on personal knowledge than based on what some person is commanding. Wisdom gained from experience is knowledge, but wisdom given by God is a gift. It's wisdom that you receive through prayer, not from the life that you have lived. Both forms combine and create a guide for your life and decisions. But only one form is birthed out of perfection, while the other is based on revisions. God will give you the wisdom to say "yes" and "no" at the proper time, as well as pull you out of situations that are detrimental. Wisdom will help you differentiate between what is good and what is sinful. Knowledge is our blueprint of life based on wrong turns and success stories. Wisdom's sole compass is living righteously and giving God glory. Ask God for more wisdom today as you navigate your twenty-four-hour journey of decisions and routines. Do not just settle for your understanding when God's wisdom could define what something actually means. Let's be wise and careful not to act out of the guise of our own knowledge. I do not want my faults to inform me; I want instruction that is faultless.

Prompt: Who is the wisest person that you know? What makes them so wise?

_____

_____

_____

_____

_____

_____

_____

_____

_____

_____

_____

_____

APRIL

April 1

Luke 2:41–52

"Age is just a number," we often hear that in relation to people of older age. But what about the people who are much younger and have lived much fewer days? I think we often times overlook the value of one's words and opinions when they have lived fewer years than us. For whatever reason, the truth exclaimed from their mouth is more difficult to trust. I am reminded of this when I read the story of Jesus being left behind by His parents in Jerusalem. It's actually kind of funny... they went to the city for the festival and forgot to take Him home when they were done. But the act of leaving Jesus behind was quickly erased in importance by the act that Jesus performed while He remained. They found Him preaching in the temple and glorifying God's name. Just a kid, preaching the truth and capturing the attention of people with far more years. What if they had allowed His age to hinder the truth of the moment that they heard? They would have missed hearing from Jesus, and I am afraid we will miss hearing from Him, too, if we allow age to dictate who we listen to. Their words are *not* invalid just because they are younger than you. You never know who God might be using to speak truth into your life at any given moment in time. God can speak through anyone, even if you are two or ninety-nine. Listen with intention, and do not prejudge words based on age. God will use anyone to help anyone else be saved.

Prompt: Who is someone that you have garnered wisdom from that is younger than you? What have they taught you?

_____
_____
_____
_____
_____
_____
_____
_____
_____
_____
_____
_____

APRIL 2

2 Thessalonians 2:1–12

There is one thing that Satan can do that God cannot, and that is a lie. Every word that Satan mutters is a false reply. Our God cannot lie because God is the truth, and He cannot deny His nature. Satan does not just "lie," but he is the best at this behavior. The problem with Satan's lies is that they never seem like a lie because he has a way of twisting them into something believable. He will convince you that you are worthless and that your hopes and dreams are unachievable. How does he do that? And why do we believe his lies so easily? It's because he listens to the negative self-talk that we tell ourselves so frequently. Satan is not "that" smart; he is just desperate for your downfall, so he uses lies to gain ground. But a lie cannot exist in the presence of truth; that is why it is so important to remain rooted in holy ground. The ways of the enemy are not new or impressive; they are repetitive and predictable. If you are unaware of your personal battle against Satan's lies, evaluate what parts of life feel miserable. Are you so used to being pushed down that you no longer have the energy to stand? Are you so used to hearing "can't" that you no longer believe that you can? Right now, say, "Satan, I will not fall victim to your ignorant lies anymore!" Then open the word of truth and allow it to saturate your life like never before.

Prompt: What is a lie that you repeatedly tell yourself is the truth? This could be negative self-talk, an intrusive thought, or a doubt. Write it down, and ask God to reveal the truth.

_____

_____

_____

_____

_____

_____

_____

_____

_____

_____

_____

_____

April 3

Job 40:1–5

We need to be careful of what we call "God's plan" because false acclamations can't quickly turn into blame. Be careful not to mistake glorifying God and using His name in vain. This might seem elementary in concept, but far too often, we place circumstances in the result category of God's plan. When in reality, the result was a by-product of human free will, not the creator's hands. When life is uncertain, we are quick to proclaim, "God has a plan for good," and cling to His will. There is nothing wrong with having hope and trusting, but we also must understand that just because something is happening doesn't mean that God's plan is being fulfilled. Have you ever heard "Our God trades beauty for ashes" and then recited it in times of despair? Do you think God's plan was to create the ashes, or does He faithfully work with the wreckage that was left there? You see, our God's plans are always good, so do not put His name on circumstances that are filled with heartbreak. Of course, God will produce a beautiful outcome but do not confuse His response with something He made. We have the ability to walk in God's plan, but we do not have the ability to understand its schedule. That is why blaming is ignorant, but trust is essential. Instead of proclaiming that a situation is "all part of God's plan," repent and pray for "His will to be done." Do not attribute trials to the Father's plan; for all we know, His plan might not have even begun.

Prompt: What is something that you have been praying for, and have you seen God make it happen? If you have not, why do you think He is holding back answering this prayer right now?

_____

_____

_____

_____

_____

_____

_____

_____

_____

_____

_____

April 4

Proverbs 28:1

I am grateful for God's commandments, but I am also grateful for His conviction. Those moments when I realize that I failed to obey and listen. We all know when we have done wrong, particularly when we begin to act suspicious and shady. We cover up our lies and run when no one is chasing. We hide our faces in shame and face our own version of heartbreak. Because even when we ask for forgiveness, we still have to deal with the consequences of our mistakes. We all know that feeling of self-loathing, and we all know the opposite feeling of doing the right thing. It's amazing how obedience allows our countenance to change. When we act righteously, we become bold and proud of our behavior. It feels good to know that you accurately represented your Savior. That is why we must pursue righteousness and avoid the trap of self-sabotage. Let's be full of freedom and not ashamed of being a fraud. Let's not hide in the shadows; let's be people who proudly stand in the light. Let's stop choosing wrong over right. God bought us for a price, and that cost was not so that we would run away in shame. It's so that we would change our behavior and break free of the chains. Do not succumb to a life of shame when there is a life of pride waiting for you. It all depends on what you choose to do.

Prompt: What does conviction mean to you? Does it have a good or bad connotation, and why?

_____

_____

_____

_____

_____

_____

_____

_____

_____

_____

_____

_____

_____

_____

April 5

Jeremiah 50:31–32

Arrogance is dangerous because it is stealthy and rewarded. It makes others seem less than because your reflection seems more important. It's easy to be arrogant, prideful, and self-seeking. If you follow the world's standards, they will, unfortunately, be misleading. We are called to dive into discomfort and take the road less traveled with confidence in our creator. We are not called to illuminate ourselves but to be a light for our Savior. God said that He would exalt the humble, and I do not know about you...but I want to be exalted by my Father. I want to desire no other titles other than "faithful servant and beloved daughter." But I would be lying if I said that is all I desired at this moment, and I hate that part of my flesh. I hate the need to be known and the desire to be the best. Even on my best day, I am only good because of God's faithfulness. I have to remind myself daily that it's because of His love, not my greatness. I want to eradicate arrogance from my heart because I know it is keeping me a few paces further from God than I want to be. I want my life to speak of Him and have nothing to do with me. It's my responsibility to avoid arrogance and actively pursue humility, not by my strength alone, only by God's grace and ability.

Prompt: What is an area of your life that arrogance sneaks in? What is fueling that sense of pride?

_____

_____

_____

_____

_____

_____

_____

_____

_____

_____

_____

_____

_____

April 6

Proverbs 14:17

Have you ever thought about the fact that we have made being quick-tempered a personality trait? Like it is some kind of badge or stitched-on nameplate. We excuse our impatience and lack of love when we adopt an irritable spirit. We tend to blame others when it makes an unsightly appearance. Why have we normalized this explicit form of sinful behavior? Why have we given it the power to claim a part of a person's nature? You are not quick-tempered; you responded emotionally and without compassion. Having a short fuse is not a genetic trait; it's you allowing your impatience to take action. Patience is a fruit of the Spirit, so if you are born again, you should not be quick to anger. It's not a minor character flaw; it's an unnecessary spiritual danger. Can you imagine if we excused other sins in the same way? Like if someone said: "I am just extremely adulterous today."
It might seem like a far-fetched example that is laughable. But why is one sin unthinkable while the other is rational? I don't know about you, but I hate the parts of myself that do not resemble Jesus. I do not want my sins to have excuses or reasons. Let's do ourselves and others a favor and stop normalizing infuriation. It must be unacceptable, not a dealt-with expectation. You are not quick-tempered; you responded with a quick temper. You choose to sin; you are not a sinner.

Prompt: What makes you angry? Why does it make you angry? How could you respond differently in these situations?

_____

_____

_____

_____

_____

_____

_____

_____

_____

_____

_____

_____

April 7

Proverbs 1:30–33

The ego is a sneaky thing. It can manifest itself in so many different ways. It can be nowhere in sight and then fully present the next day. When I think about ego, the first thought that comes to mind is self-absorption. When the lens of your world is colored with self-seeking distortion. I think about blasting, bragging, and an outward expression of self-admiration. But in reality, ego has many forms of operation. It can look like pride, but it can also look like complacency. It can resemble taking the spotlight, but it can also resemble absolute vacancy. I'm logical terms—it can look like self-guidance over listening to God's voice. But it can also look like putting headphones in to silence all of the noise. It's not just intense self-love; it's also intense self-hatred. Both are forms of keeping the ego medicated. And both are forms of pulling away from the Lord and focusing on yourself. It's like drinking from a mud puddle instead of a well. It's a way of living, but it's not providing you with optimal nutrients for life and longevity. It will follow your desires but not your destiny. You are not the center of the world, but you are also not disposable. Do not submit to complacency *or* being uncontrollable. Humility rooted in bad intentions is just ego in disguise. Be careful not to allow the foundation of your house to be built on pride.

Prompt: Do you frequently correct or criticize others (or yourself)? Do you have a hard time admitting to God or others that you are wrong? Let honesty take over in this writing.

_____

_____

_____

_____

_____

_____

_____

_____

_____

_____

_____

_____

April 8

Jeremiah 18:19–23

It's hard to forgive someone who has caused you harm and even harder to want God to forgive them. Because, in some weird way, their freedom still feels like our prison. The minute that we say "I forgive you," we are willingly releasing their transgressions. But it's hard to release them when it feels like their atonement leads to our oppression. But we do not see the full picture when we are wrapped up in the emotions of hurt. We do not want to see people be forgiven; we would rather them get what they deserve. So we often choose grudges over grace and revenge over repentance. We hold on so tight to our offenses that there is no room for forgiveness. It's like asking yourself to choose between standing up for yourself or bowing down to the one who hurt you. But that way of thinking is the wrong point of view. Forgiveness is actually choosing Jesus, which includes you and everyone else. Because true forgiveness is not just healing for the other person, it's also healing for ourselves. Revenge and grudges cause you way more harm than they will ever cause the other person, and they cause God harm too. It breaks His heart when we rejoice in choosing to make other people's life difficult to walk through. If someone causes you harm, I am sorry, that was wrong of them, but two wrongs do not make a right. Allow God to handle their judgment; that is not your role in life. Forgive other people for God and for yourself, and you will never find peace with unresolved grudges. Remember, we are servants and siblings, not judges.

Prompt: Who is someone that you are harboring resentment towards? What steps can you take to forgive them?

_____

_____

_____

_____

_____

_____

_____

_____

_____

_____

_____

_____

April 9

Matthew 20:1–16

It is often said that "comparison is the thief of joy," but I think it's more so the thief of gratitude. The constant comparison of what we have with what others have impacts our attitude. We like to blame social media for comparison culture, but it is just the newest tool that we overuse to see how we level up. And when you constantly see where you are *not* and what you do *not* have, you will never feel like you are enough. That is the parable of the workers in the vineyard; they were happy to work until they determined that their pay was unfair. When there was no comparison, there was no care. But the moment the denarius turned from a blessing into a question, it lost its value. Comparison is not just a millennial issue; it was written about in Matthew. The moment that you hold your blessings up next to someone else's is the moment that gratitude begins to dissipate. Comparing your life to others will make your life seem less great. We have to remember that we were not made to live any other life than our own and that God has a perfect plan for each one of us. Do not scroll if you cannot do so with genuine love. I do not want to live a life ungrateful for the blessings that God has provided perfectly just for me. Don't lose sight of God's gifting to you based on what you see that He gave me. You have been given your portion; hold onto that with gratefulness and excitement. If other people got "more," there is a reason that God has not provided it.

Prompt: What are you jealous of that someone else has? How would your life be better if you had that? What do you have that you think people might be jealous of? How do you show gratitude for that?

_____

_____

_____

_____

_____

_____

_____

_____

_____

_____

_____

_____

April 10

John 13:18–30

One of the most heartbreaking experiences is finding out that someone you love and trust has betrayed you. With one single act of betrayal, a trusted bond of a lifetime can be severed in two. I am sure that each of us has had moments in our lives when betrayal has taken place, so take a moment and try and remember how it felt. Then try and remember how the emotions were dealt with. Did you react in anger or walk away in silence and disbelief? Did you feel unloved and dishonored, or just deceived? Did you run to the person and demand an explanation, or did you retreat from their presence? Did you require a lengthy act of repentance, or did you instantly extend forgiveness? No matter how you answered each question above, I can guarantee that you did not dine with that person and then die for them. It was not just Judas; it's us every day, and still, Jesus went to the cross for our sins. The endless mercy of the Father was extended to us through the precious blood of Jesus Christ. Can you imagine the heartbreak Jesus felt? But He was still willing to make the ultimate sacrifice. As much as I hate to say it—we all have Judas moments where we have chosen personal gain over God's will. And somehow, God loves us even still. Take the experiences of your betrayal, and you will understand the lens of God's abounding grace. Even though we deserved to die on our own cross, Jesus *still* took our place.

Prompt: Recount an experience of betrayal. How did you react in that instance? How does it make you feel thinking about it? How have you betrayed someone in your own life? Have you asked for their forgiveness?

_____

_____

_____

_____

_____

_____

_____

_____

_____

_____

_____

April 11

Mark 1:21–28

Impurity and wickedness cannot exist in the presence of Jesus Christ. That is just another reason why it is so important to have the blood of the covenant over your life. On this side of eternity, we will experience many encounters with impurity and wicked agendas. But since we are kids of the king, we can be certain that God will protect and defend us. Our responsibility lies within the context of surrender and obedience. We must be aware of the direction in which He is leading us. And when you get that "twinge" that something is not "right," walk away and remove yourself from the situation. Do not ever underestimate the power of hesitation. If something in your spirit feels off, do not disregard it; pay closer attention to that alert. Chances are high that God either wants you to be careful or experience something and learn. You will either be called to remove the impurity or remove yourself from that environment of the impure spirit. Regardless of the approach of avoidance, God will not go near it. Not because He is scared or intimidated but because He is too holy to exist in its presence. His holiness will scatter any and everything that is unpleasant. If you are born again, then you have His presence with you everywhere you go. Pay close attention when He says "No." He will drive out the wickedness, or He will drive you away from the wickedness—both are means of protection. He has given us the Holy Spirit for power and as a means of impurity detection.

Prompt: Do you tend to rely more on your head or your gut when making decisions? When God gives you "gut" feelings, do you choose your feelings over logic? Why or why not?

_____

_____

_____

_____

_____

_____

_____

_____

_____

_____

_____

_____

APRIL 12

Matthew 5:17–20

Jesus Christ's life was a sacrificial gift, not an act to sin without consequence. We cannot lose sight of our responsibility just because we have been given a second chance. Repentance and forgiveness are merciful gifts, but they are not excuses to ignore God's laws and commands. They are not an excuse to sin; they are the backup plan. Holy Week always re-centers my focus on the sacrificial context of my life. I am reminded that each day that I wake up comes with a price. A price that I could never pay, so my Father graciously paid it for me. The absolute *least* that I can do is follow Him willingly. And following Him means listening to His voice and obeying what He has written as laws. It's not just following *some*; it's the pursuit of following *all*. It's the daily commitment of obedience and surrender to your creator. It's waking up each day and making *nothing* as important as your Savior. He set laws and commands in place for a reason—and that reason is not to my our life tediously difficult. Each one is a stepping stone to our miraculous end result. He laid the stones, and now we are required to walk on them instead of in a diverging path. Avoiding God's way will make your life docile, and it will also make God sad. Let's live like we are following God, especially because we call ourselves "followers." We are the characters... *He* is the *author*.

Prompt: What rule do you wish God would change or abolish? Why is that one rule so hard for you to follow with an obedient heart?

_____

_____

_____

_____

_____

_____

_____

_____

_____

_____

_____

_____

_____

APRIL 13

Colossians 1:3–8

I love any scripture or song that talks of hope "springing" up or arising. Because our hope in Christ Jesus is literally gravity-defying. We all have hope buried deep within our souls; it's a package deal when we receive our salvation through Christ. But we must pay close attention to not allow it to become buried too deep in the ebbs and flows of this life. It's easy to become bogged down in the "woahs" of this world, but we were made for "awe," not "woahs." We were created to look forward to the "highs," not take up residence in the "lows." That is easier said than done, but only when we choose the lens of reality over the lens of eternity. Hope can always be found if we trade our focus in for a view that does not fixate so personally. Hope starts with gratitude, so when you are in that moment of despair—ground yourself with gratitude. Take a few moments to prioritize your attention and recenter your attitude. Hope is alive and well in your soul; it's planted within you and has taken root. Even if we do not see the plant, we will still benefit from the fruit. Our portion is more than enough for us and more than enough to share. We always have the option to include hope or not—it's always there. Let hope spring up in you today, like the flowers reaching for the sun. And if you feel that you are out of reasons to hope, I can think of *one*.

Prompt: Are you a natural optimist or pessimist? If you are an optimist—how do you deal when things do not turn out well? If you are a natural pessimist—why is expecting the good in situations so scary for you?

_____

_____

_____

_____

_____

_____

_____

_____

_____

_____

_____

_____

April 14

1 Chronicles 16:34–36

How do you actually think about saying something nice to someone but actually failing to express it to them? Instead of complimenting or affirming, do you simply hold it in? We do it for a number of reasons, but I would say the most common reason is that we chicken out. We fear that we would make them uncomfortable in some way if we spoke it out loud. But have you ever been given an affirmation and walked away feeling worse than before? I am going to guess no. It always feels good when people recognize a good part of our soul. Whether it's a compliment, a promotion, or a simple "thank you for being you." It affirms a behavior and reminds you that you are someone that people look up to. The same goes for our praise and admiration of Jesus; if you think it—say it. It shows respect and admiration if we speak of His greatness. When we praise Him out loud, He gets the glory and delights in your reciprocation of love and admiration. Turn your pondering praises into proclamations! I am going to set a reminder on my phone, and when it goes off in the day, I am going to verbalize my gratitude to my creator. I want to get into the habit of verbalizing praise to my Savior. And go to other people, too; they deserve to hear affirmations, especially in a world full of so much negativity. Let's speak of others' faithfulness in a world that speaks of people's deficiencies. And let's praise God—because He is worthy of your voice. Praise Him with the meditations of your heart, then allow those meditations to make noise.

Prompt: What is the best compliment to hear from a loved one? What is the best compliment to hear from a stranger? When was the last time you complimented a loved one? When was the last time that you complimented a stranger?

_____

_____

_____

_____

_____

_____

_____

_____

_____

_____

APRIL 15

1 John 2:15–17

We are called to be in the world, not of it, which sounds good on paper, but what about in actuality? Is God's command to be set apart from the world part of your reality? I am the first to jump up and say, "Yes!" but that exclamation is a lie. There are, unfortunately, still parts of the world that my flesh can't deny. I hate that I still choose the world over Christ on a daily basis, even in ways that might seem insignificant. I don't want my minor distractions to prevent me from being diligent. And that's the exact problem with associating with the world; it separates you one degree from your calling. You risk forfeiting your birthright for a moment of belonging. I promise that the world does not need any more representatives, but our God does. What I choose to do today is what ultimately becomes. I want to get one degree closer to my Father every day, which means I am going to have to establish a redirection. I am going to have to disconnect from a few things each day in order to strengthen my heavenly connection. I want my feet to be grounded but not rooted in Earth's soil. I want my life to be the fruit of salvation, not the fruit that will spoil. What can you do differently today that will separate you from the world by one degree? What decisions are you making to become *in* the world, not *of* it your reality?

Prompt: Whose opinion matters to you most? Why does their opinion of you hold so much weight?

_____

_____

_____

_____

_____

_____

_____

_____

_____

_____

_____

_____

_____

_____

April 16

Jeremiah 23:16–22

Take a moment right now and think about where you receive your spiritual infilling. Do you seek it straight from God, or is it a product that someone else is instilling? If the majority of our spiritual food comes from the revelation of another human, then we must be certain of its accuracy. Our faith must be rooted in the Word of God, not in pulpit dictation or pageantry. We must receive our own revelation from God, which requires a time of connection. If we follow the revelation of another, we might just be walking in the wrong direction. I am not saying that pastors, prophets, evangelists, teachers, and apostles should not be listened to or trusted. All I am saying is that God wants us to dive deeper into the spiritual discussion. Instead of chewing on a piece of good fruit that you received from your pastor on Sunday, go home, open your Bible, silence the enemy, and ask God if He has anything that He wants to say. We have become too complacent upon receiving our spiritual food from the hands of everyone but Christ. We have lost our hunger for divine revelation and become satisfied with advice. God can speak through other people, and He does so often, but sometimes He just wants to speak to *you*. That way, you praise Him and not the vessel He was speaking through. Do not be satisfied with the spoon-fed Word; get in and learn to feed yourself by receiving directly. A direct connection to God's Word will keep you strong and steady.

Prompt: Who are spiritual leaders in your life? How did they earn that privilege?

_____

_____

_____

_____

_____

_____

_____

_____

_____

_____

_____

_____

APRIL 17

Romans 8:1–4

Have you ever had someone do something for you that overwhelmed you to the point of tears? Maybe they paid off a debt that you owed or released you of some fear. It's like a weight being lifted off of your shoulders that you never thought could be lifted. That moment of redemption when you never thought that you could be forgiven. I've been overwhelmed by kindness before, but this morning I write you in awe. If the sacrifice that was made rewrote the law. Of the gift of Jesus' blood that was shed on Calvary's hill. Of the faithful promise of God that was fulfilled. The beatings that Jesus endured, and the spit that He took in His face. The mockery, the hatred, and the rage. The nails and the spear that pierced His holy flesh. God loved you so much that He sacrificed His best. And He rose from the grave to fulfill the promise of redemption. God is way too good to stop at the crucifixion. He did it for you, just like friends who have served you in the past in ways that left you overwhelmed. He rolled back that stone so that you could experience paradise as well. Make the gift of the resurrection personal; it's for all of us, but focus on receiving it for yourself today. Envision yourself following Him out of that grave.

Prompt: When was the last time someone paid one of your debts (monetarily or metaphorically)? How did you react? When was the last time you paid someone else's debt? How did it feel?

_____

_____

_____

_____

_____

_____

_____

_____

_____

_____

_____

_____

_____

_____

APRIL 18

Proverbs 18:2

If you really stop and think about it, the majority of information that we hear today is just other people's opinions. We are easily convinced when we are quick to listen. I mean, really think about this…the news, the influencers on social media, and politicians' voices ring loudly in our society. We have given people platforms unjustifiably. And even outside of the scope of mass media, think about your daily interactions with other people. Think about all of the "facts" that they speak that you just accept as real. I would love to have a monitor that showed me the percentages of real truth vs. opinions that I hear on a daily basis. We must be careful of what sustenance we are allowing to sustain us. That is why reading God's Word is so important because it's the absolute truth. It is something that needs to be routinely consumed. Because consuming the truth fills you up with truth and leaves little to no extra room for opinions to occupy space. Every opinion that we take in as absolute truth is an opinion that we will eventually need to replace. How much of your foundation is built on the real, unwavering truth, and how much is built on opinions that you have heard over your life? Truth *is*, and will *always* be, opinions…might. Fill your head and heart up with truth first so that your opinions find a "no vacancy" sign. Be careful of what you allow to take root in your head, soul, and mind.

Prompt: Whose opinions do you trust as absolute truth? How have they gained that privilege in your mind and heart?

_____

_____

_____

_____

_____

_____

_____

_____

_____

_____

_____

_____

April 19

Matthew 12:46–50

Regardless of whether or not you get along with your family, you cannot avoid the deep-rooted connection. There is a realness found in relation that overlooks imperfections. Think about your own personal family for a moment...all of the differences and all of the similarities. It's a devoted kind of love, not influenced by disparities. Now think about the fact that God calls us sons and daughters, and Jesus calls us His siblings. He will love us the same forevermore as He did in the beginning. He does not roll His eyes at our quirky traits; He delights in our heart's surrender. He does not see you as a family outcast; He calls you a family member. He has set a place for you and for me at the table of family gatherings. We are invited into His home and included in all of the family happenings. What is the saying— "You do not have to like your family, but you have to love them..." that says less about preference and more about patience. It's an unwritten rule that no matter what happens, you are staying. Love for family is full of grace and consistency. Relatives depict a genuine sense of reliability. How does it change your view of God that He doesn't just call you a servant; He calls you one of His own? He has not made an eternal place for you; He has promised you a place in His heavenly home. He loves you no matter what you do because you are His son or daughter. Remember, the blood of the new covenant is thicker than that of the womb's water.

Prompt: What is your favorite trait you have been given from your blood family? What is your least favorite trait?

_____

_____

_____

_____

_____

_____

_____

_____

_____

_____

_____

_____

April 20

Micah 2:1–5

Have you ever done something "just because you could"? You did it because you felt like it, not because it was good. That, in simple terms, is the definition of free will. It's taking action in a moment that God has called you to be still. God loves us so much that He gave us the ability to make our own choices. So it is up to us whether we listen to God's call or fall into pressure from outside voices. You see, when we become born again, our personal desires begin to fade into the background. The once-raging noise of selfishness begins to make less and less sound. It's not because we become "better;" it's because we receive the Holy Spirit within. We do not become spotless, but we do become more aware of our sins. This infilling of the Holy Spirit leads to desiring God's will and not the will of selfish ambition. It is the process of practicing adoration and giving up avenues of selfish attention. It's making the choice that glorifies the Father, not the one that satisfies your own ego. It's learning to draw a hard line in the sand where your "yes" means "yes" and your "no" means "no." It's giving up your free will for the will of the God of freedom. It's choosing God's plan instead of your own without needing a reason. Be careful with free will because freedom of the flesh will lead to spiritual bondage. God's will leads to eternal freedom, while the will of the world leads you to being Satan's hostage.

Prompt: When is the last time you said "yes" to something that you should have said "no" to? What was the consequence of that "yes"?

_____

_____

_____

_____

_____

_____

_____

_____

_____

_____

_____

_____

_____

APRIL 21

John 4:39–42

Our testimonies are not just personal stories of belief; they are the foundation of salvation. You never know who may come to know Christ because of your detailed explanation. We often try and lock our story up to protect the details of our personal encounters. We attempt to show strength not through admission of our trials but through our own willpower. God gave each of us a testimony for the foundation of our own beliefs, but the power does not stop there. When He gifted us a story, He intended for us to share. Do not underestimate the power of your testimony; it might just be used to save a nation. God can use anyone or anything to open the door of salvation. If we keep quiet, we are succumbing you the power of Satan's fear-filled plan. The only way he can stop the spread of salvation is to silence our voices from telling where our story began. The Word of God will save the lost, but our words of redemption have the power to break down the walls of unbelief. Word by word, our testimony has the ability to provide revelatory relief. We must not be ashamed of our beginning or timid about our transformation because our weakness amplifies His strength. You may just realize that a few words of personal admission are all it takes. Be proud of your testimony and be willing to share it for the glory of the redeemer. Your story may just create a steadfast servant from an unbeliever.

Prompt: When was the last time that you shared your testimony? It doesn't have to be your story of salvation, but even just a testimony of God's grace, love, or intercession in your life.

_____

_____

_____

_____

_____

_____

_____

_____

_____

_____

_____

_____

April 22

Judges 5:31

True faith is found when selfish desires disappear. When you fill your mind with your own noise, the voice of God becomes extremely difficult to hear. We are all selfish to some degree, and our fleshly nature overrides our spirit more often than not. That is why being a child of God requires you to desire to be taught. Personally, I have been evaluating my prayer life, and I think it is a great place to start. The words and requests that you bring unto the Father directly reveal the posture of your heart. How much of your prayer time is spent praying for personal promotion? And how much of your prayer time is spent in pure, reverent devotion? Somewhere along the way, we blurred the lines between prayer and proclamation. We speak to the Father, always asking for more because we know that He is without limitations. But what about adoration? What about reverence? And what about praying in the posture of surrender? What if we prayed for God to use us in the battle instead of praying that He would be our defender? Prayers of selfishness feel safe and comforting, but God cannot transform you if you are not willing to be trained. Try praying one prayer that does not involve your own name. Learn to pray dangerously for God's will and allow Him to do the rest. Because at the end of the day, all that you desire will be found in the arena of God's best.

Prompt: How are you selfish? When is your selfishness most evident? How does your selfishness affect others and yourself?

_____

_____

_____

_____

_____

_____

_____

_____

_____

_____

_____

_____

April 23

Genesis 1:26–28

I have read the creation story countless times, but this morning, one single word of it caught my attention. So much so that I found myself looking up the word's definition. It comes in the paragraph about the creation of mankind, and it is used as a word of commandment. But it was so far out of the realm of our current reality that it was nearly impossible for me to understand it. The word is "subdue," and did you know we were created to subdue the earth and all that is in it? We were created for control, not just to be lowly tenants. God made us in His image and granted us authority over all other aspects of creation. But instead of using our authority for good, we have allowed it to create devastation. The definition of the word "subdue" is "to overcome, quiet, or bring under control." How much have we obeyed that order? If you need any proof, listen for ten seconds to the news reporter. We can blame it on Satan all day long, but he can't win unless we allow him to. So instead of pointing a finger at him, first look in the mirror at you. Have you used your authority to bring peace to the earth and claim back God's lost territory? Or have you abstained from interaction because the world has gotten so scary? We were created to be ruled by God and graciously given a world to rule in return. I think the world's downfall needs to be less of an expectation and more of our concern.

Prompt: In what ways are you actively trying to make the world a better place? What are some new ways you could start?

April 24

Luke 9:44–50

Our faith in Jesus Christ is not easy, but it is simple—we just tend to overcomplicate it. Instead of understanding by faith, we try and comprehend with. We see this plainly in things like denominations and religious rules and traditions. Where people major on the minor things in the Bible that were barely even mentioned. If we take our faith in its most simplistic form, it's: Love God and love people like God loves you. But it almost seems too simple to be true. I love this passage of Scripture because the disciples are trying to overcomplicate the mission. And Jesus very calmly replies with a simple nod of wisdom. You see, we like to have details and steps, and God just works in ways that are way bigger than our minds can understand. Our comprehension of everything is not part of His plan. So when He says something like, "Whoever is not against you is for you," we have to accept that as true. Even though we want to know more pieces of the equation than just the "you." We just have to trust that God has the details worked out, and we can live simply by following His lead without the logistics. Instead of trying to overcomplicate it, let's appreciate the fact that it is simplistic. Love God, love others—don't muddle your faith with overcomplications. Let's act out of obedience, not because we have been given an explanation.

Prompt: Are you comfortable taking action if you do not have the steps laid out for you? What do you wish God would tell you that could help you take the next steps? Talk to Him.

_____

_____

_____

_____

_____

_____

_____

_____

_____

_____

_____

_____

_____

APRIL 25

Hebrews 11:39–40

Walking by faith is not easy, especially when the path takes unexpected twists and turns. It can be difficult to still trust God fully when He leads you down a different path from the things that you have yearned for. Our desires are not truth; they are merely an internal compass from our broken flesh. Even when it feels like He is leading us away from our desires, we must remember that God knows best. Faith can feel like surrendering your desires, and it can also feel like closing your eyes and taking a step. It's stepping out of the boat onto the waves and into the depths. God is not faithful because He answered my prayers; He is faithful because He is God. We see now, and He sees beyond. I do not praise God because He answered my prayers; I praise Him because I am allowed to pray. My faith walk is not motivated by blessings; it's motivated by the fact that I want to obey. By faith, Moses led people through the Red Sea, and by faith, Noah built the ark. Neither of them prayed for that role when they spoke the desires of their heart. But God knows best, and His plan involved more than just them, and yours most likely does too. Remember, next time you do not get what you prayed for, that your life involves more than just you. God intends to bless you, just do not measure it up against your expectation. We see today; God sees the plan for generations.

Prompt: How have prayers that you prayed impacted those around you? What prayer do you want God to answer more than anything right now? How would a "yes" from Him impact those around you?

APRIL 26

Mark 4:26–29

Our job on Earth is to scatter the seed of the good news of God's love. Like a farmer dropping seeds onto the ground from up above. We are to scatter the news without concerning ourselves with the plowing or tilling. Our job is to plant; God's job is to do the fulfilling. It takes some pressure off of us and puts the power back into God's almighty hands when we realize that we are not responsible for harvesting the land. It's God's job to till, water, and harvest. We are not the gardener; we are the garden. But we cannot allow our lack of greater responsibility to diminish our one responsibility's magnitude. Sometimes, when we have fewer jobs to do, we think our one job's role is devalued. But that could not be farther from the case because God cannot spread the seed. We are not just a tool of His; we are a need. He needs us to spread the Word and scatter His love—and He will do the rest. He initiates and completes the process. But we have to do the "in-between;" we have to spread His Word. We have to speak it, and He makes sure that it is heard. Let's be eager to scatter seed; let's make it our life's mission. Let's be grateful that we have been given such an incredible position. God has chosen to use you and me, and He has chosen to make us essential. We are not the Almighty, but we are influential. Make sure you have a handful of seed this morning, and begin to scatter it as you move throughout your day. Let them fall out of your hand, and God will make sure that they stay.

Prompt: What do you think God needs you to do today? How do you think He wants to use you specifically on this day?

_____

_____

_____

_____

_____

_____

_____

_____

_____

_____

_____

_____

April 27

Matthew 10:24-25

Today I want to write about one of the best pieces of advice that I have ever been given. It was a simple statement from my therapist that changed the way that I was living. I was sharing about how a friendship had hurt me, but I was continuing to pour into that person because that is "what Jesus would do." And in a matter-of-fact way, she said, "Yeah...but you are not Jesus, you are you." It's not that I ever knowingly compared myself to Jesus, but I was living according to His standard that I would never be able to achieve. When she spoke these words over me, it literally set me free. I am to be *like* Jesus, but I will never *be* Jesus—my heart is not perfect. And I am grateful that I was twenty-six years old when I learned it. Because letting someone treat you poorly and loving them out of spite is not Jesus-like behavior. Serving with dread does *not* resemble our Savior. We will not be able to love everyone like Jesus does, and God understands our hearts; He does not need us to fake it. We do not need to pretend that we are righteous when we are really frustrated. I am in no way discouraging you from being *like* Jesus, and my therapist was not, either. She was just reminding me, like I am reminding you—that you are not the Savior; you are a believer. Which parts of your life are you disgusting in righteousness when the reality is that those feelings are unrighteous? If we want to be like Jesus, we would be better off being honest.

Prompt: Which parts of your life are you disguising as righteousness when the root of your heart is unrighteousness? (ex. Where are you serving with dread, who are you talking to out of obligation, etc.) and how could you change that behavior to look more like Jesus?

_____

_____

_____

_____

_____

_____

_____

_____

_____

_____

April 28

Isaiah 65:17–19

Do you ever look back on the things that used to stress you out in life and realize that they were not that big of a deal? But it's funny how, at the moment, things feel so big, scary, and real. Like in middle school, making friends seems like the most important thing that you will ever do in your life, and you stress about being included. Then in high school, the focus is on who you are dating and how to copy what everyone else is doing. College and young adulthood are about finding independence and finding a community to fit into. Then marriage and the middle years of life are often stressful trying to balance all of the things that you have to do. As I look back now on middle school, I can laugh at the things that I labeled as "stressful" because I realize that they did not have much impact. We can find the same hope in God's promises because He promised that this world would not last. Heaven will last forever, but the ways of this world will fade away, just like your middle school problems. One day you will look back on the stressors of today like you look back on final exam week in college. It does not mean that your stress is invalid; it just means that there is a greater sense of perspective. That in the greater context of eternity, our stress is ineffective. We have the eternal promise of heaven to look forward to; this world and its stressors won't last. Try to remind yourself that even tomorrow will one day be in the past.

Prompt: What are you most stressed about right now? Will that thing matter in a month, a year, or ten years? Try and recenter yourself and give that worry to God.

_____
_____
_____
_____
_____
_____
_____
_____
_____
_____
_____
_____

APRIL 29

Proverbs 23:17–18

The world will make you think that living a lifestyle of righteousness means missing out on a lifetime of fun. That if you choose to follow God, all of your "exciting" days are done. To me, this is similar to the way the world approaches people who are about to be married. Always telling people to "live it up" before the big day and turning something exciting into something scary. Committing to a marriage does not mean that "fun" is over; it just looks different than what the world deems exciting. Our world loves temporary and strays away from any commitment that is uniting. The same thing happens when we become born again; we are married to the groom of heaven. Where the world sees a boring commitment, we, the bride, see a blessing. It's amazing how much more there is in the world than what the world calls popular. You will never find joy trying to find balance in the world's "hot or not" thermometer. True love is found in commitment, and where there is endless love, there is endless joy. The world will never be able to provide that for you, and what the world can't do, it wants to destroy. When you become born again, the only thing that you are "missing out on" is an eternity in hell. It's the best "hello" to a new you and a very easy farewell. It's living in the joy of the Lord, not the happiness of the world's sin. It's loving the fact that you are missing out on fitting in.

Prompt: What parts of this world do you find yourself imitating? Why do you feel the need or desire to imitate the world?

_____

_____

_____

_____

_____

_____

_____

_____

_____

_____

_____

_____

_____

April 30

Proverbs 23:9

One of the sayings that I live by is "control the controllable." There are many parts of our life that can be decided instead of negotiable. One of those, in particular, is who you choose to surround yourself with. Because the people we do life with determine the life that we live. If you surround yourself with fools or people who walk a walk of immaturity, your life will begin to resemble their life most assuredly. I heard once that we become the average of the five people we interact the most with in our day to day. Think about who your five people are and if those five people need to stay. Maybe you think— "Well, one of those five people is my boss...and I have to be around him." And I would respond with— "Yeah...but would your soul be more righteous if you quit?" We use "have to" and "should" to preface a lot of scheduled encounters with people, but those are all choices we are choosing. Relationships with others are something we are self-inducing. If someone is causing you to stray from your walk with God, it's better to walk away from them. Do not choose a social interaction over Him. You cannot control the happenings of the day, but you can control who you invest your time into. Your five people should resemble the five best possible versions of you. Control what you can control, and that is your time spent engaging in relationships. Which relationships are encouraging your walk with God, and which should you quit?

Prompt: Which relationships bring you closer to God? Which relationships pull you away from God? Why do you choose to be involved in each relationship?

_____

_____

_____

_____

_____

_____

_____

_____

_____

_____

_____

_____

MAY

MAY 1

Daniel 9:3–6

God does not need us to speak our thoughts or express our emotions because He already knows them all. We are in constant communication with Him whether or not we initiate the call. But something happens in our souls when we speak out loud about the thoughts and emotions that we hold deep inside. It brings life to our surrender and eliminates our pride. Prayers are not confessionals; they are surgeries for the soul. Bowing your head and speaking out loud about your sins is the surrendering of control. It's the momentary realization that your thoughts are already known by the Father. But you still personally need the belief of bowing at the altar. The outward expression of the emotions that you feel creates an overwhelming release of true identity. The plea and repentance of your confessions show that you believe God is the only remedy. He knows the confessions of our hearts, but I believe the confession of our mouth is for our own welfare. Seeing that our mouth can either be our greatest tool or our worst snare. Prayer in any capacity is good, but make it a point to open your mouth daily and speak out loud to heaven. You just might realize a greater realization than you had expected. Pray from the depths of your soul and allow God to fill you up as you pour yourself out. One single spoken word unto heaven may just open the floodgates and end your devastating spiritual drought.

Prompt: What do you want God to know more than anything today? What is something that you need to release and get off of your chest?

_____
_____
_____
_____
_____
_____
_____
_____
_____
_____
_____
_____

MAY 2

1 Thessalonians 3:6–10

If you ever need to be reminded that you are not alone, read some of Paul's letters. He writes about how God is the only answer and that having a community around you makes life better. But in this time of idolized independence and virtual interactions—community is becoming sparse. It's becoming more difficult to surround yourself with people who genuinely care. I know we are all busy, but we cannot be too busy for our fellow siblings of the faith. If time is what we are lacking, then it's priorities that we need to create. Because other people are a gift, and relationships with others are actually what God called "church." Doing stuff alone all of the time will actually make your relationship with God worse. It's not that alone time is not important; it's sacred in its own way. But pulling away from people will end up harming your relationship with God at the end of the day. Because people are God's creation, and we were made to interact and intertwine. The letters that Paul wrote to the churches display that the love they had for each other was divine. Take a minute to think about your "church," and I do not mean the house of worship you attend on Sunday. Who are you close to, and who have you pushed away? Who is your church? And how are you building each other up with encouragement and accountability? If loneliness is what ails us, community is the remedy.

Prompt: Do you spend more time alone or with other people? What does an ideal community look like for you? Do you have that, or what are you missing that you wish you had? How could you cultivate that community?

MAY 3

Acts 15:16–18

God's plan from the beginning of time has consisted of forgiveness and restoration. He understands the brokenness of our fallen nation. How merciful is He that He would plan to save us before we were even created? Before Adam and Eve, Jonah, and David, He knew that perfect righteousness would need to be demonstrated. So He created human life with a plan of restoring all of humanity. He grants forgiveness for our faults, patience for our self-pursuit, and understanding for our insanity. Take a moment right now and express to the Lord the feelings you have regarding His restorative nature. Comprehend the reality that His blessings and favor are not dependent upon your behavior. What the Lord has established cannot be shaken, and what the Lord wants to restore cannot be revoked. He is faithful to grant us the ability to grow without proving past growth. His mercy and grace do not hinge on our actions; they have been established for generations. His love has been the same every moment since creation. When you walk through an uncertain time in your life where destruction seems to be the norm, remind yourself that God is faithful to transform. He has, and is, and will restore because His plan cannot be changed. He will always supply a supply of new, and He will never leave you the same.

Prompt: What area of your life do you feel you have seen the most growth in recently? What area of your life do you wish to see growth in?

_____

_____

_____

_____

_____

_____

_____

_____

_____

_____

_____

_____

MAY 4

Psalm 80:3–7

God does not need your sugarcoated truth; He can handle the real truth. If we pretend that something is not hurting, then it will never be soothed. I like reading the Psalms because David was brutally honest with God in both his praise and complaining. He called God "glorious," and he called God "frustrating." And isn't that the truth? Don't we all have those feelings at some point? I will humbly announce that my prayers are equal parts "thankful" and "annoyed." I praise God for the blessing He gave me, and within the same sentence question why He has not shown up in another part of my life. I hand my battles over to Him, and then I tell Him how He should fight. But He does not roll His eyes at me and shrug His shoulders in annoyance—He simply listens and allows me to express myself. He knows what I think before I ever even tell. He does not love me any less, just like He did not love David any less for his prayers. Our attitude does not impact His love and care. So, if you feel like God is far from you right now, maybe it's because you have built a wall between you and Him with your fabricated feelings and ungenuine words. Maybe you have sugarcoated your prayers with things you thought needed to be heard. But if it is not true in your heart, don't fake that it is; it won't put you on any special list. No feeling can rewrite the fact that you are forever His.

Prompt: How do you feel today, really? Be honest and vulnerable.

MAY 5

Proverbs 28:20

Isn't it amazing how when you stop trying to force something, it ends up falling perfectly into place? That often times we catch up to something the moment that we give up the chase. People may date a hundred different people, and then the moment they stop looking, they meet the one. The reward is granted the minute the pursuit is done. The Bible tells us not to seek wealth but to walk blamelessly, and we will receive it. Think of all of the other avenues of life that when you stop trying to attain, you achieve it. Why does God work this way? I think it's because He knows that we are people with sole fixations. We allow one particular thing to rule over our concentration. Sure, we can all do two things at once, but you cannot do them as well together as you would at separate times. This is not a personality flaw; it's part of how we were designed. That is why we have to stay focused on Jesus and not on our passion projects. God will provide your desires if you praise Him instead of fixating on an object. If the main goal in your life is anything other than serving the Lord, stop and re-evaluate your efforts. Are you living out your purpose or trying to prove something by achieving it under pressure? Do you trust God enough to allow Him to give you the desires of your heart, or do you feel the need to make it happen? Are you actively pursuing God or just really good at putting your plans into action?

Prompt: What is something you have been putting a lot of effort into lately and not seeing results? What would happen if you took a break from pushing that one thing so hard?

_____

_____

_____

_____

_____

_____

_____

_____

_____

_____

_____

_____

MAY 6

2 Timothy 1:13–14

It's easy to feel alone in this world, even when we know that God is always with us. It's hard to feel even when we fully and completely trust. I think that God knew that we would feel that way, and so He sent the Holy Spirit to dwell inside our hearts. Knowing that having little reminders of His presence would remind us that we are never actually apart. I do not know about you, but I often take the Holy Spirit for granted as I go throughout my day. I am more attentive to the connection when I worship or pray. But the Holy Spirit is there for so much more; in fact, the Holy Spirit is there for it all. The Holy Spirit is a helper and is closer than a call. This passage, in particular, encourages us to use the Holy Spirit as a guard to protect the things that we have been taught. Because Satan loves to attack our spirits by making us second-guess our thoughts. Allow the Holy Spirit to protect your mind, your heart, and your spirit too. There is a reason that God made the Holy Spirit dwell *within* you. It was not for occasional help; He knew that we would need it all of the time. Do not choose your independence over God's design. Lean on the Spirit, and trust the guidance and protection that God has graciously provided. It just is; you do not have to find it. Lord, I ask You right now to grant me the awareness of the Holy Spirit's presence and allow me to lean on Your power and not my own. My soul is not empty; it is Your permanent home.

Prompt: When do you feel most alone? When do you feel most connected?

_____

_____

_____

_____

_____

_____

_____

_____

_____

_____

_____

_____

_____

May 7

1 Corinthians 6:19–20

We are called to love God and love others as we love ourselves. But have you ever connected your ability to love with your personal health? I am not talking about unexplainable diseases like cancer or other tragic illnesses. I am talking more about your daily nutritional choices and fitness. Your body was created *by* God, *for* God, it's a sacred temple. But our view of ourselves has become *way* too simple. This has nothing to do with your weight or your clothing size, but it has everything to do with how you view and treat your body. Negative self-talk and a poor diet can be spiritually costly. It's easy to separate our spirit from our flesh, but God gave us this body for a reason as a gift. We show honor to Him by the ways that we choose to live. If you have no concern for your health, then isn't that a slap in your creator's face? It's about caring about what goes in your body, not just what goes on your plate. It's about what you eat, how you move, and the care that you show yourself. You have to be healthy in order to love well. Your body is not your own, so treat it like a rental that you will one day have to return in good condition. Health and wellness are not part of being trendy; they are part of being a Christian. Do you treat your body like it's a sacred temple, or do you treat it like it's your own? If you are loving to yourself, love to others will be shown. Don't compare yourself to others, but just ask yourself if you are treating your body with care. It's never too late to start the journey towards physical repair.

Prompt: In what ways do you take care of your body? In what ways do you harm your body? Think holistic here...not just physical. It could be negative self-talk, substances, a sedentary lifestyle, too much screen time, etc. Let God reveal it to you.

_____

_____

_____

_____

_____

_____

_____

_____

_____

_____

MAY 8

2 Peter 3:3–7

Waiting for God is the best way to spend your time. It's better to wait and trust than it is to set out looking for something that you will never find. What makes waiting hard is when everyone around you is not stopping to wait, they are following their own lead. So then, you equate your patience to not attempting to succeed. We have to remember that God's timing is perfect, so waiting on Him is the ultimate plan of success. We can rest in His present tense and trust what He has next. It does not matter if people scoff at your schedule or ridicule your patience. We do not have to be anxious with anticipation. Other people will scoff at your faith but is their degradation more valuable than your faith?

Would you rather have God's approval or gain the world's acclaim? It is hard to be laughed at and pitied for your beliefs, but it's absolutely worth it. The roots of faith run much deeper than what can be destroyed on the surface. So if people come and pick off your petals, don't stop watering the roots. Faith is not about popularity; it's about a reckless pursuit. You will never miss out on opportunities if you are waiting on the Lord's direction. Do not waiver in the face of blatant rejection. God has a perfect plan for today, tomorrow, and the rest of eternity. Do not forfeit your faith in the name of insecurity.

Prompt: What mountain is standing before you right now? What would it feel like if God moved that mountain? Ask Him to.

_____

_____

_____

_____

_____

_____

_____

_____

_____

_____

_____

_____

May 9

Luke 19:37–40

The whole earth is singing God's praises all of the time; it's our job to determine if we want to join in too. Because if your choice is to remain silent, some part of nature will take the place of you. It says here in this passage that if the disciples stopped praising Jesus, then the rocks would have cried out in their place. Praise will always inhabit space. The wind sings a song of a low hum of worship, and the trees reach for heaven's embrace. The ocean bows as it ebbs and flows with gratitude for His grace. The sun exudes a warmth of an overabundance of thanksgiving. Even the rocks cry out in silent tones, though they are not "technically" living. What about you? Does your body cry out in praise as you go about your day? Does your praise increase or begin to fade? Do you exclaim words of worship, or do you simply fill the air with noise? Are you contributing to the choir or filling the void? Does your body praise your creator as it moves in daily motion? Do you exude humanity's design or surrendered devotion? Are the stones, the trees, the rocks, and the oceans praising more than you? Don't just praise Him with verbal affirmations; praise Him with everything that you do. If you need inspiration, take a walk out in nature. Watch how everything praises our Savior. Let's bow like the ocean, let's reach for heaven like the trees, and hum His praise as the wind does. Let's make our life the reflection of His love.

Prompt: In what ways (other than your voice) do you praise God?

_____

_____

_____

_____

_____

_____

_____

_____

_____

_____

_____

_____

_____

MAY 10

Acts 26:24–29

It's hard not to like someone when they are genuinely nice and caring towards you. No matter what runouts you might have heard in the past about someone, that can all change with one experience of their truth. Like Paul, during the time of his ministry—he was widely known and greatly disliked by the masses. But those opinions were formed by looking through rumor-tinted glasses. Paul would enter a new town and be beaten and imprisoned, not because of what he did but because of who he spoke of. But instead of hatred and objection, the guards would be met with surrender and love. People would mock his presence and then later follow him like a shadow. They would attempt to smother his flames, and then before they knew it, they were putting wood on the fire to help it grow. It might seem counterintuitive, but that is because it is. It's hard for people not to like you when you are His. Because His love exudes and permeates the environment in which you inhabit. It is not just the garment that you wear; it saturates the fabric. Your smile isn't just a smile; it's a direct line to Jesus's face. Your touch isn't just a touch; it's a feeling of the Father's embrace. So if people don't like you because of rumors...let them believe it until they meet you. Reality will prove them to be radically untrue. Chase after God, and then watch as others begin to run in your direction. When others expect a beating, hit them with a blessing.

Prompt: What is something that most people don't know about you? How would knowing this affect the way that they look at you?

_____

_____

_____

_____

_____

_____

_____

_____

_____

_____

_____

_____

_____

MAY 11

1 John 3:23–24

We toss around the word "love" so often that we actually forget that it is unconditional. It is not a mood; it's a miracle. We were given the simplest yet greatest commandment of all, which is to love Jesus and love one another. We were not called to be partial; we were called to be lovers. But our vocabulary is full of *things* that we "love" instead of *people*. Favoritism or preference does not equate to a love that is real. Love is deeper than passion or feelings of satisfaction. True love is loving someone no matter what happens. Think of all of the people that you claim to love; do you really love them no matter what? What happens if they stop meeting your needs or break your trust? It's okay to admit that your sentiment would not withstand the trials. But be upfront with yourself that what you felt for them was never true love because love doesn't have cycles. It's steadfast, and it does not waiver based on circumstance; it's merciful and grace-filled. It's not an endless brick wall that is chipped away and rebuilt. Do not toss the word "love" around if you do not truly feel the unconditional sentiment towards the person. It cannot be contingent or uncertain. If the feeling of love isn't there for a person, ask God why and for a greater understanding to be provided to you. Love needs to be who we are, not what we do.

Prompt: How do you show love to others? How do you show love to yourself? What does love feel like in your body?

_____
_____
_____
_____
_____
_____
_____
_____
_____
_____
_____
_____
_____

MAY 12

Luke 18:15–17

Have you ever thought about the fact that children are the newest thing from heaven that we experience here on Earth? That they are nine months removed from the creator's hands at the moment of their birth? Children innately have faith, trust, and an abundance of love because they have no reason not to. They see with God's vision because they have not developed a worldview. Scripture tells us countless times to have child-like faith, but how often do we actually? We become way too structured and pessimistic with reasoning and practicality. God never told us to increase our intelligence for a greater measure of faith. Children believe and love without the need to persuade. The longer you are in this world, the more cyclical you can become. It's not your fault; you are just reacting and creating barriers to the dangerous place the world has become. We need equal parts wisdom, maturity, and child-like wonder. Do not let the dark world keep you from seeing in color. The energetic life of a child is a miracle on display. They have just been handed the baton by God as their lifelong relay. Instead of thinking we have the answers, let's watch them ask the questions. We can teach them, but they can help us learn a lot of lessons.

Prompt: Think about yourself at five years old. What were your favorite things to do? What excited you most? How could you incorporate some of those things into your life today? (Bonus points if you print out a picture of your childhood self and keep it somewhere you can see it every day.)

_____

_____

_____

_____

_____

_____

_____

_____

_____

_____

_____

_____

_____

MAY 13

Proverbs 31:8–9

You have been given a voice to use; are you using it with purpose? Do your vocal cords resound pride or service? Do you speak with intention or mutter words without any prior thought? Do you concern yourself more with your conversation, or are you just concerned that your words won't be caught? Our voices are powerful, and not just for spreading the good news of the gospel, but for helping others in need. Your voice has the tangible power to intercede. You can speak for one who has no power; you can encourage someone who is filled with hopelessness. You have the power to dispel lies that people think and replace them with what they actually *are*. But are you using your voice for that, or are you just using it for literal conversation? Or even worse...are you regularly using it for defamation? Maybe use today as a barometer and pay closer attention to your voice. What we say is not a reflex; it's actually a choice. How many times do you gossip in a day? How many times do you curse? How many times do you verbalize something before thinking first? If you are anything like me, I am embarrassed to answer those questions. I am not always proud of my message. But the only way to fix it is to fix it. Maybe speak only after I am certain that I have listened. Because I have a powerful gift, and you do too. Let's be people who speak, not people who spew.

Prompt: If you had the chance to give one last sentence of encouragement to the world, what would you say? Why would that be what you chose?

_____

_____

_____

_____

_____

_____

_____

_____

_____

_____

_____

_____

MAY 14

Ecclesiastes 8:5–6

I do not like not being in control...I like knowing and planning everything out completely. I do not like when things get messy; I just want them to happen nearly. I struggle when my plans get changed and the events become out of my control. But what the control really covers up is the fear in my soul. The fear of the unknown, the wild and dangerous sense of ambiguity. Feeling like I am the only one in a situation who does not speak the language fluently. It's scary, and it makes me feel like I am slipping and falling into an abyss with no way out. But that is the presence of fear and the absence of doubt. I know in my head that God has control of it all and that His timing is perfect, but it's hard to believe at the moment. When things do not add up, it can feel like you are God's opponent. But that is simply not true, and the truth is that your plans were not aligned with God's plans. He is not reprimanding you with change; He is just taking the control back into His hands. And it still feels uncomfortable and hard, but that is 100 percent okay. Trust does not always feel good along the way. But God is good, and He will protect His children from any and all harm or distraction. When we are on the wrong path—God takes action. So we trust, even though it's scary and frustrating. One day you will praise Him instead of complaining.

Prompt: What feels out of control in your life right now? Who is in control of that? Why do you want control of that?

_____

_____

_____

_____

_____

_____

_____

_____

_____

_____

_____

_____

MAY 15

Job 3:20-26

Complaining is not seen as a positive attribute, and there is good reason to back that thinking. But instead of dismissing the sighs of your soul, allow yourself to hear what your heart is explaining. Masking complaints with ingenuine satisfaction is encouraged by society, but it's not scriptural. God never told us to rid ourselves of negative feelings by way of dismissal. If you feel slighted but do not express it, that does not alleviate the actual feeling. Complaints do not disappear with concealing. If you think complaining is unvirtuous, read the pages of Scripture. The act of complaining does not forfeit your faith; it sometimes makes your relationship with God richer. God does not delight in our fake praise; He delights in our authenticity. He knows that when we trust Him enough to come broken, we also trust Him enough to be the remedy. When feelings are suppressed for the sake of sanctity, resentment is established. When you feel as if you cannot be your full self, masking yourself becomes a habit. God never told us to come to Him with perfect praise and a mended heart. He wants the fullness of every piece, not just certain parts. Don't hide your emotion from God; He already knows it anyway. You are not protecting His authority by censoring what you say. I am not encouraging you to be a negative person; I am just encouraging you to be authentic with God with every emotion. Your genuine struggles will not steal your devotion.

Prompt: What is something that you find yourself complaining about often? Why do you feel the need to continue to take part in this thing? What would happen if you let it go?

_____

_____

_____

_____

_____

_____

_____

_____

_____

_____

_____

MAY 16

2 Corinthians 7:1

We will never be perfect, but we can strive to be pure. We must try to avoid being contaminated instead of waiting on the cure. God gave us the guidebook to life, and He has promised us to help along the way. He even sent us His Son to be perfect righteousness on display. We cannot passively wait around and expect God to provide us with a perfectly easy life. Just as He has promised us hope, He has also promised us strife. We must actively seek purity in every area of our life so that we may, one day, experience righteousness. In areas of our life that need explaining, we must ask God to enlighten us. Being a Christian is not a noun; it's a verb—it takes a change of heart and a change of lifestyle. It must not be a title; it must be the main part of your profile. If purifying yourself seems overwhelming, start with one single area and actively decontaminate that portion. That could mean ridding yourself of habits or teaching your eyes aversion. It is not meant to be easy, but it will improve your relationship with the Lord. In your quiet time with the Lord, ask Him what you need to turn from and what you need to run toward. A life of purity will lead to a heart of contentment and a spirit of peace. Don't forget that when you ask God to take something from you, it is your responsibility to release it.

Prompt: What do you need to run from right now? What do you need to run towards? In other words—what do you need to give up, and what do you need to do more of?

MAY 17

Joshua 2

Don't ever base your ability on the labels that the world has given you. If Rahab had denied the call because of her title, she would have never done what God was calling her to do. If Jesus had behaved according to His social status, can you imagine the miracles that would not have been accomplished? If you succumb to your earthly position, you might just miss out on your heavenly promise. We all have labels, titles, and statuses associated with our names, and they have the ability to gain momentum and take control. That is why we must remember that a title does not exist in the innermost part of our soul. We are God's children, and His workmanship on display for the whole world to see. That is why we must not be what the world tells us we should but actually pursue what God is calling us to be. We must trust God's plans more than we trust the world's perceptions. One will lead to the fulfillment of kingdom work, and one will lead to a lifetime of deception. So as you ride and go about your day today, remind yourself that your purpose outweighs the world's titles. Your labels have no authority over your ability, but your purpose is necessary for your spiritual survival. Do not be the person that the world calls you to be, be the person that the Lord created. We were made to inspire the world, not live intimidated. Your calling is greater than your self-confidence because you were made to do works that outweigh your ability. You weren't made to be defined; you were made in the hands of divinity.

Prompt: What titles do you have? Out of those titles, which one is most important to you? If you could give yourself any title, what would it be?

_____
_____
_____
_____
_____
_____
_____
_____
_____
_____
_____
_____

MAY 18

Proverbs 11:24

My dad has told me my whole life to give more away every year than I did the year before. He has done it his whole adult life, and it has resulted in him being blessed enough to give more and more. I believe that it's true because it's biblical, but my dad's life is a testament to its proof. So I have committed to the same action and believe in its truth. We hear it all the time, don't we? "The more you give, the more you will receive." But is it something that you say, or is it something that you actually believe? Do you give more than you are comfortable with, or do you only give when you have more than enough? Is it given out of sincerity or merely out of surplus? These are questions to ask yourself; they are not questions of accusation. Do you give out of kindness or with regard to compensation? There is a different feeling in your heart when your wallet is full and you give versus when you give your last cent. One is based on trust, and one is just a gift. Give what God is calling you to give, do not base it on your financial status. Don't make it an occasion; make it a habit. I want to give more than I ever have before and then continue that practice until I pass. Kindness will be rewarded, but money will not last. Do not worry about your welfare; trust that God can handle you and all of your finances. Do not waste it all by saving it or spending it; invest it.

Prompt: If you won the lottery, who or what would you give money to? Why?

MAY 19

Proverbs 27:17

Other people's actions are not our responsibility, but our actions around others are. We must be responsible for the way that we act and the life that we live. Whether we believe it or not, our actions have an extreme influence on our peers and onlookers. Because by nature, we are all consumers. My actions will influence my surroundings, regardless of my intent. Our lives are a public show that our peers have the opportunity to attend. That's why choosing who you surround yourself with is so important to who you will become. You will end up doing what the people around you have done. As iron sharpens iron, so does one man sharpen another. So although you cannot control another's actions, you can control not being a stumbling block for your brother. Live your life with intentionality and be purposeful with your actions. Take absolute responsibility for what you allow to happen. Be intentional with your pursuits and take your influence seriously. Take a step back from self-centered thinking and have a little humility. You are not responsible for me, but you are responsible for yourself. You can influence how I live my life by what you do. You have one life to live, but remember that your one life has an exponential influence on other people. Peer pressure is not just a young adult phenomenon; it's always real. Your actions have the ability to encourage, uplift and inspire. So ask yourself this question...are you iron?

Prompt: What things are you doing that could be a stumbling block for another person in your life? What things are you doing that might be a positive influence on another person in your life?

_____
_____
_____
_____
_____
_____
_____
_____
_____
_____
_____
_____

MAY 20

Ephesians 2:1–7

Living in shame of your past mistakes will hinder your future, but living aware of them will increase your gratitude. It all depends on how you approach it and with what attitude. Being born again means that your previous self has died. But there is a thin line between seeking righteousness and living in pride. When you look back on your unsaved past, it's common not to even recognize the person that you once were. Your past might become more distasteful the more that you spiritually mature. This is the time when Satan tries to inflict shame on our hearts and ridicule us for our past sins. He is really good at pointing out our past losses and making us forget about all of our wins. It's not healthy to live in the past, but it's also not healthy to avoid it. We have to have enough confidence in our salvation that our past does not destroy it. I think having a healthy relationship with your past self will allow for a greater appreciation for your salvation. Learn to confront your past self without heaping on self-condemnation. God has called us to walk in freedom, so lock the prison doors behind you. You do not have to pretend they never existed in order for them not to confine you. Claim the mistakes of your past as a trophy of the transformation that God has provided. The past should not be depressing; it should make the future *that* much more exciting.

Prompt: What part of your past are you still ashamed of today? How can you show forgiveness to your past self?

_____

_____

_____

_____

_____

_____

_____

_____

_____

_____

_____

_____

_____

MAY 21

1 Corinthians 10:1–13

Generational wisdom is one of the most precious commodities that we have today. Most of the time, we take for granted the knowledge that is shared because we underestimate the price that has been paid. Think on a secular level about how many lessons have been learned by our ancestors that we just accept now as common knowledge. They learned by doing, and now we learn what they did through lessons in school and college. Think about Albert Einstein, Isaac Newton, Sigmund Freud, and Thomas Edison. They are not just names of theories; they are people who discovered and taught us lessons. If Albert Einstein's discoveries are important, how much more valuable are the lessons of Moses? Or Samson? Or Jonah? Think about how much we have learned from Daniel, David, and Noah! Their lives each represent a lesson or lessons that we have the privilege of knowing the details. We know what happens when you disobey God without having to spend three nights in the belly of a whale. We get to walk in freedom but look back on the history of sin's chains. We get to read about the beginning of time and how times have and will change. That in itself shows the precious grace of God, that He would allow us a front-row seat to all of life's lessons. He has provided us with every example and took we need to face the unexpected.

Prompt: If you could have dinner with three people (living or dead)—who would you choose? Why would you choose them? What is one question that you would ask each of them?

_____

_____

_____

_____

_____

_____

_____

_____

_____

_____

_____

_____

_____

May 22

Proverbs 11:13

We all have the tendency to talk about others, but the moment it's labeled gossip, we claim we would never participate. Too often, our conversations are something that we underestimate. The value of our words goes much deeper than just a nonchalant chat with a friend. We have to remember that our pursuit of righteousness has no stop or end. When you speak about someone else, what good does that accomplish? All it does is include them in your sin as an accomplice. It's backward to think that "venting" to someone could actually make any situation better. Do not confuse relief with pleasure. Speaking about another when they are not present only hurts everyone involved. It does not solve a problem; it just creates more problems that will need to be solved. Because your ability to speak about another only increases the more that you do it. It is a hard habit to break but easy to abuse it. Once it becomes a norm, no one is safe from your judgment. And it's extremely difficult to be simultaneously critical and loving. It's best to hold your tongue about others unless they are present or unless, of course, it's an issue regarding personal safety. There is no such thing as righteous gossip; it's all degrading. It breaks trust, it hurts hearts, and it decays your soul. The more your tongue dominates the conversation, the less you are actually in control.

Prompt: Who is the last person that you talked about behind their back? What good came from doing that? Does gossip ever produce good fruit?

_____
_____
_____
_____
_____
_____
_____
_____
_____
_____
_____
_____
_____

MAY 23

Psalm 20:6–9

If you are following the Lord, do not ever doubt if you will walk in favor. Being blessed is just one of the many by-products of surrendering to the Savior. Will life be easy? Certainly not, but ease does not equate to blessed. In the same way, that favor does not equate to God granting you all of your requests. The favor of God runs much deeper than surface-level "yeses." It comes in ways that you needed but could have never expected. For me personally, it's often the "bonus" blessings or the "cherry on top" moments. The extra special additions that no one else notices. The "no" to my request, but the "yes" to the prayer I was too timid to pray. My dreams are like snacks, but His plans are entrees. All because of His grace, love, mercy, and sacrifice. He continues to give me bonuses even though He has paid my debts price. That is what you call *favor*, blessings, and victory. That is why I will humbly and willingly call Him my king. I have seen His generosity way too many times to doubt His goodness. He took me from empty to overflowing fullness. He allows me to experience victory even though I do not deserve it. You gain way more than you could ever lose from a life of service. Take heart in knowing that you are walking in the favor of the creator of all that is, all that was, and all that is to come. You get to walk in victory because your God has already won.

Prompt: In what ways has God shown favor in your life? Think of the little and big ways.

_____
_____
_____
_____
_____
_____
_____
_____
_____
_____
_____
_____
_____

MAY 24

2 Chronicles 6:40–42

It's important to learn the behaviors of being a good host, not just in the physical but also in the spiritual concerning the Holy Ghost. God has graced us with a companion that is closer than any friend we could ever encounter. But if we do not welcome Him in, we will never fully experience the measure of His power. Have you ever been to an event or gathering and felt out of place? Like maybe, at that moment, your presence was not desired in that space? If you can think back on that moment in time and try and remember your behavior during this situation. Did you feel comfortable enough to open up, or did remaining quiet seem like an obligation? If we do not feel invited, most of the time, we will not feel comfortable enough to express our true selves. Suppression of identity is not good for anyone's health. If we do not welcome God unto our hearts each day, He will not act to the fullness of *our* potential. He does not want to be acknowledged on occasion; He wants to be essential. Examine your heart right now. Is it hostile or hospitable? Is the relational love one-sided, or is it reciprocal? Are you willing to clean the rooms of your heart and allow the Lord to move in? Don't ignore the empowering relationship with God because you are too busy hosting selfish sin.

Prompt: What places have you felt most welcome? What made you feel welcome in those places? How can you incorporate those things into your life to make others feel the same way?

_____

_____

_____

_____

_____

_____

_____

_____

_____

_____

_____

_____

_____

MAY 25

Luke 15:8–10

It's easy to forget, so I am here to remind you that you are extremely significant. I know it's sometimes hard for you to believe when the world tells you differently. You are not just one out of billions; you are God's only you. Your uniqueness is a representation of your immense value. It's so easy to get caught up in the vastness of the crowd that you lose your sense of worth. But God has set you apart from all others since the day of your birth. If you did not matter, you would not be breathing in this very moment. God loves you, and your inhale and exhale show it. When you hear the negative voices in your mind convincing you that your life is not valuable, cite the source of the voice. You might not be able to silence it, but be sure to label it as just noise. Because the truth is that God loves you, every single part of you—from your quirks to your courage. He does not see our perceived withering petals; He sees a flower that has yet to flourish. You are a unique piece of the puzzle, and without you, it would be incomplete. You are not just a want; you are a need. He created you, He formed you, and He made you on purpose. So when you hear any voice telling you that you are insignificant, remember that God would never call you worthless. We were each created with distinction to do specific work for the kingdom. Instead of focusing on all of the ways that you are unworthy, focus on that one reason.

Prompt: Write at least three things that you love about yourself that are unique to you. Bonus points if you can think of more!

_____

_____

_____

_____

_____

_____

_____

_____

_____

_____

_____

_____

MAY 26

Ecclesiastes 10:4

Have you ever experienced the agitation of someone who was just trying to get you worked up? Maybe they approached you with a bad attitude or accused you of bad stuff. What is your initial reaction in those moments? Are you ignited or reserved? Do you dismiss their accusations, or do you view them as concerns? Being influenced by others' opinions is not always wrong, but it should always be held beneath the opinion of our Father. Sometimes other people's aim is just to disrupt and bother. But our response speaks volumes about our focus and our belief. Are we more concerned with what God says is true about us or about how we are socially received? Because the hard truth is—we will not be liked by everyone. Jesus was perfect and loving and was still hated for the things He had done. But did Jesus explode at accusations or gossip? No, He calmly continued on with His work. Instead of convincing others that they were wrong, He taught those that wanted to learn. We are called to be like Him—calm, caring, and focused on what is important. If we are doing the work of Christ, we will not always be socially supported. Is it hard to remain calm when the world around you is stirring up chaos? Yes, but it is worth it. You can be polite, but you will never be perfect. Chase after the will of God and allow the world to spin at its own speed. Stay calm and carry on following God's lead.

Prompt: When was the last time you interacted with someone who was rude? When was the last time that you acted in a rude way? How could you have acted instead?

_____
_____
_____
_____
_____
_____
_____
_____
_____
_____
_____
_____

MAY 27

Job 9:1–11

We are privileged to serve a God that is ever-present and full of grace. We do not have to perform for an encounter; we simply can rest in His embrace. The same God that spins the planets is the God that walks with you throughout your day. The same God that moves the mountains is the God that hears you when you pray. I know that we all know these facts on a practical level, but let it sink in a bit deeper and permeate your heart. The God you have the opportunity to live for is the one who created the start. How cool is it to think that the hands that hold the earth are the same hands that comfort you when hard times come? The breath that creates the wind is the same breath that fills your lungs. The one who calms the roaring waves is the same one who calms your anxious thoughts. The one who sees you in times of struggle is the same one who died for you on the cross. Sometimes we get so relaxed around God that we lose sight of His magnitude. If we can regain our perspective, I think we will regain our gratitude. We are blessed with the opportunity to have a personal relationship with our God and Savior. But if we become too fixated on our personal relationship, we will lose sight of the magnitude of God's favor. When your relationship with God feels monotonous, step back and regain perspective. Spending time out in God's creation can be highly effective.

Prompt: What are your three favorite natural places? Be specific. How could you spend more time in these three places, and if not—what natural places could you spend more time in?

_____

_____

_____

_____

_____

_____

_____

_____

_____

_____

_____

_____

MAY 28

Proverbs 16:24

Have you ever expected a harsh reply and been met with unexpected grace? In a moment of head-hanging shame, someone kindly lifted your face. Words might seem small in the grand scheme of life, but they are more powerful than any weapon. I believe the reason is because they are the purest heart-revealing expression. A harsh word can hurt for a lifetime, and a gracious word can heal a lifetime of scars. As followers of Christ, we must be aware that the words we choose to speak are not solely ours. We are servants of the creator of grace, and our responsibility is to be His extension. Sometimes the most gracious thing you could possibly say is simply to be silent and listen. Our world has enough bitterness, and it is more judgmental than an appointed jury. Nine times out of ten, you will receive either mockery or fury. It's easy to grow accustomed to this behavior, and we harden our hearts so easily toward kindness. So in a world full of dark and dreadful judgment, let's be the response that ignites some form of brightness. Let's be the words of honey that are soothing and sweet on our lips. Let's focus less on calculating judgment and more on building relationships. Let's extend grace where it is least expected so that we may resemble our Father's abounding love. Instead of pushing people down, let's point them to the Father above.

Prompt: When was a time that you were shown unbridled mercy? When were you forgiven for something that you felt was unforgivable?

_____
_____
_____
_____
_____
_____
_____
_____
_____
_____
_____
_____

MAY 29

Exodus 8:5–15

Signs, wonders, and miracles are not provided by God for dramatic entertainment; they are provided for a purpose. They are not just some kind of reward for our dedicated service. They are meant to provide revelation in the unbeliever's hearts and confidence in the hearts of Christians. They are a tool to *get*, not to *keep* people's attention. When God allows the miraculous to take place, it's as if He is letting down a divide from heaven. It's truly always an incredibly important lesson. It's God's way of meeting people where they are and trying to fast-track them to where they should be. But we cannot convince others that it's a miracle if they just believe it is a mystery. If their hearts are committed to coincidence, then we cannot persuade them otherwise. Some people will surrender to God without sight, and some people will not believe even after seeing Him with their own eyes. The miraculous works of God are gifts, but those who refuse to open them are out of the realm of our personal responsibility. Sometimes the most miraculous thing we could do for another is to pray for them on bended knees. The Bible is full of people who witnessed God's miracles and still refused to believe. Do not become discouraged; just pray that their hearts will be made complete. And as believers, we must be grateful for the miraculous works of God that He so graciously pours out on us. Miracles are not for show; they are just another expression of God's love.

Prompt: Think of a time when you witnessed a miracle happen. It could be big or small. How did this impact your life?

_____

_____

_____

_____

_____

_____

_____

_____

_____

_____

_____

May 30

1 Timothy 1:12–17

We are more inclined to make excuses than we are to take responsibility. It's like we need to make excuses for our own stability. The excuses can range from minor to life-altering lies. But the scariest part of them all is that our mind can so easily convince us of something and allow fiction to wear a "reality" disguise. Excuses are never ideal, but they specifically ruin God's gift of mercy. How can you accept this free gift if you are convinced that you are not worthy? You can tell yourself all of these lies and make excuses for your lack of surrender all you want. But just know that the fullness of God's plan cannot take place in a heart that's nonchalant. There comes a point in time with specific maturity that excuses begin to become outdated. It would become a lot easier not to make mistakes if you simply slowed down and concentrated. But in a high-speed world, excuses have become expected. Reality has become a mirage, and authenticity has become neglected. Instead of accepting responsibility for our sins, we simply excuse ourselves from the occurrence. The truth of the matter is it's less about character and more about a lack of courage. Do not miss out on eternal freedom because you were too busy trying to find reasons why it's "not for you." God's grace solely depends on who He is. It has nothing to do with what you do.

Prompt: What is an excuse that you make often? Why do you feel the need to use this excuse? What is one thing that you want to stop excusing?

MAY 31

James 2:12–13

It is so easy to jump to judgment instead of being patient in understanding. We jump ahead to conclusions like a plane extending its wheels long before it lands. We can blame it on human nature all day long, but that is a pretty lousy excuse if you ask me. Our habitual stance should not be judgment; it should be one of mercy. And not a "bless their heart" kind of mercy that is shrouded in underlying judgment and personal opinion. But rather the type of mercy that will always answer with "you are forgiven." Not because others "deserve" it but because mercy is given when you do *not* deserve it. It is what we receive from God and what we are instructed to give to every person. I do not want to hold a posture of judgment; I want to walk with a cadence that exudes mercy and grace. I do not want others to feel condemned when they see my face. The world has enough judges, it does not need me and you to be a judge too. Do not concern yourself with other people; just worry about being the best version of yourself. God can handle the judgment; it is our responsibility to handle leading people towards Him. Let's encourage and construct, but let's not condemn. Choose mercy, choose understanding, not because they "deserve" it, but because none of us do. When others think of Jesus, let them also think of you.

Prompt: Are your actions more often based on pride or humility? Why do you think this is the case?

_____

_____

_____

_____

_____

_____

_____

_____

_____

_____

_____

_____

_____

_____

JUNE

June 1

Philemon 1:4–7

Having a relationship with God is nothing short of a miracle, but relationships with people are a unique gift. They are an integral part of the kingdom of God and the life that you live. Sometimes we can be flippant with the relational ties we have been given and forget the magnitude of their importance. It goes much deeper than receiving support and being supportive. God has entwined your lives for a reason, and the intricacy of the weaving cannot be disregarded. From the beginning of time, God has sown seed and reaped harvest, but He chose to plant you and your peers in the same garden. So it's not just the intricacy of who you meet; it's the importance of their lives timing also. That God thought it right that each of you walked the earth on the same todays and tomorrows. Your friends are not choices. They are purposed by God for a reason. Every interaction is a gift to help strengthen what you believe in. We are all occupying the earth at this specific time because God wanted us to. We recognize the gift when we realize that it is so much more intricate than just me knowing you. Each and every interaction has been planned by God from the beginning of time. Our days become much more important when we realize we are part of God's design. Cherish your peers; do not disregard their extraordinary importance. We each have the honor of attending the same life service.

Prompt: Name three people you are thankful that God brought into your life (outside of family members). Why are you grateful for each one? Bonus points if you send them a text or call them and tell them what you wrote!

_____

_____

_____

_____

_____

_____

_____

_____

_____

_____

_____

June 2

Luke 8:26–39

The devil cannot steal what God already owns; Satan's cunning tricks will never win. The only way Satan can gain ground is if he can make you doubt the Spirit's power from within. Satan uses tactics of deception, confusion, and oppression. He knows that he cannot sever the ties of God's love, so he tries to distract you from the connection. Satan works hard, but he cannot outwork our God, and God will always prevail. But in order to avoid the tactics of Satan, we must stay alert and in tune with the details. No matter what your current spiritual status is, you are still a target of Satan. As long as we walk in the love of God, we will be a product of Satan's hatred. This world will always be a battleground because his attacks never cease. The Lord Almighty is our only hope for righteousness and relief. We must not fear Satan, but we must recognize his attacks. We must keep moving forward but always stay aware of the target on our backs. When we fall into one of Satan's traps, we must ask God for the strength to escape. Knowing that only God can make things right when we make a mistake. Our responsibility is to turn those mistakes into testimonies and expose the tactics of the enemy. We must boast about the mercy of our Lord while highlighting Satan's tendencies. Don't allow your life to be dictated by Satan's lies; stay grounded in the promises of truth. Next time Satan comes dangling doubt in front of you, demand him to show you proof. The authority you speak will send him into a downward spiral that will result in his retreat. But he will keep trying and trying and trying to trick you until you demand he recognizes his defeat. You are a product of heaven, do not allow lies and deception to derail you. What God has bound in eternity, Satan can never undo.

Prompt: What has you feeling defeated lately? Have you allowed God into this battle? If so, how has He helped? If not, what is keeping you from allowing Him to help?

_____

_____

_____

_____

_____

_____

_____

_____

_____

_____

June 3

James 1:13–18

Do not mistake a difficult season for an unloving God. When things are not going according to plan, we tend to assume that the plan has flaws. Does God want you to experience hard times? No, but He also did not want you to choose sin. When we choose to disobey God, we welcome the chance of misfortune. God forgives us of our past sins when we repent, but we still have to deal with the repercussions of our actions. Just because our slate is wiped clean in the spirit realm does not negate the fact that it happened. For instance, if you were drinking while driving and wrecked your car, God's forgiveness would not repair your vehicle. Do not blame God for being unfaithful when what you are expecting is unreasonable. Every good and perfect gift is from above, which means that the bad things are not. If we commit a sin, we must deal with the consequences of being caught. God mends our hearts and heals brokenness, but He is not to blame when we are left to clean up the pieces of something that we shattered. Just because He does not make everything instantly perfect does not mean that you do not matter. We have the gift of God's unending love and unfailing mercy. Don't you dare blame your bad situation on the King of kings. This season might be hard, but if you have surrendered to Him, there is good up ahead. Do not blame Him for bad directions when you did not walk where He led.

Prompt: What is something that you are hoping God will do in your life that maybe your actions are preventing from happening?

_____

_____

_____

_____

_____

_____

_____

_____

_____

_____

_____

JUNE 4

Lamentations 2:19–21

It can be tempting to fall into self-pity and feel like no one could ever comprehend what you are going through. And in some sense, I guess that is true. Your story is unique, but it's not set apart from the hand of God. But it's easy to give into the self-indulging facade. It is true that no one has ever lived life in your shoes, and they have not walked every mile of your journey. Self-pity will make your story seem clear, and a relation to everyone else seem blurry. God wants us to feel unique, but not to the point of self-indulgence. Our life does not need to be filled with "our woes," although it's okay when we have moments. Because the truth is that God understands absolutely everything that you are going through, and there is never a moment that He won't. So you can find confidence in the fact that He understands you when others don't. It might not make your "woes" feel any easier, but it will provide a sense of peace that transcends self-pity. His love and understanding allow us to go from "gripe" to "gritty." It's not about *not* feeling unique or set apart; it's more about not being absorbed by your feelings to the point that you are all you think about. Your story is unique, but you will never be left out of God's crowd. Don't allow self-pity to steal your affection away from praising God, who is infinitely understanding. God will do the peace-giving, the pacifying, and the planning.

Prompt: Are there any parts of your life that you feel self-pity about? What makes you feel sorry for yourself? What could be done to change this mindset?

_____

_____

_____

_____

_____

_____

_____

_____

_____

_____

_____

_____

_____

June 5

Romans 1:21–23

Speaking and acting are two totally different things. They complement each other, but in no way are they the same. I can say stuff all day long, but if my actions do not match my words, then my words are void. It's like boasting about your salary while being unemployed. We must match our actions with our words; it's not enough to just speak. The action portion of our faith is what confirms belief. If you believe in Christ, you will not only speak about it; you will act out your faith. It goes deeper than your vocabulary; it's how you behave. We must be careful of what we speak, and we must guard our hearts and mouths with our discipline. Often times that means a lot less speaking and a lot more listening. But the additional aspect is the action; we must also replicate our pursuit of righteousness. Glory is not given in idleness. It's movement, it's "doing," that produces growth and expresses faith. Your testimony can be understood just as much by what you do—not just what you say. Speak about the goodness of God, but allow that goodness to permeate your life. Let it not only be known by hearing but also by sight. God commands us so many times to "go" or "do," and that is not by accident. He does not just want us to claim faith; He wants us to practice it.

Prompt: Who do you *want* to be? What actions are you taking to become that person?

June 6

2 Corinthians 4:1-6

I just heard a sermon preached where the pastor was talking about how some say the Bible is not all true. And his response was, "It has no errors, but even if it did...it has a lot less errors than you." Talk about humbling, right? Talk about being confronted with absolute truth. God's Word is worthy of our pursuit. It's easier than it's not to become "high and mighty" in your understanding of God's Word. Before you know it, your foundation of beliefs is based on what you have heard. Hearing the Word of God can be good, but it has the chance of being distorted as it passes through different conduits. But when you read it on your own—it's just you and God present. We are called to be the light in a dark and desperate world, so that's just it...be the light. Do not allow others to convince you that it would be better for them if you were not so bright. Humans are the problem, and we always tend to mess up God's perfection. We need less innovation in faith and more reflection. If the Word of God says something—it's true. It's amazing how plainly God speaks when you simply allow Him to. You are a conduit of His Word, but you (or anyone else for that matter, besides Jesus) are not His Word incarnate. You are the artwork, not the artist.

Prompt: How does it feel when you realize you are not right? Name a recent time that you have had to admit that and how it felt to do so.

_____

_____

_____

_____

_____

_____

_____

_____

_____

_____

_____

_____

June 7

Luke 22:1–6

Satan has no bias, and he works overtime to try and take control of believers. He works his way into situations and disguises himself as the leader. He can take a disciple and turn them into a demonization as he did with Judas. He likes to convince people that they can be used for glory, but without him, they are useless. How do we protect ourselves as believers of the Almighty King? The first thing that we must do is protect our minds and be aware of what we are hearing. Are you hearing the voice of God, or have you been following the voice of the dark spirit? Do you avoid Satan and his tactics at all costs, or do you find yourself drawing near it? Are you offensively making a game plan but avoiding defense? Are you actively pursuing a deeper spiritual understanding, or are you satisfied with mere common sense? Are you desperate for closeness with God? Are you desperate to be used by Him? Or are you more concerned with your selfish desires from within? We all make mistakes, but there is a difference between a mistake and a stipulation. Are your sins truly mistakes, or are they rooted in selfish foundations? Did you become led astray by accident, or are you willingly submitting to Satan in exchange for a desire? Satan might light a flame under sin, but he will extinguish your spiritual fire. The reality is that none of us are immune to the attacks of Satan, but we have all the immunity that we need in the blood of our Savior. But instead of walking through life unaware, we must take responsibility for our behavior. Chase after God to the point that you are also running from Satan. Satan isn't just occasionally attacking; he is always waiting.

Prompt: What areas of your life do you think Satan might be influencing? Why? What can you do to give God back control of that instead?

_____

_____

_____

_____

_____

_____

_____

_____

_____

_____

June 8

Ecclesiastes 10:12–14

Our predictable routine of life has provided us with a false sense of control. We no longer depend on the pieces from God to make us whole. We set our calendars well in advance and plan our days down to the second. We leave little to no room for the unexpected. It's not only a rigid way to live, but it's also opposed to Christ's design. We cannot even stop and pray for someone else because we do not have "enough time." We "know" the future because we have planned the future far in advance. We do not think about the Spirit's lead; we think about our plans. We can joke and say that we are "type A," but what we really are is a "little god." Consumed by control but using a personality type as a facade. This is humbling because I would consider myself the poster child for being "type A." But I realize the more that I take control, the more my faith fades. The more that I plan the future, the further away I get from the plans He has for me. When I plan every moment, I am becoming the Spirit's enemy. I get that society operates off of schedules, but you should not allow society to permeate your entire life. Just because it's what everyone else is doing does not make it right. You do not need to plan the future; I promise that it will be infinitely better if you allow God to. He will always fill your schedule with meetings and experiences that are actually right for you.

Prompt: Are you a planner, or do you like to "go with the flow"? Why does this way of living bring you comfort? What would life be like if you were the opposite way? How do you think it would change your life for the good or bad?

_____

_____

_____

_____

_____

_____

_____

_____

_____

_____

_____

June 9

Job 12:13–23

God's will will be done. The only question is will you be in agreement or opposition? Are you bound to your desires or committed to God's mission? Often times I find myself making plans that I think are righteous without asking God if they are right. A burning fire is not the same as daylight. I can burn with zeal and passion, but if it's just a fire, it will eventually burn out. I can water my garden with a watering can, but if there is no rain, it will eventually end in drought. The same is true for a life lived outside of God's will; the ending will lead to darkness and devastation. We were promised eternal life, not a life that met all of our expectations. If I got everything that I wished for and all of my greatest plans actually came true. It still would be a fraction of perfection compared to what God has planned to do. So we each have a choice to make—submit to God's will or stubbornly drag our feet in disdain. God's will is not dependent upon your approval or complaints. How much easier would it be to find faith instead of all of the reasons His will is wrong and harmful? How much more enjoyable would your today be if you trusted Him with your tomorrow? What reason do you have *not* to trust God? Has He not always been faithful? Surrendering to His will is not just about faith; it's about being grateful. His will *will* come to pass; do you trust that it will be better than your plans? You can either be certainly insecure in your ability or perfectly safe in His hands.

Prompt: Do you believe that God will provide you with the desires of your heart? Why or why not? Have you seen Him provide for your desires before?

_____

_____

_____

_____

_____

_____

_____

_____

_____

_____

_____

_____

JUNE 10

Job 29:1–6

Hindsight really is 20/20, especially when it comes to seeing God's blessings. Because they often come in ways that you were never expecting. But when you look back on your life and see the way that God has put all of the pieces of the puzzle together, it builds your testimony. Recounting the past can become somewhat of a sacred ceremony because you can look back on years past and see how *that* connected to *this*, how *that* hard time led you into the beauty of what it currently *is*. How even in times of trial, God's love was still so remarkably evident. But a lot of the time, it's easier to see it in the past than it is to see it in the present. God does not fault us for this, but He does hope that we will pay attention to His never-ending work. So that maybe we will see Him working today because looking at the past has allowed us to learn. If you are having a hard time seeing God move, start journaling today. Then, in a few months, look back and read the words that you wrote on the page. I guarantee you will see God's hand in and around every thought, feeling, and circumstance. But it requires an intentional focus, not just a glance. If counting your blessings seems hard today, recount yesterday's instead. Sometimes you do not even realize how full you are until you count all of the times that you were fed.

Prompt: Do you journal or keep any account of the past? Take a moment right now and think back on the last time you saw God evidently show up in your life.

_____

_____

_____

_____

_____

_____

_____

_____

_____

_____

_____

_____

_____

June 11

Amos 5:12–17

I think our view of justice has been confined to the corners of a courtroom for far too long. It is not a judge's responsibility to deem something "right" or "wrong." It is our responsibility as Christians to uphold the commandments of our Father and represent justice. But it seems that responsibility has lost its luster, and the laws have lost their substance. We can make excuses all day long, but we all know what is right and what is wrong. It is easy to recognize which behaviors do and don't belong. But we have conditioned ourselves to sit back on the sidelines and allow justice to be shown and handled through appointed authorities. But how can "justice" operate in the same vocabulary as "minority." God calls us to love what is good, and in the same breath, He calls us to hate what is evil. Unfortunately, "good" and "evil" are not synonymous with "legal" and "illegal." We must stand up for what is right, even if it means being labeled as rebellious. Faith and justice require us to be bold and zealous. Do not wait around for worldly justice; walk through your day with God-appointed righteousness. This lifestyle of responsibility will not allow for an attitude of idleness. When justice is not being delivered by our leaders, then we must stand in the gap and proclaim the just acts of our Father. We need to have an attitude of boldness, not an attitude of being unbothered. Love what is good, hate what is evil, and live your life according to the standards of God's commands. We must stop sitting on the sideline. It is time to take a stand.

Prompt: When was the last time you spoke up for someone who did not have a voice? When was the last time you noticed someone who was overlooked?

_____

_____

_____

_____

_____

_____

_____

_____

_____

_____

_____

JUNE 12

Romans 11:25–27

I never want to be ignorant in a situation where the Word of God needs to be shared. I do not want others to miss Him simply because I did not bring Him there. I want to study my Bible and seek after God with absolute reckless abandon. Maybe my comprehension of His goodness can help with others' sense of understanding. As Christians, we are called to bring God everywhere we go, not as a chore but as a part of ourselves. And having God with us is more than just for *our* help. It's for sharing the Word of God and actually being able to explain it well to others. Your discipline will help others discover. But it takes time, it takes effort, and it takes a willingness to learn and listen. It requires slowing down and waiting on God's provision. Were you ever asked a question in class, and you were ashamed when you did not know the answer? Like you had fallen short of a *very* clear standard. God mercifully understands our lack of knowledge, but He wants us to *want* to know. Our curiosity and dedication are proof that we *want* to grow. And not only for ourselves but to allow the Spirit to work through us to help others too. But in order to help others learn, you must first start with yourself.

Prompt: What is an area of life that you feel ignorant about? How could you become more knowledgeable in this area? Who could help?

_____

_____

_____

_____

_____

_____

_____

_____

_____

_____

_____

_____

June 13

Isaiah 33:15–16

No matter what is happening in the world, we must remain steadfast in our attitude of positivity. Our boldness must be rooted in God's consistency, not bound to the confines of our timidity. We must remain pure and upright even when the world is crumbling around us. Not because we are "great" but because of our great trust. In moments of difficulty, we must work extra hard to be sure that we do not give in to mental stagnation. We must always be uplifting and never give in to degradation. Not just the degradation of others but the degradation of ourselves. Because speaking negatively is bad for everyone's health. We must be eager to listen to the world around us so that we may help provide relief in the current situations. Our job on Earth is to provide ease to the lifestyle of frustrations. God promises to fulfill our every need if we will exemplify His goodness in our every action. He will allow us eternal paradise if we will work to bring Him satisfaction. His satisfaction is not earned; it is given freely. But in order to receive it, we must be willing to live for God wholly and completely. So as we navigate this Naples world, we must use the compass of the Lord. We must be willing to walk in the Ford Rion that He is calling us toward. We must remain positive even when the world around us is drowning in negativity. Being an outspoken outsider is just part of God's ministry.

Prompt: Think back to a time when you went against the "popular opinion" and stood up for something you believed in. Write about why you did it and what it felt like to be steadfast in your beliefs.

_____

_____

_____

_____

_____

_____

_____

_____

_____

_____

_____

_____

June 14

Psalm 107:10–16

"Bondage" can come in many forms that exceed just physical restraint and an absence of freedom. If you have lived any amount of life, you will have walked through a bondage season. It could have been spiritual, mental, emotional, or physical restraint that you have experienced. Each presented its own challenges that were harmful and serious. But the truth is—God is the God of absolute freedom and the destroyer of chains. He refuses to leave you bound and unchanged. But it's up to us to accept His mighty love and to fully receive it. We will remain in bondage until we accept that we are free and actually believe it. Just like many of God's followers who were thrown into prison for their beliefs...Satan wants us all in prison. Taking people captive is how He makes a living. So do not downplay your bondage or avoid your chains—confront them and allow God to help. You will never be free if you attempt to do it yourself. Allow Him to break the chains of emotional bondage and spiritual restraint. Accept change and surrender your chains. You were not created to be a prisoner, so do not settle for that being a part of your identity. Bondage is not a punishment from your heavenly Father; it's a tactic of the enemy.

Prompt: What area of your life do you feel "shackled"? Ask God to help reveal how you got there and how to get out.

_____

_____

_____

_____

_____

_____

_____

_____

_____

_____

_____

_____

_____

June 15

Hebrews 6:4–8

Paul writes in the book of Hebrews how it is impossible to come back to God if you have truly known Him and fallen away. At first, this caught me off guard because I have always believed that God would forgive any and all mistakes. But turning from God after truly knowing Him has nothing to do with God's grace and everything to do with personal judgment. And when a decision has been made, you must deal with the repercussions. The truth, in all honesty, is that once you have experienced the fullness of God, it's impossible to go back. You might sway to the left or right occasionally and need God's help to get back on track. But to completely withdraw surrender after knowing Him seems absolutely unimaginable. To have tasted the bread of life and choose to eat stale crumbs seems unfathomable. God's heart breaks over the lost souls of this world, but I cannot help but imagine that losing a saved soul does not hurt a little more. That betrayal stings because of the trust you shared before. If you are a believer and struggling with your faith because of hurtful church experiences or opinionated Christians. Do not make God pay for the world's poor decisions. Give up on church, give up on a friend, but please do not give up on your creator. The hurt of the world is not the responsibility of your Savior. If you are born again, why would you want to crawl back into your decaying corpse? If you refused to turn the tap on, you would not blame the lack of water on the source.

Prompt: What are you blaming God for right now, or have you blamed God for in your life that is actually a product of human frailty?

_____

_____

_____

_____

_____

_____

_____

_____

_____

_____

_____

_____

JUNE 16

Hosea 6:6

God desires our willing surrender; He does not want us waving the white flag in despair. We don't obey because we have to out of force; we obey because we care. He desires our hearts, not our tails tucked between our legs—bound up in fear. He does not get glory when we feel shackled to being "near." If your time with God is centered around the feeling of dread, then please stop and talk to Him about that feeling that you are having in your heart. Creating a relationship that is founded on "force" will only drive you farther apart. And you might read that and think, "That's not me," but just spend a moment taking inventory of your relationship. Let me speak about a few possibilities, and you can see if the shoe fits. Do you love sitting down and reading your Bible, or do you quickly scroll through a devotional because you "have to"? Do you look forward to worship on Sunday, or is it just "what you do"? Do you intentionally talk to God about your life or just say a quick "amen" before you eat a meal? Do you say "God is good" because it's "what everyone says" or because it's how you actually feel? God wants our genuine affection, not our fake, forced servanthood. He desires our surrender, not a relationship based on "should."

Prompt: What are things that you do on a weekly basis because you "should"? What if you changed your posture towards those things to "I get to"? Or what things could you let go of that aren't serving your body, mind, and soul?

_____
_____
_____
_____
_____
_____
_____
_____
_____
_____
_____
_____
_____

JUNE 17

Romans 15:1–4

If life seems predictable and easy, I am here to tell you that you might not be living up to your full potential. A life lived in surrender is a lot of things, but it's never simple. If we are living like Christ, our life should be full of moments spent outside of our comfort zone. We should spend more time in the ambiguous than we do in the known. We were created to be a team of believers constantly pushing and encouraging our teammates to become a little stronger. Instead of a life of routine, we are meant to live a life of honor. But how often do we stop at the feeling of complacency and fail to reach our potential? How often do we avoid the big things in life and grab hold of the little ones? God has so much more for you and me than we could ever imagine. But in order to experience them, we have to make them happen. God is not going to send lost souls to your front door; you have to go out and find them. Do not miss out on life because you are content with dying. We have hope and peace that transcends our circumstances. Let go of your scheduled calendar and give God your plans. Focus on building the kingdom of heaven and encouraging your fellow believers in their own walks. Let's live big instead of small. Do not squander your potential for a life of complacency; chase after your purpose with passion. Our life is not a noun; it's a verb that means—*action*.

Prompt: What is the most exciting part of your life right now? What would make life more exciting? How can you incorporate more of those things into your life?

June 18

Galatians 5:1

Christ has set you free! I think it's time that we rejoice and start living like it. So many Christians today walk around sulking, complaining, and quiet. I know life is not easy and that things happen on a day-to-day basis that cause stress. But instead of magnifying our hardships, let's try and focus on all of the ways that we are blessed. Our call in life is to love God, love others, and lead them into the arms of Christ. But why would someone want to follow Jesus if you seem miserable in life? Walking with God entails new morning mercies, grace upon grace, and redemption. Live like you are free, not like you are still in prison. Following Christ includes being filled with joy, and not fabricated joy...the real, genuine, kind. It's something that just *is*, not something that you must find. So if you feel like you are still in bondage but have given your life to Christ—talk to God about it! God does not want you in bondage; He wants you to feel genuine joy from within. Your feeling shackled might just be an attack from Satan, and I promise that God can fix that. You are worthy of joy, don't settle for sad. You are a chosen, saved child of the utmost God; walk around like you actually believe that it's true. Allow others to see the joy of Christ when they see you.

Prompt: Make a list of the ten things that bring you the most joy. Big or small. Then write beside them how often each one is included on a weekly basis. Are you happy with the frequency of each?

_____

_____

_____

_____

_____

_____

_____

_____

_____

_____

_____

_____

June 19

Proverbs 2:1–8

This world is hard to navigate, and it often seems like the moment that you get it "figured out," something else falls apart. That is because this world is as fickle as a false start. It will entice you into believing one thing and then flip the script in an instant. If there is one thing that the world is good at, it's being consistently inconsistent. So how can we be steadfast when our world is so unstable? How can we be faith-filled when the world is so unfaithful? The truth is—Jesus—everything is dependent upon our dependence on Him. Your walk has more to do with your desire to do better and less to do with your countless sins. As inconsistent as this world is, God is *that* much more stable. He will take us from our clumsy cowardice and turn us into someone that is graceful. He can take our one-dimensional minds and establish a three-dimensional nest of wisdom. He can take our short-sighted lenses off and give us 20/20 spiritual vision. He can establish an unshakeable foundation upon the sand of our broken beliefs. He can teach us how to give with a joyful heart, far more than we will ever receive. He can instantly grant you more wisdom than you could ever learn in a lifetime. He will provide you with the information you have so desperately been trying to find. Do you see the repetitive keyword here? "He, He, He." The faster we realize the importance of "He," the easier it is to let go of the importance of "me." Life is too short to only live up to the potential that we have established when God's plans for us are far greater! Why waste your energy being the curator when you can trust the creator?

Prompt: Name five things that make you feel stressed. Write out beside each one how God could intervene and alleviate the stress.

_____

_____

_____

_____

_____

_____

_____

_____

_____

_____

June 20

James 2:1–12

It's not enough to not discriminate; we must also not show favoritism. Having a level head and an equality-driven soul takes humility, love, and wisdom. We are quick to understand the sin of hate but slow to realize the sin of positive bias. If you are increasing one, then the other is consequently getting a minus. Favoritism masks itself as intense love, but in reality, it is an unfair devotion. Having that much more love for one thing over another will only lead to commotion. God loves us each uniquely, but He loves us all equally. We must learn to love in the same way and stop loving unevenly. Can it really be a sin to love too much? As crazy as it sounds, yes, it can be. Because when your love is waited to one side, it distributes unequally. You cannot love God with all of your heart but then only love the neighbors that are nice to you. Love is an unconditional emotion; it cannot be based on what others do. Can you imagine having the true heart of Christ and viewing everyone through the same lens as the people you love the most? How much better would our world be if we didn't just love people who are similar or close? Can you imagine the conversations that would happen if a billionaire and a beggar shared a meal? What if our first instinct wasn't to hate but to heal? We must pray for the vision to view everyone as equal and then love them all the same. Love is the ignition of peace and the smolderer of pain. Let's set a table in our hearts and invite everyone in for a meal and conversation. Love out of instinct; don't hate out of hesitation.

Prompt: When was the last time you shared a conversation with someone who had beliefs that were different from yours? Recount that interaction. How did it feel to hear another's thoughts and beliefs? If you cannot recount a time, who could you grab a coffee with that might broaden your perspective on life?

_____

_____

_____

_____

_____

_____

_____

_____

_____

June 21

Acts 16:14–15

Have you ever thought about the words that people use to describe you to someone else? How important adjectives can be, and how much descriptive words help. Think about this right now, how do you think others describe you? Do you think the words that they use give an accurate and holistic view? Are you known for one attribute but feel that your identity is established in so much more? Have you become what others describe, or have you willingly allowed your soul to explore? What is the first description people use, and does it have anything to do with your devotion to Jesus Christ? Or is it linked to something merely based on materialistic sight? We cannot control what other people think, describe, or see. But we can control our ability to be the best version of "me." We can make our faith the most important part of our identity so that people have no choice but to identify us by our faith. If we make God our number one message, there will be no room for guesses or mistakes. This is not so much the case of "what people think;" it's more about your inner identity being displayed outwardly. Descriptions can have an impact, and that impact can be felt powerfully. It's not so much about gaining righteousness through others' descriptions; it's about living a life that brings God recognition. So if you feel that others may identify you by worldly markers, start making God your number one identification. It won't take long for others to realize that He is your identifying obligation. If we do this right, then we will be known because of "Him," not "me." Pure surrender and servanthood results in Him being your one and only identity.

Prompt: How do you think people would describe you? How would you want to be described?

_____

_____

_____

_____

_____

_____

_____

_____

_____

_____

_____

June 22

Proverbs 29:20

The words that we speak alter our credibility both in a positive and negative direction. They either draw us closer or further from forming a real and genuine connection. One false word or aggressive outbreak can destroy a lifetime of trust. That is why we must be extremely careful of what we choose to discuss. We must think about the words that we speak before we allow them to escape our lips. One unrestrained word has the power to ruin multiple relationships. Words that have been spoken are hard to take back because what is said out loud signifies authentic feelings that are real. Because, as broken people, we cannot help but say what we feel. But what about when those feelings are bound in ill will or frustration? How can those words lead to anything other than devastation? How can we associate ourselves with the Prince of Peace unless we resemble that same peace? How can we speak about the Love of God and allow words of hatred to be released? The reality is—we cannot—and God expects us to bridle our mouths to words of negativity. We cannot preach words of misery and expect to have a ministry. We cannot act out of a flesh-centered response and expect spiritual authority. How can we be trusted with more power when we have given our feelings top priority? We must think before we speak—better yet, we must pray before we speak. Our words must flow with truth and mercy, not spew with an unexpected leak. We are the body of Christ, and being part of the body means being the mouth and the voice. Let's make sure our words are uplifting and true, not just useless and destructive noise.

Prompt: What is one problem that you are thankful you do not have?

_____

_____

_____

_____

_____

_____

_____

_____

_____

_____

_____

_____

June 23

Exodus 22:25–28

A gift is not a true gift if it comes with conditions. Too often, we view gifts as business acquisitions. We have become so accustomed to only receiving what we have earned or what has been paid for. That the idea of a free and gracious gift does not seem possible anymore. But what about the free gift of mercy and salvation? Do you claim it without question, or are you approaching it with hesitations? Are you afraid to accept the gift because you are uncertain if you will be able to provide some type of back payment or interest? Or do you worry that maybe God's love will not be consistent? Are you scared of accepting the free gift because of what it will cost you in return? What if I told you that it is not something that can be bought, paid for, or earned? What if I told you that this was a gift you could keep for eternity, not something that had to be returned? What if we viewed gifts through the lens of salvation instead of through the lens of a world's view? What if we gave out of the kindness of our hearts, not just when things were expected or due? What if we began to see gifts as a translation of love instead of a product of expectation? What if we chose to give freely regardless of the situation? To be more like Christ requires us to become less like the world—in every way, shape, and form. We must make graciousness our priority and stop attempting to match the norms. We are called to be an example and a representation of God's love on Earth. Which means we must reveal that everyone has worth. Gifts cannot be paid for, returned, or conditional. They must be free, absolute, and intentional.

Prompt: What is the best gift you have ever received? Why was it so special? Who gave it to you?

_____

_____

_____

_____

_____

_____

_____

_____

_____

_____

June 24

Psalm 62:1–2

How many times is the answer to: "How are you doing?" "I'm good! Just really busy!"? We have gotten pulled into the lifestyle of getting things done and doing them quickly. Our high-speed environment has taken root in our soul and established residence. If you need proof, I bet your schedule will provide the evidence. So how do we live in a chaotic world but remain peaceful in our spirit and mind? How do we establish contentment in a world of discontent design? The one and only way is by seeking the one and only Prince of Peace. Jesus is the only one who can provide true rest and release. Surrendering to Him won't stop the world from being busy, but it will calm the urgency of your soul. It's amazing the freedom you receive when you give up the need for control. The busyness of life becomes a lot more meaningful when you are doing the work for His purpose. Suddenly acts of repetitive work become simple acts of service. Your days will become filled with what He has in store instead of what you think you need to do, which might look like a schedule you recognize or something completely new. The difference between us being in control of our schedule and God being in control is that He schedules time for rest. We make our schedule based on our to-do list, and He makes it for our best. So in the midst of the chaos and the high-speed status of the world, allow God to guide your steps. It's amazing the peace you will receive when you trust Him with what is next. A busy heart produces busy work, whereas a willing heart produces servanthood. Let's trade the busyness and false productivity for a life of work and rest that is meaningful and good.

Prompt: Is your busyness self-inflicted or out of your control?

_____

_____

_____

_____

_____

_____

_____

_____

_____

_____

June 25

Deuteronomy 27:15

Idol worship is evidently detestable in the eyes of God our Father, and it pains me to realize that I myself am not innocent. In fact, we all have been and currently still struggle with being idol-worshipping participants. It might not be displayed as a golden calf; maybe it's just your cell phone. You see, idol worship does not mean that you have to have statues of other gods in your home. Idol worship is putting *anything* before God and worshipping it with our focus, time, and energy. It's anything that fills our minds and occupies our memory. Maybe it's your phone, a love interest, money, or even a fixation on your physical flaws. Any time and energy spent *not* focusing on God is time and energy that is lost. When something becomes a habitual focus, do yourself a favor and fast it for a week. Even if you think it's not an idol, just do it and see. Give up that daily drink, the nightly scrolling, and the pursuit of another. Step away for a few days so that your heart's worship can be uncovered. It takes diligence and discipline to do personal pruning. But obedience and righteousness are always worth pursuing. It hurts to realize you have elevated an object onto a throne, but it will hurt worse to kneel before God's throne and have to explain your idol worship. Doing the hard work now is absolutely worth it.

Prompt: What do you think might be an idol in your life right now? How do you think it would feel to give it up for a week? Ask God to help you.

_____
_____
_____
_____
_____
_____
_____
_____
_____
_____
_____
_____
_____

June 26

Exodus 31:7–10

Accountability is an undercover gift, although it might not always seem that way. It's the action that is needed when people go astray. It's not about being bossy; it's all about being helpful and caring. If we held each other accountable, we would have to do a lot less repairing. But our pride so often gets in the way of accountability because we either *think* we are the boss or we feel like we are being judged. We roll our eyes at other people trying to get involved with *our* stuff. We puff our chests out in defense of our actions, even if we know they are wrong. Our spirit may feel convicted, but our flesh is stubborn and strong. We need each other—we need accountability, but more importantly, we must accept it. Without help from others, we will never pursue righteousness; we will neglect it. We need to seek humility in order to receive criticism without feeling attacked. So often, what is meant as a pat on the shoulder, is felt as a smack. Let's be more willing to be held accountable, and let's be bold enough to hold other people accountable too. So that I can be the best me, and you can be the best *you*.

Prompt: Do you have an accountability partner? If so, who are they, and how have they helped you? If not, who could be that person for you?

_____

_____

_____

_____

_____

_____

_____

_____

_____

_____

_____

_____

_____

_____

June 27

Romans 12:3–8

Our culture perpetuates popularity by elevating people to an untouchable status. If we are not careful, we can call into the same dangerous habit. There are celebrities, athletes, influencers, and leaders that have been put on a hierarchical pedestal and deemed "more important." But from a biblical view—that thought pattern is distorted. We are all sinners that need a Savior; not one of us has more value in the eyes of the kingdom. We are *all* brothers and sisters...take a moment and let that sink in. From the man on the street asking for money to the woman performing songs for packed-out arenas. Everyone is equal, apart from Jesus. We all make up the body of Christ, and we each have been given distinct gifts and talents. It might seem like someone's role is more important, but I promise we are all balanced. God never said that we must achieve a certain status because status to Him does not exist. We are not called to fantasize about others' lives; we are simply called to live. If you are busy focusing on someone else's gifts, how will your gifts be used to their greatest potential? We need to remember that we all have importance, and we are all influential. It's hard to stand in opposition to society, but as Christians, we must be willing to let go of societal ranking. We need to be less concerned with society's standards and more concerned with saving.

Prompt: What celebrity would you be intimated to meet in person? Why do you feel intimidated by them? What makes them have such a high status to you?

_____

_____

_____

_____

_____

_____

_____

_____

_____

_____

_____

_____

_____

_____

June 28

Hebrews 4:1–13

How often do you feel tired and worn out from the nonstop repetition of each day? How often do you wish that you had a time out from the game that was being played? Not a day of momentary rest but a day of true stillness. Because you know that rest and recovery lead to restoration and resilience. Do you know that God knew that we needed rest too, and that's why He created the Sabbath? But unfortunately, we have viewed it as an option instead of a habit. The Sabbath is not an option for rest; it is actually a proper command. It was not something that God established haphazardly; it was thought out and planned. When was the last time that you acknowledged and abided by a true Sabbath, where you truly did nothing but rest? If you were graded on how well you performed on Sabbath, would you pass or fail the test? Do not spend another week complaining about being tired if you refuse to partake in the rest that God is offering you. Do not disobey the commands of God by filling up your Sabbath with things that you have to do. God designed us to work hard for six days and then to have one full day of rest and recovery. We cannot mask disobedience with the facade that work is a luxury. You are not impressing God by working harder; you are disrespecting Him with your disobedience. You are not proclaiming your devotion; you are showcasing your deviance. Start today and learn to rest just as hard as you have learned to work from Monday to Saturday. If you poured the same energy into resting as you do with work, you would be astounded by the restoration you would receive and the words that you would pray.

Prompt: What would the ultimate day of rest look like for you? How could you make this day a reality?

_____

_____

_____

_____

_____

_____

_____

_____

_____

_____

June 29

Lamentations 1:20

The Lord knows your true feelings even when you try your best to cover them up. He can handle *all* of your "stuff." But too often, we try and cover up our dark feelings and hide them from other people. And in the process, we convince ourselves that our anguish is not real. But that is a lie, and those true feelings will come out eventually because we cannot keep them repressed forever. Sometimes we have to get real about the "bad" to accept that we need better. Repressing emotions is not holy; it's harmful. You are not always "fine;" you are carnal. We need to stop lying to ourselves because when we lie to ourselves, we are lying to the Lord too. He does not ask you to be artificially okay; He asks you to be you. And being you includes feelings that range from happy to sad. One is not inherently good or inherently bad. Repression leads to resentment, and we need to avoid resentment at all costs. Instead, let's bring our emotions to God so that any problems might be resolved. He knows what you are feeling; give all of those feelings over to Him in surrender. No glory comes from you being a pretender. So, if you are feeling joy, sadness, frustration, passion, or anguish—let it be felt honestly out loud. Do not suffer in silence. It is okay for your feelings to make a sound.

Prompt: Who do you vent to? How often do you allow yourself the space to be emotionally vulnerable with someone else?

_____

_____

_____

_____

_____

_____

_____

_____

_____

_____

_____

_____

June 30

James 2:20–26

You cannot just claim the title of "Christian;" you must actually act like Christ. Our actions must be indicative of our gratitude for His sacrifice. Works without faith are pointless, but faith without works is only half of a surrendered life. It's like wearing a wedding ring but never interacting with your husband or wife. A surrendered heart cannot help but take action for God because it beats for His purpose. If you are a born-again believer, you cannot help but take part in service. Once He changes your life, it's impossible not to live out your love for Him. Your outward life becomes a display of what has happened within. So if your only representation of God in your life is your title, stop and examine your heart. Surrender requires everything, not just a small part. It's time that Christians act like Christ Himself and not what society has deemed appropriate for the title of Christianity. We should identify more with our spirit than we do with our humanity. We can call ourselves Christians all day, but would other people call us Christians? If we only care about the label, then our surrendered heart is missing. Action is required in the service of God. It is not forced; it's instinctual. It's just part of the nature of being one of God's people. Action over acting, and loving over labels. Putting your faith into action is a fantastic way to show God that you are grateful.

Prompt: If someone did not know you, would they know that you are a Christian by the way you lived your life? Why or why not?

_____

_____

_____

_____

_____

_____

_____

_____

_____

_____

_____

_____

_____

JULY

July 1

Psalm 25:9–11

Receiving instruction is a blessing unless you allow your ego to block it. It's critical that we fill our minds and hearts with good and righteous knowledge. And we are blessed because walking with God includes walking under His perfect instruction. It's a never-ending dance of learning to grow out of our dysfunction. You have to be coachable in order to be a Christian. You have to be willing to lay down your price, change, and listen. Like an athlete in a game, we sit under the instruction of our coach and our creator. But instead of pats on the back and playing time, we gain wisdom and favor. It's a full-time job...this "following God" thing...it's a daily grind that requires practice. It's commitment to the process and dying to our habits. It's giving up "our way" for the way of God Almighty. It's trusting His instruction, our conviction, and His timing. Instead of being defensive, let's assume the posture of gratitude. Let's give Him our admiration instead of our attitude. Let's accept instruction because we have a perfect God who is willing to instruct us. He does not do it because He wants to make our lives difficult; He does it because He loves us. Let's be malleable people who are willing to change and grow under instruction. Let us be coached out of our corruption.

Prompt: Name the best coach you have ever had, and what made them such a good coach? It does not just have to be sports, just any person who you feel has "coached" you in some way.

_____

_____

_____

_____

_____

_____

_____

_____

_____

_____

_____

_____

_____

July 2

Luke 8:38–39

Sometimes we want what is *not* God's plan for us, even if it seems completely righteous. We have to remember that we are still a bit selfishly biased. When we make our plans, we still tend to allow our flesh to dictate what sounds best at that moment. And in times like that, we realize we can be our own worst opponent. Take this story in Luke as an example—a man was saved from demonic oppression and asked to follow Jesus. He decided that it would be best to dedicate his time to what he now believed in. But Jesus said "no," and to go back home and share his testimony there. He did not send him away out of hatred; He sent him away out of care. But in our eyes, following Jesus made sense and seemed like the most righteous course of action. But that is not what would have brought God the most satisfaction. The same goes for you in your life and me in mine. What do I *think* is part of God's design? And what *actually* is? And am I willing to be patient and obey? Are my decisions based on my feelings, or are they anchored in what I hear God say? What choices will I make today that I label as God-ordained when they are really my idea? Are they rooted in commands or just how I feel?

Prompt: Think back to a time in your life when you made a decision based on selfish ambitions. What came from that decision? It does not have to be all good or bad—just examine what flowed from that choice and what you learned from it.

_____

_____

_____

_____

_____

_____

_____

_____

_____

_____

_____

_____

July 3

Proverbs 17:13

Revenge is approved by the world and even expected in moments of a decision. It's because our world loves the drama of a sustained division. But repaying evil for evil will never end in a positive way; it will only result in greater destruction because it is, by nature, the opposite of the Lord's instruction. Mercy and grace cannot exist in the same atmosphere as revenge. That is like building a relationship of trust with the intent to only pretend. We cannot stoop to the level of another just so we feel equally repaid. We are supposed to model Jesus, and if Jesus had lived a life of revenge, He never would have gone to the cross or risen from the grave. We must be bigger than our desire to repay evil for evil by repaying evil for mercy. Not because the other person is "worth it," but because we are all unworthy. If you refuse to extend mercy to another, you will never comprehend just how magnificent God's mercy is for us. It's made to withstand the test of time through all of our sins and mistrust. If God can extend endless mercy to us, then we must do our best to extend the same mercy to others, even when they cause us harm. We must reach out to shake their hand even before we know that they are completely disarmed. Forgiveness does not mean much when there is nothing to forgive. That is why we must make it a foundation of the life that we live. No more revenge or repayment, just mercy and abounding grace. Take revenge out of the fabric of your life and put empathy in its place.

Prompt: Do you feel like revenge is deserved? What does "revenge" mean to you?

_____

_____

_____

_____

_____

_____

_____

_____

_____

_____

_____

July 4

Job 5:8–11

No matter what you believe or hear in this lifetime, this is the one truth that withstands the test of time: you want to be on God's side. It is impossible to live a life of abundance and blessing without having God along for the ride. Our world preaches a lifestyle of independence more than it preaches a lifestyle of surrender. It teaches you to learn to take the offensive approach instead of trusting the great defender. While being able to support oneself is beneficial, it's not spiritually sound. Without God, our foundation will be built on uneven ground. We must commit to Him and be willing to follow His perfect plan. With the understanding that without Him, we would not be able to stand. You may be able to walk through this life, but you will be missing out on the greater measure if you do not walk through life with the Lord. Without God, there is a possibility of misdirection, but with His help, you will always be moving forward. Pride is a waste of time and energy, especially if it is keeping you from living a life of surrender and commitment. It's a lot easier to be participating instead of being resistant. At the end of our life, we all will answer to God for the choices and commitments that we make. Don't miss out on eternity in heaven because you are too independent to be saved. Give up control and trust the Lord's mighty and miraculous ways. If you want the promised eternity of heaven, you must give God your present days.

Prompt: Do you consider yourself an independent person? What makes you think that? In what ways could you be more independent, and in what ways could you be less independent?

_____

_____

_____

_____

_____

_____

_____

_____

_____

_____

_____

_____

July 5

Hebrews 2:1–4

Sometimes it takes more effort to listen than it does to speak. That is because listening requires a certain level of respect, whereas talking is cheap. As Christians, we are called to speak the name of Christ and bring the gospel to light in every situation. But not all of God's commands are intended for dictation. Sometimes the most eloquent thing that you can say is absolutely nothing at all. Sometimes it requires only your ears to respond to God's call. Having ears that are eager to listen produces a heart that is willing to serve. How else can you comprehend your mission if you are not willing to listen and learn? Silence isn't always comfortable, but comfort will never produce miracles. It's better to be silent than be accidentally satirical. In order for us to become more like Christ, we must be willing to listen to His instruction and talk less about our opinion. Our desires will never outweigh His dominion. Now—don't get me wrong, there is a time to speak, and God gave us the ability to use our voice for a reason. But it's our responsibility to make sure our words are adding to His glory and not leading to depletion. If we fill the air with words, we will only be able to hear ourselves speak. Silence provides much-needed relief. Listening is more important than any word or sermon you could ever preach. It's a skill that shows empathy and has a personal reach. Serve God with every part of your being, especially with your ears. God can only reveal to you as much as you want to hear.

Prompt: Who is the best listener that you know? How do you feel when you leave time spent with them? How can you show up for people in the same way that they show up for you?

_____

_____

_____

_____

_____

_____

_____

_____

_____

_____

_____

July 6

Isaiah 9:18

Acts of wickedness are like sparks ignited in a dry forest. It might seem small, but its repercussions are enormous. One single spark can set the entire world ablaze if it is not smothered or extinguished. Flames are not willing to relinquish. We can see the figurative wildfires being ignited and causing destruction everywhere that we turn. It seems that almost everything has been or is at risk of being burned. We must assume the responsibility of spiritual firefighters and work to eliminate the flames. We can do that by extinguishing fires as well as by cleaning up what remains. Wickedness does not get to win; our promises are not littered with smoke and ash. We are here to bring fresh air to the areas that have been smoggy and overcast. We are here to end the flames as much as we are here to educate against starting the fires. It's our responsibility to explain the destructions that come from our sinful nature and selfish desires. It's more productive to educate against flames than it is to spend a lifetime putting them out. That is what sharing the gospel is all about. Once the water of life engulfs a soul, no spark can be ignited. A fire will not start if it is not lighted. Wickedness will not spread if wickedness is not started. Instead of teaching how to clean up ash, let's first teach how to plant gardens. The fires will continue to burn, but we have the authority to put them out and stop new ones from lighting. If we commit to instructing, we will limit the igniting.

Prompt: Where do you see evil around you right now? How could you potentially help alleviate this evil?

_____

_____

_____

_____

_____

_____

_____

_____

_____

_____

_____

_____

July 7

Matthew 15:35–39

We live in such an over-abundant culture that sometimes we forget the kindness of God's provision. We have been given so much that we actually believe the opportunities and gifts have to do with our decisions. But if we humble ourselves, we will realize that God is the provider of every single thing that we have. It's all that is offered, not just what we grab. Take, for instance, the loaves and fish. You would not just fill your plate, but your mind would be blown seeing the abundance. You would not just focus on your fish; you would be mesmerized by the hundreds. The same is true in our life. We grab our portion of blessing without paying attention to the thousands of blessings that have been provided already. We disrespect the miracle when we label provisions as ordinary. Your food is not on your table because it's what you ordered; it's there because God provided it. And it's not just food; it's *everything*. We need to step away from our narrow-mindedness. Your breath is a provision, your clothes are provisions, and your spouse is a provision too. All of the beautiful things in your life are gifts God has given to you. Do not become so focused on your portion that you lose sight of the miraculous abundance. Your life is made up of a million little pieces of what God's love is. Your life is not a piece of fish and a loaf of bread; it's the feast of the five thousand. Your life isn't sparse with blessings; it's actually crowded.

Prompt: Name five blessings God has given to you in the past week. They could be as big as getting your dream job or as small as finding a parking spot on the front row when it was raining.

_____

_____

_____

_____

_____

_____

_____

_____

_____

_____

_____

_____

July 8

Job 9:28–31

It can be really tempting to fall into a pit of sin temptation and succumb to its power. If you are not actively disciplined, you are at risk of being devoured. And I am not just talking about "messing up;" I am referring to the mental game that is going on in your head. We need to be careful of what we buy into and what we believe is said. For instance, when the narrative surrounding sin turns from "repentance" to "rest," there is a problem. When you start to believe that you have too many issues and that none of them are worth solving. That you are a sinner, so why would you not act out in sin? That you are already a loser, so why would you even try to win? Why ask for forgiveness when you will just sin again tomorrow? Do you see how that narrative will lead to stagnant faith and sorrow? Yes, you will sin again, but that does not stop you from redemption *now*. God knows you will mess up; it's part of the vow. But to give up on Him because you have placed your identity in sinning is the wrong path to take. He *wants* to resurrect you, so stop jumping back into the grave. It's not about you being perfect; it's about you seeking Him. Stop ignoring His ways and succumbing to sin. You are worthy of righteousness because He hung on a cross for your unrighteous nature. Your identity is not "sinner;" it's "child of the Savior."

Prompt: What is something that you are holding onto because you refuse to let God take it away?

_____

_____

_____

_____

_____

_____

_____

_____

_____

_____

_____

_____

July 9

Lamentations 1:16

Loneliness is the deepest longing a human can feel, in my opinion, because we were not created to experience it. That is why God sent us the Holy Spirit. The truth is, only the lost are lonely because they do not have the Spirit residing within their hearts. So when people fall away, their lives fall apart. Relationships are vital to believers as well, but they are not bound up in dependency. Loneliness cannot co-exist with a God that is with you unconditionally. So if you are a believer and your heart is aching with loneliness, can I ask how much attention you have been giving the Lord? Have you stifled the sacredness of your spiritual reward? Have you claimed loneliness but ignored God's unconditional company? Have you disregarded the Holy Spirit in the midst of dependency on somebody? If you are not a believer and you are experiencing loneliness, I would love for you to meet my friend Jesus. You never have to be alone again, and He is the reason. Not only did He die on your behalf, He sent His Spirit to live within your heart. So not only will He never leave you, you actually physically cannot be pulled apart. He is the remedy to loneliness and the piece of the puzzle that is missing. Loneliness is a tool from the enemy to distract you from living. I am not saying relationships are unimportant or easily disregarded. I am just encouraging you to fill the gaps with Jesus before the loneliness gets started.

Prompt: When do you feel most alone? What do you need in order to feel less alone in this life? Be honest with God—see what longing your pen reveals.

_____

_____

_____

_____

_____

_____

_____

_____

_____

_____

_____

_____

July 10

Psalm 9:7-10

The Lord is so many things; in fact, He is everything to us if we will let Him be. He is our Savior, our strength, and our security. He is our ending joy and our peace in times of chaos. He is our shelter in the storm and our compass when we are lost. He is our refuge, and He shelters us from the pursuit of danger or trouble. He carries us out of the burning building and protects us from the rubble, like an armored guard protecting a castle and keeping out trouble from getting in. That is Jesus defending your body, mind, soul, and spirit from harm and sin. But we have to allow Him to protect us; we cannot just put up our own armor and disregard our need for His. Because it's not just what we keep out, it's what we already have let in. And if left up to us, our armor would deflect a few things but also suffocate us with danger from underneath. We need protection from things that are unheard of and unseen. We need God for everything, and we need Him all of the time. We need Him when the storms are raging and when the sun shines. Because the three basic necessities of life are water, food, and shelter—and guess what...He is all three. The fountain of unending water, the bread of life, and the boat on the raging sea.

Prompt: Describe home. What makes you feel at home? In what ways does God resemble home to you?

_____

_____

_____

_____

_____

_____

_____

_____

_____

_____

_____

_____

July 11

Matthew 12:25

Division creates weakness in every area or situation in our life. Things begin to deep through the cracks when we are not held together so tight. My first thought is the childhood game red rover, where you would lock arms and try and withstand someone's all-out charge. It would not work if you held hands at arm's length apart—*only* if you locked arms. And not just because arms are inherently stronger but also because there was less space in between. The closeness made you a stronger team. And that is the mental image that God is giving me for families, churches, countries, and communities. Where there is empty space, there is no unity. So when the opponent comes running, the weak spots cave in immediately. There is no fight; it happens easily. And those weak spots look like addiction, denominations, politics, and racism. It is when power becomes more important than people and sympathy dies to the rat race of the social system. It's when medication becomes more important than family, and recognition becomes more important than relationships. When the space in between becomes greater, the human bond cannot withstand the enemy's hit. The void space is present in every part of our society today, and it is our job to bring it back together. To pull people closer and make our grip better. Instead of hanging on by fingertips, let's lock arms and hold each other close. That way, we can handle the pressure when the enemy begins to oppose.

Prompt: What weak spots do you see in the world or in your own life that are causing disunity? What is the solution to those things?

_____
_____
_____
_____
_____
_____
_____
_____
_____
_____
_____
_____

JULY 12

John 15:9–14

Love is the greatest command of them all, so why do we overcomplicate it? We are slow to show it and quick to say it. We jump to judgment so quickly and wave our love around with unending conditions. But that is not how our love is supposed to look as Christians. We are to love like Jesus, which means unconditional and relentless. It's a love that's rooted in patience, grace, and forgiveness. Not because another person earned it, but because they just *are* a person. Their humanity makes them 100 percent deserving. It has nothing to do with their lifestyle or their personality; they are worthy to be loved regardless of those details. Unconditional love does not require balanced scales. It just is, regardless of any other circumstance or behavior. We must love people wholeheartedly if we want to love like our Savior. Examine your heart. Do you feel love for others, or is it a process that you go through? Is it based on who they inherently are, or just how they treat you? We could all use a little more love in our lives, so let's be the change that we wish to see. Let's start releasing what we wish to receive. Let's lead with love, not judgment or question. If we truly followed that command, Earth would feel a lot more like heaven.

Prompt: What makes you feel loved? What do you think that you do that makes others feel loved? How often do you do those things?

_____

_____

_____

_____

_____

_____

_____

_____

_____

_____

_____

_____

_____

JULY 13

Proverbs 15:4

We all know that words hold weight, but we often sling them around like they mean nothing. Words are heavy when they are hateful and when they are loving. Think of all of the things that you can remember people saying in your life; I bet the list is long. From compliments to people saying things that make you feel like you do not belong. It is crazy how much I remember about conversations, or even passing comments, even the slightest things I can recall. Moments when people affirmed me and moments where they made me feel one inch tall. The point is, regardless of the context, words are extremely influential. They are written in permanent marker, not an erasable pencil. So we must be careful what we speak out loud to others because you never know the impact until they have received it. The minute it becomes a verbal word, others will believe it. And I don't know about you, but I want to be an encourager, not a spiteful speaker. I want to magnify all of the ways in which someone is like Jesus, not be a hateful word repeater. Don't speak words that are hateful, and do not speak words that are not true. Choose silence when it's necessary and speak boldly when you need to. Our voices are a gift, but only when we use them as such. Our world is really good at making people feel less than; let's use our voice to encourage people that they are enough.

Prompt: I want you to think of three to five people that you interact with on a daily basis. Write their names down, and then out beside their names, write one sentence of intentional encouragement to each one. Now, at some point today, I want you to speak those things to each person. See how they react and how it makes you feel.

_____

_____

_____

_____

_____

_____

_____

_____

_____

_____

_____

_____

July 14

Romans 4:16–17

Confidence does not equal faith, but where there is faith, there is also confidence. Just because you feel a certain way about something does not mean that it is God's providence. Faith is much deeper than a feeling; it is an intense sense of knowing the unknown. It is the trust in seeing what is yet to be shown. Confidence is abundant in our world today, but I would argue that faith is less so. We are bold to speak about what we see but more timid when things are unknown. But as Christians, our cornerstone is not confidence; it's faith. It's not the assurance of proof; it's the empty grave. It's not about being zealous for the past; it's about trusting God with your future wholeheartedly. It's not the answer to the prayer; it's the muttered words on bended knees. The more that we rely on faith, the more confident that we will become in our Lord's love for us. The more that we depend, the more that we will trust. The more that we lean on faith, the more confident that we will become in that faith coming to fruition. The less we depend on our eyes, the more we will see with God's vision. Confidence from proof and experience is shallow, but faith in God is as deep as an unending well. Let's be more of a "trust and see" person and less of a "show and tell."

Prompt: What have you not seen but know is true? Think outside of the context of spirituality. Why do you *know* this is true?

_____

_____

_____

_____

_____

_____

_____

_____

_____

_____

_____

_____

_____

July 15

Nahum 1:5–6

It's important to relish in the love of God, but we also must remember how powerful He is. The whole universe and everything in it is alive because He lives. With one word from His mouth, the mountains fall, and the oceans roar. God is the only one who can look at a finished product and instantly make it into something more. I get lost in God's love, and I tend to fixate my attention on our father-daughter relationship. I'll admit that I sometimes forget about His authority as I focus on our intimate acquaintanceship. It's not that I am viewing God wrong; it's that I am only viewing half of His glory. Like I'm only reading the chapter titles of an extremely detailed story. God is loving, but He is also the Almighty creator. God is your closest friend, but He is also your Savior. He delights in your honesty, but He also demands reverence. He doesn't just want you to welcome Him in; He wants you to bow in His presence. It's hard for our human minds to comprehend the supernatural spirit of God; that's why it's important to ask God to remind you. Ask Him to give you the proper lens to see His glory through. Do not be content with half of His nature when His totality is so much more intricate. Do not be content with the flesh when He has graciously given you His spirit. He is the alpha and omega, and He is also your best friend. Do not be so stuck in the middle that you forget He is the beginning and the end.

Prompt: In what ways do you see God as a friend? In what ways do you see God as the Father? How do you interact with Him as both a companion and a creator?

_____

_____

_____

_____

_____

_____

_____

_____

_____

_____

_____

July 16

Psalm 34:8

The small things in life are really easy to miss, especially when you are focused on the big picture. It's easy to miss spontaneous blessings when you only remain focused on the things of life that are fixtures. Take a moment and reflect back on a time in life when you truly savored every moment. You took in every sight, every smell, and every word that was spoken. Maybe it was a time spent away on vacation or just a simple day at home with the person that you love the most. But regardless of the scenario, your heart, mind, and soul were completely engrossed. The colors seemed more vivid, the smells were delightful, and the joy seemed to be endless. You left that environment wishing that the moment could be extended. What if I told you that it was not the place—it was actually the Spirit within you? Your heart, soul, and mind all aligned into a moment of exactly what you desired to do. The details became so important because the moment itself had meaning. What would happen if we approached our every day with the same type of joy-filled seeking? In every situation of life, you can taste and see that God is good. From the mountaintop views to the simple walks around your neighborhood. God's blessings are endless, but it's up to you to recognize them and soak up the benefits. Often times that requires utmost focus on the details of the present tense. Do not postpone joy for moments that are out of the ordinary; soak up the blessings of today. It might seem monotonous to be in the same place with the same people but enjoy the sights that you see and the words that others say. We should not have to escape the norm to soak up each moment. It's not about where you are; it's about where you are focused.

Prompt: What are things that delight you in your day-to-day life? What are things that delight you that *could* be included in your day-to-day life?

_____

_____

_____

_____

_____

_____

_____

_____

_____

July 17

Hebrews 2:6–8

It's a beautiful realization when you understand that God chooses to be merciful. He does not have to, but He chooses to make His love unique and personal. He doesn't just love us; He gave us the whole world and promised us paradise after death. He gave us a life to live, and He sustains us with each breath. How does it feel to know that the God of the universe is mindful of you? Based solely on who you are, not what you do. He has crowned you with honor and glory because of His mercy, not because of your righteousness. He can still pour out blessings in the midst of your idleness. How can we doubt God's love for us when He has given us the world and more? He has given us what we need and promises us all that we hope for. He is aware of the most intricate details of your life because He created you and purposed each one. He loves you as you are, whether you are laced up in perfection or chaotically undone. How can we worry about anything when we have God's love which is greater than everything? How can we doubt our purpose when we are His offspring? How can we lean into more of Him without realizing that He is all of us? A relationship has to be built on more than just trust. You must trust God blindly but clearly see the depth of His love for you. Being a believer is something that you are, not just something that you do. It takes faith and trust as active notions, but it also takes introspection in conversation. God has granted us the ability to come to Him in each and every situation. You are a child of God, chosen for eternity and given a crown of honor and glory. The God of all creation is interested in each and every word and page of your story.

Prompt: How does viewing yourself as a kid of the king change your mindset about God? Write what it feels like to be considered His offspring.

_____

_____

_____

_____

_____

_____

_____

_____

_____

_____

July 18

Ecclesiastes 1:12–18

I think we have all heard some version of the saying, "With great power comes great responsibility." But have you ever associated the same terminology with your sense of spiritual dependency? With great reliance on the Lord comes great expectations of behavior. With great devotion to God comes the expectancy to resemble our Savior. With great intelligence comes the opportunity to share knowledge and instruct with leadership. With great courage comes the opportunity to showcase how to be fearless. With great wisdom comes the responsibility to teach and spread advice. The gift of wisdom is that you can share with others how to be wise. But see...it's all our responsibility because we have been given such abundant gifts. If we ignore our responsibilities, our purpose will be missed. It's not a question of if we should, it's a question of if we will. How many gifts will we use to their full advantage, and how many gifts will we let Satan steal? Do you feel an urgency in life to share, instruct, and lead? Or are you happy with focusing on your current wants and needs? As children of God, we have accepted the responsibility of being an advocate. It's not up to you to determine whether you are good or bad at it. Wear it with a badge of honor, and let's get to work. Start fulfilling the task that is uniquely yours.

Prompt: Who is the best teacher you have ever had? What qualities made them a good teacher? How do you implement techniques of teaching on a daily basis?

_____

_____

_____

_____

_____

_____

_____

_____

_____

_____

_____

_____

July 19

Micah 5:4

It is in our biological nature to crave a sense of security and feel protected. None of us enjoy feeling vulnerable or neglected. So we attempt to find security in people and hide under the shelter that they have created. But resting under the shelter of a human is unstable and complicated. That is why we are so blessed to have a God who provides us with endless comfort and protection. He is faithful to provide us with care, comfort, and direction. But we will not feel that presence unless we fully depend on Him instead of depending on people for our security. We can easily get wrapped up in others' unstable immaturity. We have all done it, right? Put another human in God's place? We ignored our walk and took off running at their pace. But then what happens? They let you down...not because they mean to, but because they are human. They cannot be the provider because they are too busy consuming. Examine your life—who are you depending on right now, a person or the one true God? Are you putting your life in perfect hands or hands that are flawed? I have been putting my life in the hands of others, and I am ready to give it back to my king. I do not want Him to have pieces; I want Him to have everything.

Prompt: Who have you been putting in place of God? How can you give that title back to Him and still continue in a healthy relationship with that person?

_____

_____

_____

_____

_____

_____

_____

_____

_____

_____

_____

_____

_____

_____

July 20

2 Peter 2:9-12

When you are in opposition to something, it's easy to become outspoken in your disapproval. But our disdain for something can often be brutal. There is no greater evidence of this behavior than the unbelievers who heap words of condemnation on Christians. It's one thing to choose not to believe, but it's another when you make ridiculing others your life's mission. We see these people and experience their hatred, but we still mimic some of their negative dialogue. Ours can't be right if all of it is wrong. Will they have to answer for their outspoken heresy? Yes, they will be judged and punished. But just because we believe does not mean that we will be spared from judgment. We may not be blaspheming God, but if we are judging others, then we are still choosing sin over righteousness. We have to obey the standard that has been required of us. Is it sad to see unbelievers slander God? Yes, it is absolutely heartbreaking! But judging them for their slander will not lead them any closer to their saving. We have to guard our hearts, minds, and mouths from any words or thoughts that are in opposition to the Word of God. We do not have the right to run our mouths just because we are flawed. Do not mimic the behavior of the unbelievers; mimic the behavior of Christ. Do not heap more ridicule on others—be an exhibition of mercy and sacrifice.

Prompt: In what ways do you resemble the world in your actions and speech? How could you change those to be more Christ-like?

_____

_____

_____

_____

_____

_____

_____

_____

_____

_____

_____

_____

_____

July 21

1 John 2:8–10

The most dangerous lie we could ever tell is a lie that we tell ourselves. Not only does it cause problems in our life, but it has the ability to wreak havoc on our mental health. A lie takes root like an unwanted weed in the garden, slowly taking over and gaining more and more ground. Until one day, you go to reap your harvest, and no fruit can be found. As Christians, the lie that we most often tell ourselves is a life of self-righteous achievement. It is easier to sweep our sin under the rug of confusion than it is to own up to its completion. Claiming that you have not sinned does not make you sinless; it makes you blind to your sinful reality. Often times our intentions leave us absent-minded to their actuality. Our attempt to please God with self-righteousness leads to us getting in our own way. That is why in every situation, truth must be the melody of every word that we say. A lie will only deceive you, but God will never be deceived by your lie. We must live a lifestyle of "conviction and self-discipline," not "make mistakes and deny." God will always be there to forgive you, but a lie makes it hard to forgive ourselves. Because once we realize the lies have taken root, we have to dig up all the weeds around it as well. It's easier to take in conviction one sin at a time and repent for the mistake at the moment. By covering up our sin with a lie, we are creating a massive conviction postponement. Be honest with yourself because if you're not honest with yourself, you will not be able to be honest with anyone else. A lie might feel good at the moment but hurt for a lifetime, but the hard truth always helps.

Prompt: What is a lie that you are still in the midst of living? How can the truth take its place?

_____

_____

_____

_____

_____

_____

_____

_____

_____

_____

_____

July 22

James 4:13–17

It does not matter your personality type or way of life; we are all caught up in the humanness of planning for the future. And somewhere along the way, we have been told that our plans provide God with humor. Have you ever heard the old saying: "Tell God your plans if you want to make Him laugh"? This notion implies that God finds humor in what you want but do not yet have. It's an inconsiderate and harsh attitude to place on the God of empathy, love, and mercy. It implies that all of your hopes and dreams are pointless and unworthy. Should we plan for the future? No, not unless we have received absolute confirmation from the Lord. But just because we cannot explicitly plan for the future does not mean we must never look forward. We were created to hope, we are called to dream, and we innately have desires. But what we cannot forget is although we construct our dreams, God is the dream provider. He created us with a purpose, and in that purpose, He placed dreams, hopes, and desires that we would yearn for. He did not create these emotions in us to let us down; He established them so that we would recognize that He always gives us more. Instead of making plans for tomorrow, share your plans with God and then let Him rewrite your schedule. Trade in the expected for the miraculously special. Do not hide away your hopes and dreams; show God how much you desire the purpose that He instilled within you. Turn your plans into a conversation with God instead of something that you just "do." Instead of having a schedule full of plans, let's have a schedule full of purpose. Our dreams are not reached with an agenda; they are secured with a heart of service.

Prompt: What is one dream that you are holding onto hope for that you have never shared with anyone? Why does it scare you to share it? Do you trust God to make it happen, or are you quietly trying to make it happen yourself?

_____

_____

_____

_____

_____

_____

_____

_____

_____

_____

July 23

Lamentations 3:10-12

Satan isn't too busy to bother you; he is always patiently waiting. He doesn't set traps and forgets to check them; he is constantly reeling and baiting. It's not something to be scared of, but it's something we need to be constantly aware of. Because every day, we are living in a moment when "push comes to shove." The thing about Satan's temptations is that they often look innocent at the start. A lot of the time, they do not send up any red flags in your body, mind, or heart. But then, before you know it, you are trapped in his snare or flailing about on his hook. You are taking his bait before you even have the chance to stop and look. But from what I have learned in my lifetime, I have realized that he is completely predictable. He is not smart, creative, or even that original. He just doesn't play fairly, and if life was a game, he would be the poor sport cheater. He uses the same bad tactics over and over because he is a repeater. Our life doesn't need to be spent looking for him; we just need to be aware. That way, we avoid his bait and his snares. He makes a living destroying our lives, and I want to do everything that I can to pick his snare up, throw it in his face, and roll my eyes. He isn't scary; he is just really good at being in disguise.

Prompt: If you take a moment to examine your past week, can you pinpoint any traps that Satan was setting? Did he catch up, or did you avoid it? In what way can you allow your past to inform your future?

_____

_____

_____

_____

_____

_____

_____

_____

_____

_____

_____

_____

July 24

Luke 3:4–6

When you have a houseguest coming into town, don't you take time to prepare? You spend hours cleaning to make sure everything looks nice when they get there. You clean up the rooms and straighten things up that are not even out of place. You make sure that every piece of art is dusted and every book is straight in the case. Is it because the houseguest cares if everything is in order? Ninety-nine percent of the time, no. You do it because you care about the guest, and tidying up is how that care is shown. Well, what if we looked at our heart as a home? Because in the spiritual realm, it is. It's where our soul resides and the Holy Spirit lives. Do you prepare your heart each day like you are about to welcome royalty into your home? Are you taking the time to intentionally place things, or are things scattered and thrown? Are you cleaning up your heart with repentance, and are you putting flowers on the table with praise? Prayers are the paintings on the wall, and your worship is the bouquet in the vase. The homemade meal is the relationship with God, like a conversation with someone that flows with ease. The opening of the door is the falling to your knees. Is your house prepared, or are you content with hosting the King of kings without intention? He will show up no matter what, but wouldn't it be nice if you had something waiting for Him in the kitchen?

Prompt: What does "being a good host" entail to you? In what ways do you show hospitality to others? In what ways do you show hospitality to God?

_____

_____

_____

_____

_____

_____

_____

_____

_____

_____

_____

_____

_____

July 25

Mark 6:45–56

When reading the Bible, you are given page after page of miracles to digest. I think we would all be lying if we did not have them ranked in our minds from "mediocre" to "impressive" to "best." Now, explicitly you may have never ranked God's miracles, but you cannot tell me that some are not more impressive than others. But we must step back and try and comprehend the vast ground that God's miracles cover, from walking on water to filling jars with oil to raising the dead from the grave. With every miracle, God's intention was to save or lead someone to be saved. It's easy to read the miracles of the Bible and say, "I wish that I could have experienced that!" When in reality...you will, and you probably already have. Not every miracle is a resurrection or a gravity-defying feat. Sometimes it's just the small instances that He makes the broken complete. He may have never allowed you to experience walking on water, but what about all of the steps that He has guided? You may not ever see 5,000 people fed by one lunch, but what about the never-ending nourishment that He has provided? What if some of your life's miracles were written in the Bible? Would you rank them high on the list of miracles? Or are you too busy demanding God to produce greater evidence that is physical? The reality is: God produces miracles every moment that you take a breath. Look for the miracles happening in your life, not just ones that involve conquering death. He is the God of details, and He shows up in ways of magnitude and subtlety. His miracles are not few and far between; they are being poured out abundantly!

Prompt: What miracles in the Bible stand out to you? What miracle do you wish you could have experienced in person? What miracle have you seen in your lifetime?

_____

_____

_____

_____

_____

_____

_____

_____

_____

_____

July 26

Mark 1:9-13

God's love for you is not temperamental; it is steady and consistent regardless of the season. God is love, so He shows us love. He does not need a specific reason. It's easy to think that God has withdrawn His affection from you in seasons of trial and persecution. It can feel like God has turned His back on you in complete and total seclusion. But read this scripture and realize that God told Jesus how much He loved Him and then immediately sent Him into the wilderness for forty days to be tempted. Jesus did not bask in the peace of His anointed authority; He was relentlessly tormented. Now, to us as humans, we could easily label this as being "thrown to the wolves" and question God's motives. We could quickly fall into the natural inclination of assigning God our human emotions. We could question God's love for His Son because of our own opinions of what love looks like. But wouldn't that make God wrong and us right? God cannot be wrong, and His love is far greater than any love you have ever given or received from another. God is love itself; He is not just a perfect lover. So if your circumstances are tough, don't blame God's affection; draw closer to His embrace. He has a plan for you at this moment and in this place. He didn't banish Jesus to a life of torture; He just sent Him into a tough forty days. He did not love Him any less or more—God's love is simply *always*.

Prompt: Describe a season of wilderness in your life, and then describe how God showed you love even in that season.

_____

_____

_____

_____

_____

_____

_____

_____

_____

_____

_____

_____

July 28

Luke 3:11

"Sharing is caring." It's easy to say but harder to actually do. Our world has taught us that it is okay to only focus on "you." To remain fixated on your needs past the point of actually needing. It's no longer about sustenance; we are just flat-out greedy. If you need any proof of that, just think back to 2020 when every aisle of the grocery store was absolutely empty. Was it empty because everyone bought *one* package of toilet paper? *No*—we all bought as many as we could. Because as long as *we* were taken care of, we were good. But what about the person who just desperately needed one, and there was none left? How did this scarcity mindset go to our heads? And it's not just the result of the pandemic; we were selfish far before COVID-19. We need to refocus on the fact that we are actually part of a team. I am not saying "give everything away," but we do need to be more mindful of our overabundance. Is it providing you satisfaction and safety or just sustenance? Do you have *so* many of something that you know others have none of? What would it look like to not live out of selfishness and rather out of selfless love? Let's be more mindful of our abundance because abundance can often lead to idolization or, at the very least, a false sense of control. Nothing you buy or have will complete you...only God will make you whole.

Prompt: What is something that you have in abundance that others have little of? How could you share this commodity or at least become more aware of your privilege?

_____

_____

_____

_____

_____

_____

_____

_____

_____

_____

_____

_____

JULY 29

Isaiah 32:6–8

Just because everyone else is doing something does not mean that it is okay for you to do it too. Just because it works for them does not mean that it will work for you. We do not receive permission from the world around us; we just obey the commands of our Father. Instead of finding our identity as a peer, let's find it as a son or daughter. Because the truth is, if we follow God, we should oppose the societal norm. Not because we are rebellious but because we will *not* conform. When everyone else is acting foolish, we must stand firm in righteous discipline. Let's have a farsighted vision. Where the close influence of humanity is blurred, but the view of heaven is crystal clear. Our allegiance is *there*, not here. And as a child of God, we must recognize when the world is gaining our allegiance and attention. Instead of acting and imitating, we must surrender and listen. God is so good to us that He allows us to act like a fool and still be His. But let's not just praise Him with our mouths because He forgives. Let's chase down righteousness and throw off foolishness. Life is more than just social status or inclusiveness. Let's be disciplined enough to be set apart and not with grumbling but with gladness. Let's be influenced but the Almighty King of kings—not the world's madness.

Prompt: In what ways do you blend into the world around you? In what ways do you stand out?

_____

_____

_____

_____

_____

_____

_____

_____

_____

_____

_____

_____

_____

_____

July 29

1 Corinthians 1:26–31

God does not need you to behave in ways that are outside of the realm of "you." Let me explain what I mean. He created you with intention as an integral part of a team. He does not need you to play every role or act out in ways that exceed your unique gifting. Because what role would God play if nothing in your life was missing? You see, if we had it all figured out and felt as if we had the means to handle every situation, our ego would be enormous. We would not be grounded in the reality of our imperfection; we would be caught up in our own personal performance. If we knew it all, our inclination would be to constantly boast about our abilities. But we get to focus on our God's goodness when we are honest about our deficiencies. And once we come to terms with that, we realize that we can only boast about God because He is all the good that is within us. We don't boast because of who we are; we boast because of what God gives us. Because without Him, we are nothing; that is just the true reality. It can be incredibly liberating to admit your lack of capacity. Because God is our all in all, and *that* is worthy to be boasted about. We are everything with Him and nothing without.

Prompt: What do you view as your greatest strengths? What do you view as your greatest weaknesses?

_____
_____
_____
_____
_____
_____
_____
_____
_____
_____
_____
_____
_____
_____

July 30

Micah 3:5–12

We are quick to blame others for misleading us but slow to examine why we were following them in the first place. It's not fair to blame others for their stench when we are choosing to occupy the same space. Is it wrong for people to spread false information? Of course, but it's also wrong for us to be dependent on their words. We were not created to find absolute truth in any part of this world. The example that automatically comes to mind is the media. I think we can all agree that it is pretty corrupt. Half of what they tell us is over-exaggerated, and the other half is junk. But the media does not owe us truth or morally biased news; it's their job to be that way. Instead of pointing the finger at them, maybe we need to uncover why we feel the need to believe everything that they say. This is not just a media problem; this is any and all speech that guides you away from morality and God's commands. But once again, do not blame the person with the microphone; examine why you put the microphone in their hands. It does not make their lies any less sinful; it just gives you the power to overcome the false teachings. You should not just believe what everybody is preaching. Guard your mind against misinformation by lending your ears to what God is speaking. Listen to the fountain of life, not just whatever water is leaking.

Prompt: Who have you given access to a microphone in your life that you need to silence instead?

_____
_____
_____
_____
_____
_____
_____
_____
_____
_____
_____
_____
_____
_____

July 31

Luke 6:37–38

I recently heard someone say that "we judge ourselves by our intentions, but we judge others by their behaviors," which can lead to a judgmental mindset. Of course, we will be quick to judge if we view others' "worst" and only view our "best." I would be willing to say that 90 percent of the time, people are giving life their best effort. We just only have access to the displayed information. In other words, we get the action, just not the narration. So often, we default to judgment instead of defaulting to mercy. Because it's easier to come up with the 500 ways they don't deserve grace instead of the *one* reason they are worthy. God explicitly tells us to judge others in the same way that we would want to be judged. We throw out sucker punches when we expect in return only a little nudge. It's easy to view our sin through the lens of reason because we have lived the backstory. But when others sin, we simply write them off as falling short of God's glory. How would you feel if God judged you in the same way that you judge others' mistakes? Aren't you grateful that His automatic response is grace upon grace? So if we are willing to take His grace, then shouldn't we be willing to give some in return? Because grace is a free gift that is not deserved or earned. Make today the first day that you view others' actions through the lens of intention. Allow grace to be an automatic gift that has no conditions. Learn to be a member of the jury, and sit back and learn to dissect behaviors and truly listen. Nine times out of ten, we all have good intentions.

Prompt: How does it feel to be misunderstood? What does it feel like to be judged by people who do not really *know* you? How often do you do this to others?

AUGUST

August 1

Psalm 42

Take a moment and think back to a time when you were extremely thirsty, and your body was crying out for fluids. Maybe it was after an extreme event, or maybe it was just a day that it was really humid. Regardless of what comes to your mind, I believe that we all can relate to the desperation of dehydration. A simple glass of water becomes extremely underrated. The moment that the water hits your lips, you become unable to stop drinking the quenching liquid. Like a drooping flower after a rainstorm, suddenly, your head is lifted. Now what would happen if we treated the Word of God like a cure for dehydration? What if God's Word gave us the same quenching sensation? The reality is that it does; we just have to need it the same way that we need water. Instead of running to the stream, we have to run to the Father. If you are a child of God, then the Word is already a necessity of your soul. Without consistent nourishment from Him, you will never be healthy and whole. Without the daily inpouring of spiritual hydration, you will become a dry, barren soul dependent on yesterday's portion to sustain you. We are built to receive more with each day that is new. Every day we must be like the deer by the stream panting for water, desperate for the spiritual hydration and sustenance that only God can give. If we know we can only go three days without water in the physical, how do we expect to occasionally drink from God's Word and still live? Run to the quenching waters of God's Word, do not become content with being dehydrated. Your harvest cannot come if your soil is dry, and God's intention is for our soil to be saturated.

Prompt: What does it mean to be in a spiritual drought? Have you or are you currently experiencing it? How did God rehydrate you?

_____

_____

_____

_____

_____

_____

_____

_____

_____

_____

August 2

Philippians 2:12–13

Faith is a uniquely personal thing that is shared only between you and your creator. Only you have control over your faith; no one else is the curator. Is your faith rooted in your personal relationship with God, or is it rooted in your relationship with another human being? Does God define you, or is it others that give you meaning? Is your faith the same on a Tuesday morning as it is on a Sunday afternoon after hearing a sermon preached? Are you following Jesus for yourself, or are you following someone else's lead? Are you bowing down to the Almighty, or are you kneeling before a disciple instead? Are you getting the bread of life from the source, or are you blindly being fed? You see, Paul wrote and inspired a generation of people to become Christians, but he was not Christ. He wanted to be sure that all those who learned from him knew who gave true life. Humans are fallible, and ego tends to take over when influence combines with wisdom. And if you are not careful, you can start seeing the Word of God through someone else's vision. It's *your* faith, not your parent's, or your preacher's, or your spouse's. We all have an individual room in God's residence; it's not a neighborhood with many houses. Take control of your faith, and claim a sense of wonder, do not rely on the faith of someone else. Salvation does not come from being near a saved person; it comes from being saved yourself.

Prompt: Who helps you make sense of Scripture? It could be a pastor, mentor, parent, friend, etc. In what ways do they help?

August 3

Proverbs 19:15

I think we can all agree that laziness is not a great trait to have. Actually, in all accounts of the word—it's just bad. It's a "do less, expect more" mentality that leads to an attitude of entitlement. Once it occupies one area of your life, it begins to envelop every environment. Then suddenly, movement becomes treacherous, and all work becomes something that you avoid. Suddenly you aren't just a "bad life employee;" you ate completely unemployed. And I think this abundance of laziness has stemmed from a confusion about self-care and Sabbath. Rest and self-help are critical, but there still has to be a balance. We are called to be hard workers who put their hands on the plow and rest *hard* once a week. We are called to serve, not spend our days asleep. We are called to spread the gospel and set an example for others, not blend in or avoid interaction. We are called to take part in God's plan of action. We all have ways in which we are lazy, but let's do our best to make sure it's an isolated incident. Where in your life are you spectating where you should be a participant? God has not called you to sit on the sidelines, but I promise He will provide you with adequate opportunities for rest breaks. He doesn't need you to wear yourself to the bone, but He also doesn't want you to sit around and wait. Let's be aware of our laziness and work to rid our life of this cancerous habit. Let's work really hard and truly rest really hard on the Sabbath.

Prompt: Do you Sabbath every week? If not, why? What does Sabbath look like for you/what do you want your Sabbath to include?

_____

_____

_____

_____

_____

_____

_____

_____

_____

_____

_____

_____

August 4

Psalm 78:13–16

If God will split the sea and move mountains, I promise that He will mend the broken pieces in your life too. If He did it for them, He will do it for you. One of Satan's favorite lies is to convince us that we are unworthy of God's redemption. He does not want us to believe that we are free, so he keeps us caged in conviction. But that stronghold is not of God; it's of the enemy, and it's a lie. It's easier for Satan to burn us if we are convinced that we are already on fire. But you are not "too far gone," and there is no obstacle too big for God to overcome. God is just getting started when we say that we are "done." He will move the mountains in your path, and He will split the Red Sea that is blocking you. When it needs to be done, that is exactly what God will do. He does not require you to be perfect; He just requires your whole heart. He wants to tear every lie from the enemy apart. Because God can do anything, and by grace, we are His. So we must remain steadfast when Satan is doing his best to convict and convince. We are children of the most high king. Satan has no authority over our lives unless we allow him to have it. Let's make trusting in seas to be split our habit. God wants to "wow" you again and again. Do not allow Satan to stop your right to a life of wonder by mocking you with sin.

Prompt: What mountain do you need to be moved from your life? How would your life look different if it was moved?

_____

_____

_____

_____

_____

_____

_____

_____

_____

_____

_____

_____

_____

August 5

Mark 10:17–31

It's always easier to say than it is to actually do. It's easier to give advice to others than it is to take the advice for you. It's easy to read the Bible and roll your eyes at the lack of obedience or willingness to lay down their own personal desires and follow Jesus without question. But how many times daily do you choose Earth over heaven? The humanity of people is laid out so perfectly in this verse when the rich man asks Jesus how he can inherit eternal life. Jesus plainly states that in order to gain eternity, he must be willing to sacrifice. And not just sacrifice a little, but sacrifice the very thing that he valued the most. You see, God does not need the things that we hold at arm's length—He needs what we hold close. And to this man, his wealth was everything to him; it defined him to the core. He could have what he needed with room for even more. But Jesus said, lay it down at the Father's feet, and that is exactly what was hardest for him to do. It's easy to read and say, "Just do it!" But what if that were you? Would you give up what you cherish most if God was asking for it? Be honest with your answer to yourself and to Him. Is your identity rooted in what you have or what He has placed within?

Prompt: What do you cherish the most? What do you think you would do if God asked you to give that up? Would you be able to trust that He would provide if taken away?

_____

_____

_____

_____

_____

_____

_____

_____

_____

_____

_____

_____

August 6

Proverbs 28:2

Unification can only happen if people share a common goal. We will never mesh together as a unit unless we are all satisfied with our individual roles. It's hard to be a team if you do not have a trusted leader to guide and make decisions for the whole team. But in order to trust a leader, you have to share common beliefs. That is why we see division in our world so often today because we do not all share the same desires. It's hard to reach an intended outcome when we all want different events to transpire. How can we expect to reach the finish line if we are all running in different directions? It takes more than just a willing spirit; it takes a mutual connection. Today we have so many different groups, finish lines, and leaders that it is nearly impossible to find unity. We each have become satisfied and passionate about our own community. Having a community of like-minded individuals is not a bad thing, but it is bad if it encourages hatred of another group. It's okay to have a team meeting as long as it doesn't encourage excluding others from entering the room. The only way our world will successfully find unity amongst all of the division is by all sharing a belief in Jesus. Without God as the ultimate goal, we will continue to shatter into a million pieces. As we shatter, we are becoming more and more difficult to put back together. It's hard to mend a connection that is continuously severed. The world's leaders have importance but not near as much importance as the ruler of creation. If we would all surrender to God's plan, we would find unity regardless of the differences between our nations.

Prompt: What is the best team you have ever been part of? What attributes did that team have that made it so great?

_____

_____

_____

_____

_____

_____

_____

_____

_____

August 7

Psalm 4:1

It's heartbreaking to be ignored, overlooked, and pushed aside. Knowing that someone does not care no matter how hard you have tried. It can feel like a heavy pressure or a sinking feeling in your chest. You worked up the courage to express your feelings, and they could not care less. If we seek to find peace in the assurance of others, it's sad to say, but it will never be found. You cannot build your foundation on crumbling ground. If you seek for others to grant you peace, be ready to live a life that is unsatisfying and exhausting. It will be a constant battle of climbing up and then falling. The only one who can listen, guide, and provide full assurance is our Father in heaven. He will listen to your cries, your joys, and all of your confessions. You can be certain when you go to Him that your heart is safe from any form of breaking. No matter what time of day you go to Him, He is patiently waiting. He hears your every thought and listens to the unraveling of your heart. He is the only one that can put you back together when the world tears you apart. It's unfair to place expectations upon people that only God can attain. So let's comprehend the reality instead of living a life full of complaints. God is the only one who provides perfect love, understanding, guidance, and affirmation. He will grant you security in exchange for your hesitations. Unlike people of this world, God cannot be selfish, so He pours all of His soul into us. He is greater than your greatness and worthy of your trust. So cry out to God in the quiet, in the chaos, and in the times of joy and despair. He was, and is, and will always be there.

Prompt: Think back to a time that you were overlooked or ignored. How did you react in the moment, and how did it settle and stay in your spirit? Has God ever made you feel that way? It is okay to be honest with Him.

_____
_____
_____
_____
_____
_____
_____
_____
_____
_____

August 8

Psalm 113

How often do you really trust God to do the impossible? How often do you pray for a miracle instead of praying for the probable? It's one thing to say that you trust the Lord; it's another thing to live that trust out loud. It's one thing to say that Christ is king; it's another thing to humbly bow. I want my faith to be big enough to go against logical actions. I want to pray prayers that exceed what I can logically make happen. We serve the God of endless miracles, the resurrected King of kings! Why do we settle for asking Him for the smallest things? When was the last time that you prayed for something to happen that was way out of your control? Do you talk to God with your head or with your heart and soul? I want to see a revival of miracles, but those miracles will not happen if we are content without them. We have to have an unquenched desire within. I have seen miracles with my own eyes, and it feels like a glimpse of heaven on Earth. It was as if I had been given something for which I yearned. I want to see miracles today, tomorrow, and every day after that until miracles are no longer needed. God is not just here to meet a need; He is here to exceed it. Do you trust Him for the miraculous, or are you content with the conventional? Why not seek spectacular instead of simple?

Prompt: When was the last time that you prayed for something *"big"*? How did God answer that prayer?

_____
_____
_____
_____
_____
_____
_____
_____
_____
_____
_____
_____
_____

August 9

Mark 7:31–37

Jesus was perfection in flesh and spent His entire life performing miracles, yet still, He was criticized. The same people who loved Him and fell at His feet later had Him crucified. It's maddening at best but confusing as well to read about such seemingly hypocritical people. My biggest question is, how in the world could you ever be that evil? But Jesus' satisfaction was not rooted in humanity; it was rooted in the supernatural. He did not base His worth on man's popularity; He based it on God's Word, which is factual. He did not gain a massive ego when times got good and miracles were being poured out of Him left and right. He also did not sulk in self-loathing when He was the center of everyone's fight. What can we learn from His devoted consistency and His steadfast focus? I think that we are supposed to realize that we should not base our world around things that are merely supposed to be noticed. Did Jesus feel heartbroken when He was misunderstood? Yes, but He knew He was understood by God, and that held more weight. People's opinions of your worth seem to fade into the background when you focus on a God who is great. It doesn't make hatred or condemnation acceptable; it just gives you a defense mechanism. If you are confident in the Lord, you can deal with others' cynicism.

Prompt: Who or what do you find your worth in? Why?

_____

_____

_____

_____

_____

_____

_____

_____

_____

_____

_____

_____

August 10

Daniel 3:16–30

From the time I was a little kid, the story of Shadrach, Meshach, and Abednego has always been my favorite. I love the reassurance that when we need to be saved, God will do the saving. But there is something about the mental image of the great big fiery furnace and the three steadfast servants that always gripped my heart. I guess it's proof that no matter what, God will meet you where you are. Although I have never physically been in a fiery furnace, I have metaphorically been in one many times in my life. And most of the time, it was because of sin—not sacrifice. But just like the story of the three turning into four, my one turned into two. He came into the furnace for me, and He will do the same for you. He loves us so much that He enters into our most painful moments with us and protects us when we are at our weakest. He will not allow anyone to pull us down or defeat us. And there is just something so reassuring about having Him sit with me in it, not just help me through. He is in the midst of it, not just sitting in a bird's eye view. He is kind enough to be *with* us, not just for us. It's just another representation of His incredible love. So if you are in a fiery furnace, or if you feel the heat increasing—trust in the one and only God to come and be with you in the flames. He will never leave you in the furnace alone, and He will never leave you unchanged.

Prompt: How did your life change when you came to know the Lord? Think of the tangible ways and how you have evolved since.

_____

_____

_____

_____

_____

_____

_____

_____

_____

_____

_____

_____

August 11

Luke 10:1–12

We have all heard it said 1,000 times, and we will hear it said 1,000 more that we live in a world of "instant gratification." We want it, and we want it *now*, and if it's not going to happen *now*, we succumb to frustration. What we need to understand is that instant gratification is not biblical; it's actually quite the opposite. We were created to work hard and persevere, and now we have become quite incompetent. We expect to reap a harvest after planting one seed and watering it for one day. We expect God to produce miracles when, in return, we will not even take the time to pray. Our world has changed dramatically from "slow and steady" to "fast and immediate." Even if a video takes more than ten seconds to download, we swipe it away because we do not have the time to see it. We have shaved seconds and minutes off of our daily tasks, which add up to hours that we should have free. Then we spend those hours creating a chaotic to-do list or binge-watching TV. If time really is the greatest commodity, then who and what is important enough to gain your time? What invitations of tasks do you accept, and which do you decline? No one is "too busy" for anything; we are only "too busy" for things and people that we do not prioritize. That is why the Christian lifestyle isn't called "comfort;" it's called "sacrifice." The harvest is plenty, but the workers are few, so are you going to get to work or sit back and watch? Are we going to priories our Father's work or allow excuses to claim our cause? Are you willing to trade a life of the instantaneous for a life of sacrifice and perseverance? Are you willing to give up present desires for an eternal heavenly experience?

Prompt: Make an honest list of the top five things that occupy time in your day. Beside each thing, write if it invigorates you or drains you. Examine your list and ask God if there is anything that needs to be added or taken away.

August 12

Joel 2:21–27

We are living in dark and uncertain times, and each day, it feels like we are moving in the wrong direction. But what can we expect when our world has severed all ties to God's connection? Just like it is written in the Word of God, the world has become self-loving and judgmental. The popular lifestyle has proven to be spiritually detrimental. Do you know what else is written in the Word of God? It's going to get *way* worse. Persecution will come to all of those that serve. Hatred will fall upon *all* of God's children, and the life of sacrifice will become more than just a metaphor. But we can find comfort in knowing that God also promises us more. He will send earth-quenching rain to our dry and desolate soil and provide us with more than enough to eat. Where the world has sent famine, God will produce a feast. In the midst of suffering, God promises us a hopeful future, but we must be willing to live through the pain with faithful trust, which includes remaining unwavering even when life is unjust. In times of trial, it's good to run to His Word. The stories of overcoming trials are in black and white for you and me to observe. Has the world changed since the Bible was written? Yes, but our God is unchanging. He cannot be anything other than perfect, faithful, and amazing. The Word of God is a tool to help us walk through life; it provides all of the information that we need. God also gave us the Holy Spirit to step in and intercede. So do not allow the broken world of the present and future to cloud your hope of eternity. Cling to the promises that God has spoken about with certainty.

Prompt: What scares you most about the world right now? Why is this the thing that scares you most? Ask God to come in and calm those fears.

_____

_____

_____

_____

_____

_____

_____

_____

_____

_____

August 13

Amos 5:21–27

God is not impressed with your outward display of emotion if it is not a true reflection of your heart. He does not desire you to throw festivals and revivals if you are just doing it to somehow see yourself set apart. He doesn't need your offerings if they are just merely offerings from the earth. He wants your *all*, not just what you have established that He is "worth." Why give God a festival on Earth if your heart has no intention of celebrating Him? Why would we display false advertisements of something that is clearly not happening within? God knows everything about us, from every high to every low. Even the things we keep hidden deep within, God knows. He does not need your fake offerings, He simply wants your heart, and that comes at the price of surrender. He wants your broken and genuine, not as some perfect pretender. Our world has made "fake" a reality and allowed disingenuine actions to become acceptable. To the point that even in our spiritual walk, we have become susceptible. We must run after God's heart with every ounce of our being, knowing that when we find it, we have found reality. We must seek our satisfaction through spiritual growth and stop settling for superficiality. Our life is His, so if we live in any other way than His truth, we are actually becoming a false representation. And "false" and "representation" in the same breath lead to a deadly combination. Stop trying to "do" for God and just allow His will to be done. Stop giving Him false gifts because, in reality, you are giving Him none. Just give Him your heart and watch reality begin to unveil itself in truth. You can love God with all of your heart genuinely without displaying it using ornate offerings as proof.

Prompt: Okay, honesty hour here...in what ways are you "fake"? Who/what/when/how do you show up as a false representation of yourself or ingenuine? How can you change this behavior to be more genuine?

_____

_____

_____

_____

_____

_____

_____

_____

_____

August 14

Colossians 1:9–14

There is something that is so encouraging about reading Paul's letters to the churches in the New Testament. He was not just a leader to them—he was invested. He was like a coach or a big brother, providing encouragement and instruction. His words were not degrading or demeaning; they were helpful and loving. Reading this passage made me think about my spiritual role models and the people that I am discipling. Who has provided guidance for me, and who am I guiding? Think about that question for yourself because we all need people on either side of our spiritual equation. God created us for community, not isolation. The New Testament laid the groundwork for the church, and it was completely based on family dynamics. Trying to do anything on your own is too difficult to manage. God knew our weaknesses as humans; that is why He established the church to gather in love and accountability. God is the foundational structure, but people are there for stability. If you are doing life on your own, I encourage you to find a community of believers who will point you toward Christ. Then find someone younger than you to have faith and pour into their life. We are one big family of believers. I think we need to be reminded of the simplicity of the church in the New Testament. Community and discipleship are essential for our spiritual development.

Prompt: Who are you discipling? Who could you be discipling? How are you discipling them?

_____

_____

_____

_____

_____

_____

_____

_____

_____

_____

_____

_____

AUGUST 15

Proverbs 21:2–3

How often do you check yourself and examine your everyday actions? It's good that we come to God when decisions need to be made, but what about the things that just happen? For instance, what about your habits and routines that you say yes to each day without realizing that you are saying yes? What if those things you deemed right were actually inhibiting your progress? Sometimes we go to God for the big things but ignore Him in our day to day. We blame it on being busy, but maybe it's because we fear the truth of what He would have to say. Instead of defining your life by routines, ask God which routines are righteous first. He will show you what parts of your day to day that are the best and which are the worst. This is not a one-time check-in; this is just a part of being a Christian. It requires obedience and listening. Do not compare your routines to the world; the world is not seeking righteousness. Right and wrong are only defined by God's decisiveness. But how will you know what He says is right if you do not ask Him or approach Him? How can you know you are pursuing righteousness if you do not know Him? Do not assume your actions are righteous—ask God instead. Do not go along with the world—do what God says.

Prompt: Do you tend to ask for permission or forgiveness? Whose permission do you require to make choices? Why or why not?

_____
_____
_____
_____
_____
_____
_____
_____
_____
_____
_____
_____

August 16

Isaiah 53:4–12

When we are going through hard times, we often lose sight of the beauty that can come from trials. We become fixated on our difficulties and become a creature of survival. But when you look back on your life, did anything good ever come from easy instances? Or did the most rewarding moments of your life come after some unexpected expenses? We try so hard to make our life comfortable that we run away from hardship the moment it arrives. We avoid what might just be a blessing in disguise. There is a reason that the Bible is full of stories of suffering and accounts of personal hardship. Sometimes our armor will be broken no matter how strong we are guarded. Do you think Jesus wanted to endure all of the humility, suffering, and torture? No, even He pleaded for another way, but He knew His temporary pain would lead to so much more. If He had avoided the pain, the greatest promise of all would not have been completed. Instead of rising on the third day with restorative powers, He would have simply been defeated. So if every story from Noah to Paul, Jesus to John, Abraham to Job included suffering, then why would ours be any different? It is vividly clear that without suffering, it is unlikely we experience anything significant. God does not cause suffering, but He does use it to produce the greatest blessings. We must learn how to disengage from chaos in the moments when we are distressed. If you are walking through a hardship right now, do not rush the moment; feel it deeply and ask God for a greater measure of strength and understanding. Trust in the full process of what He is planning.

Prompt: What valley are you walking through right now, and what would it look like for God to pull you out of that valley? Do you believe that He will?

_____

_____

_____

_____

_____

_____

_____

_____

_____

_____

August 17

Genesis 9:1–3

I feel closest to God when I am surrounded by nature, but it still blows my mind that He created it for me. The hills, mountains, deserts, forests, oceans, and seas. We were not the afterthought to His creation; He created the earth just for us. He made sure that the earth was perfect before He formed Adam from the dust. Protecting the earth is not political; it should be engrained in our hearts and acted upon with purpose. We should take care of nature because it's God's gift to us, not because we feel the need to do community service. We should care for the earth because God created it specifically for our pleasure. It's not an allotment—it's a treasure. When I go on a hike or swim in the ocean, I like to remind myself that God made each element for me. Every grain of sand and every leaf on each tree. He laid down green grass for your comfort and spoke mountains into existence for your awe and wonder. He created an infinite amount of species and creatures for you to discover. Are you aware of His gift, or are you too busy to be appreciative of nature? When was the last time you enjoyed the outside without labor? Get amongst it—and I promise you will feel closer than ever to your creator. The earth was made for you to explore, enjoy, and savor.

Prompt: When was the last time you walked barefoot outside? God created us to be one with the earth, to feel connected and grounded. Take five minutes today to stand or walk out on the ground barefoot. Use the time for prayer or meditation.

_____

_____

_____

_____

_____

_____

_____

_____

_____

_____

_____

August 18

Psalm 78:1–4

How annoying is it when you are talking to someone, and they refuse to listen? They are not even attempting to pay attention. I know, for me, it feels blatantly disrespectful, but mostly, it makes me feel extremely unimportant. When you make an effort to speak, but they make no effort to absorb it. If we know how it feels to be ignored, how much more do you think God does? How often do we ignore His teachings but demand His love? How often do we sit and actually listen for Him and to Him with open ears? When He speaks, is it something that we actually hear? Because the words that God speaks are mighty and powerful, and they contain life in abundance. Every word that He speaks has meaning and substance. So when we ignore Him, we lose out on the knowledge, and we hurt His heart when we refuse to absorb what He is attempting to impart. How is this true in your life? In what ways are you ignoring your Father's voice? Listening is not a perpetual action; it is a choice. How can you be a better listener today than you were the day before? In what ways can God's Word be something that you absorb, not something you ignore? God's words are the bread of life, so stop chasing crumbs when you can have a feast. Don't expect to reap a harvest if you refuse to receive and plant any seeds.

Prompt: How much of your day is spent in silence? We often complain about not hearing God, but the volume of life is turned up so loud that we can't hear Him even if He is speaking.

_____

_____

_____

_____

_____

_____

_____

_____

_____

_____

_____

_____

_____

August 19

Mark 1:1–3

"Proper preparation prevents poor performance." Have you heard that one before? "Failing to prepare is preparing to fail" is one that I love even more. Both mean the same thing, and both require a healthy dose of discipline. It's an attitude of taking initiative, not just being a participant. I am "type A" to the core; self-discipline and organization come naturally to me. I am regimented about planning what I need to do or where I need to be. I will backward plan my day down to the minute and keep myself on schedule to be sure that I accomplish all that I need to accomplish in the day. I firmly believe in the statement, "If you are on time, you are late." But other than writing this journal every morning, I do not prepare a way for Jesus in my routine. Even though out of everything in life, He is the only one that I need. I do not want my faith to become regimented, but I also do not want to become so casual with it that it gets pushed to the bottom of the priority list. If I am not intentional about my pursuit of God, I do not think that my schedule will magically create room for Him to fit. We must prepare and plan our walk to God to be included in our day-to-day. I think all of our faith could use and bit more intention and "type A."

Prompt: Are you intentional with making time for God? In what ways could you be more intentional?

_____

_____

_____

_____

_____

_____

_____

_____

_____

_____

_____

August 20

1 Thessalonians 2:1–7

No matter our upbringing or personality type, we all have a little bit of "people-pleasing" within us. We may try and avoid confrontation or difficult topics that need to be discussed. We are taught to avoid the topics of politics and religion, especially in a new relationship. Because differences of *that* magnitude can be difficult to dismiss. What this has done is provided an excuse for silencing our testimony. Instead of leading with our faith, we are taught to approach the topic slowly. We have allowed society to influence our behaviors in conversation. Instead of freely speaking and leading people to Christ, we have cowered to the world's rules and regulations. There is a time and a place for political discussion, but the time and place for God is everywhere and always. It is disrespectful to put God's name and our world's leaders on the same topics page. The name of God is only offensive to the unbeliever's ear. Isn't that all the more reason to make it something that they hear? You do not see the world slowing down to be sure that they are not offending Christians. If anything, they are yelling slanders louder so that we have no choice but to listen. Do not conform to society's norms and risk losing your relationship with the Almighty. It's far more important to preach truth than it is to speak politely. If you find that you have offended someone by speaking God's name, do not apologize for their reaction to His righteousness. What they blame on your words is probably just a conviction of their own consciousness. Don't hold back—speak God's name! You never know if a friend will be lost or a child will be gained.

Prompt: Would you consider yourself a "people-pleaser"? In what ways does this show up in your life? In what ways is it beneficial to you, and in what ways is it harmful?

_____

_____

_____

_____

_____

_____

_____

_____

_____

_____

August 21

Psalm 25:14

If you want to know more about a person's life, wouldn't you invest more time into getting to know them? You wouldn't wait for them to walk through the door; you would invite them in. Think about your friends or even your relationships that are meaningful to you. You do not just expect closeness to occur; it's something that you actually must pursue. Just like our pursuit of friendship, we must also pursue our relationship with our Father in heaven. It takes work; it cannot just be expected. If you want to get to know someone, don't you invest time into their life and ask them questions about their passions and interests? You find curiosity is sparked about the things that are different. Because the bottom line is that you care, so your actions and investments prove that adoration. So, if it's important in our society, how much more important is it in our salvation? Jesus is our closest friend, and I think it's time we start treating Him like He is. Instead of taking His presence for granted, let's intentionally welcome Him in. Let's ask Him questions in prayer and read about His life story in the Holy Bible. Let's be more inviting and less entitled.

Prompt: What actions do you take if you want to get to know someone? Do any of those reflect how to pursue God?

_____

_____

_____

_____

_____

_____

_____

_____

_____

_____

_____

_____

_____

_____

August 22

James 2:14–17

What good is having a title if there is no action behind the name? For instance, what is the difference between a CEO and an employee if they are treated and behave the same? The same goes for the title of Christian; there has to be action in order to claim the title. We cannot be complacent waiting for God's work to be done when we were called to start the revival. Following Christ is good, but what happens if you follow so closely that you ignore others' desperation for direction? It's great to have a relationship with Christ, but what if your unawareness leads others away from making a connection? We are called to be people of great faith, but great faith also needs action. One without the other will not bring God satisfaction. God loves when we pray for people, but if there is more that can be done in the physical, why do we *only* pray? We are not showing much compassion if we see someone's needs and walk away. In order to be more like Christ, we must assess each situation with a heart of empathy. And we must be patient and caring enough to provide the hurting with any and all known remedies. Faith without deeds is lazy, and deeds without faith are self-pleasing. But when you combine the two and pursue God's purpose, you will live a life of greater meaning. Do not become complacent with the title of Christian if it is based solely on your faith. The title should be used when it aligns with the way that you behave. Allow your faith to take root, and then allow the branches to extend into action. Our faith is more than a personal decision; it's also what we make happen.

Prompt: How is your faith a verb? In what ways do you act out your faith? In what ways could you act out your faith?

_____

_____

_____

_____

_____

_____

_____

_____

_____

_____

August 23

John 21:25

The Bible is a blessing that provides us with a detailed story of Jesus' life on Earth. We have four accounts of His thirty-three years of life, each starting from birth. These accounts include healings, instructions, parables, and examples for each of us to follow and imitate. We can read the Gospels, and by understanding the Savior's life, we can learn how to be saved. But isn't it crazy that we have sixty-six books in the Bible, all of which point to God's truth? Thirty-nine books in the Old Testament foreshadow the Son, twenty-three of the New Testament describe how we should act like Jesus, and the four Gospels give us proof. Yet even still, all of the information of the Trinity is not written down in the Bible. If all of the works of God could be contained on paper, what we have now would be the equivalent of just a title. His power and goodness are just too great to be contained on paper. Yet, part of being saved is knowing the story of our Savior. Reading the Bible should not be seen as a chore; it's a delight to learn more from Him and about Him. It's hard to know the text and doubt Him. Do you cling to every word of the text, or do you allow the tangible proof to slip through your fingers and fade from memory on your bookshelf? It's not there to give you a "feel good" verse every now and then; it's there to sustain your health. Challenge yourself to open the pages every day and read a piece of Scripture. Before you know it, what once was not part of your routine will become a fixture.

Prompt: What stops you from reading your Bible? What barriers in life do you have that are preventing you from reading more of His written Word?

_____

_____

_____

_____

_____

_____

_____

_____

_____

_____

_____

August 24

Romans 6:8–14

Sin is a mistake, not an excuse. Too often, we sin and allow God's grace to become something that we abuse. Are we saved by grace? Absolutely! But God's grace is a gift, not a right. It's the gift of having a protector, but that doesn't mean we should always subject our protector to a fight. We have become comfortable with God's forgiveness to the point of living the life that *we* desire. When in reality, we are taking advantage of the kindness of the supplier. How would you feel if you offered to clean up someone's spilled soda, and then the moment you finished cleaning, they intentionally spilled it again? Would you put up with their disrespect or bring that behavior to an end? Why do we do the same to God and wonder why our relationship with Him is not growing deeper? Is God your Almighty creator or just your sin cleaner? The difference between our capacity for forgiveness and God's is that God does not have a limit. He promises mercy and forgiveness in exchange for our commitment. But His mercy is not a scapegoat for our decision to sin and live a life full of sinful behavior. Every time that we choose to sin, we choose to disrespect our Savior. We must make righteous living our priority with the understanding that we will make mistakes daily. But there is a *big* difference between choosing to sin and falling into sin mistakingly. You are not a "sinner;" you are a Child of God. Don't mistake your occasional action as a title. Sin is a byproduct of being a human, but it should not be a routine of our daily cycle. Don't sin because you "cannot help it"—God can help it, so ask Him and then address the sinful action. You will not be judged on your sin, but you will be judged on the sin you continuously allow to happen.

Prompt: What is something that you repeatedly do that you know is unhealthy for your mind, body, or spirit? Why do you keep doing it, and what is preventing you from stopping? Have you asked God to help you with this thing?

August 25

John 20:19–21

How beautiful is it to know that Jesus is present with us at all times? Even when we doubt His presence, He is never hard to find. It's easy to feel lonely in this big, wide world, but do not allow the world to convince you that you are alone. You are loved, cared for, and fully known. How kind was God when He sent the Holy Spirit to live inside of our souls? How gracious is He to send a helper for our spiritual self-control? Walking through life alone is hopeless, but thankfully we never have to experience that hope-sized void. We receive peace and comfort while the world is paranoid. If you are walking through a season of loneliness, do not blame God; adjust your priorities. God cannot be the author if you do not allow Him to be a part of your story. The Holy Spirit was made for you, specifically to be a helper and a guide. Do not seek loneliness out of the pursuit of independent pride. Doing something on your own does not impress God; it breaks His heart. He does not want to just cross the finish line with you; He wants to be there from the start. He will never leave you, but in order for you to feel Him, you have to acknowledge His presence. We have to live on this earth with our hearts tied to heaven. He is closer than you know and never plans on leaving you, no matter what you do or do not do. He is not there because of circumstances; He is there because of you. So do not claim loneliness as a title; claim God as your always-present companion. He is with you now and forevermore. He is incapable of abandonment.

Prompt: If you could title the chapter of your life that you are in right now, what would it be named? Now, what title do you think God would give it? How do they differ, and which one do you prefer?

August 26

Proverbs 13:12

Hoping for something that will never come will only set you up for disappointment and heartbreak. It's like convincing yourself that a person is coming to your party, but they are just running late. When the truth is that they are not planning to come at all, they never even looked at the invitation. Yet, our heart is fixated on the possibility of their affirmation. It's said in Proverbs, "Hope deferred makes the heart sick," and I think we all would agree. It can feel like a dagger to the heart when things do not happen that you thought were meant to be. That is why we must put our hope in Jesus and not in humans or things of this world that we have no control over. Jesus gives us "it is finished" security while everyone else struggles to provide any type of closure. Have you been experiencing heartbreak lately? And if so, think about why? Is it because one of your desires or expectations was denied? Or are you so rooted in hope in Jesus that you do not think twice about how others influence that hope? If expectations are the crosshairs, who is the scope? It's easy to say, "Put your hope in Jesus," but what does that actually mean to you? How can He be the focal point and end goal of everything that you do? And how can we take the pressure off of other people and expect less out of humans that will never be able to meet our needs in totality? Let's put our hope in fewer places of uncertainty and instead root it in reality.

Prompt: What were you hoping for that you did not see come to fruition, and what happened instead? What are you currently hoping for that you are praying will come to fruition?

_____

_____

_____

_____

_____

_____

_____

_____

_____

_____

_____

August 27

Isaiah 52:5–6

I think we have all heard it said, or we have said it ourselves before, that "You can't speak badly about my sibling, but I can." I think it is part of a deeper feeling that closeness allows us to fully understand. So it seems normal to make fun of your sibling, but the moment someone else does, you get angry and defensive. For some reason, it strikes a nerve that is sensitive. Maybe because you know the underlying love behind the words of oppression. But when they come out of another's mouth, they simply are filled with aggression. Whatever the reason is, we all turn into bodyguards ready to battle against the opposition. We will make sure that they *never* speak those words without our permission. If we get this fired up about defending a loved one, why are we not as fired up about the one who first loved us? When constantly His glorious name is being slandered and flippantly discussed. How can we be so defensive of our siblings but so passive when it comes to our Father? How can our hearts be still while God's name is slaughtered? God's name is the most glorious name in all of creation. Yet we sit back and allow it to experience repeated defamation. God's name is not just one that we are called to worship and praise; we are also called to preach it and protect it. Any disregard for malicious words is us participating in neglect. It may not be an outspoken slander, but we experience His name being used in vain every day. This is because our world has taught us to disrespect God so much that it has become the norm of things to say. We must defend His name and stand up for the righteousness of His perfection. Defensive behavior is sometimes the most powerful form of affection.

Prompt: Who do you feel protective of? How do you show protection?

_____

_____

_____

_____

_____

_____

_____

_____

_____

_____

August 28

Psalm 51:1–2

Every day I find myself sinning, yet some days I find myself more desperate than others to repent. It's funny how some sins feel like the rules have been broken while others just feel like they have been bent. But sin is sin in God's eye...there is not one sin that is worse than another. Yet sometimes I expect God to strike me down with lightning, while others I just expect to hear loud thunder. When the reality is that He does not see levels of sin—it just is all opposed to righteousness. None is more necessary than another to confess. They all must be forgiven; we must repent for each and every one that we commit. Because it's the fact that we sinned, not necessarily what the sin is. I find reassurance in His equality of grace, but I want to feel that equality in my own conviction too. I do not want society's standards of "acceptable" to cloud my own view. It's easy to fall into that trap and forget to repent because society has deemed it okay. So it's critical that we ask for His forgiveness each and every day. Let's chase righteousness like we want to catch it instead of it being an unexpected action. At the end of the day, let's be aware enough to own up to the occurrences of the day that we allowed to happen.

Prompt: What sin have you deemed "okay" because the world has given it its stamp of approval?

_____

_____

_____

_____

_____

_____

_____

_____

_____

_____

_____

_____

August 29

2 Peter 3:17–18

Righteousness requires action, but it's both an offensive pursuit and a defensive endeavor. It's easy to comprehend action by correlating it to being the aggressor. But what about the game of defense as it relates to your own righteousness? What does that entail to you? What is righteousness if it is not just what you do? We are taught many times throughout Scripture to be "on guard" so that the world would not carry us away with its influence. Our defensive game is important when we are currently not in an offensive movement. So what does that look like practically in your everyday life? What does defense look like to you? For me, it's awareness, discernment, and protection of what I allow my ears to hear and my eyes to view. Defense for me is not the choices that I make; it's the awareness that I even have choices. It's not the silence that I choose; it's the recognition that there are noises. It's not the prayers or the praise—it's the understanding of why I choose to do that. It's not the act of being good; it's the predetermined commitment to not be bad. Allow your own faith and spiritual walk to come to mind, and truly allow God to show you the dichotomy of positions. The offense is deciding, and the defense is the consequences of that decision. Which part of your spiritual game needs more work, and are you willing to be coached to improve? Allow God to tell you if you need help with realizing that you have them or actually making moves.

Prompt: Do you feel comfortable acting out your faith in front of others? If so, how often do you do so? If not, why and what would make you feel more comfortable?

_____

_____

_____

_____

_____

_____

_____

_____

_____

_____

_____

_____

August 30

Matthew 7:15-20

Do not put your trust in people based on what they say; put your trust in people based on what they do. If you allow people to use words as their measure of reliability, there is a chance that they will take advantage of you. Someone's word is reliable when it aligns with their actions, but words on their own are empty. Especially when the person speaking uses *plenty*. It's not our job to point fingers at people, but it is our job to protect our hearts and minds from false information. If we are not protecting ourselves, then we can easily fall into persuasion. When in reality, the only voice that we really need to listen to is the voice of our Father and His perfect guidance. But too often, we tune Him out because of false information that someone is providing us. I am not discouraging you from listening to your trusted people, but I am encouraging you to find those people and vet them honestly. Because the price of living in the pursuit of a false promise can be costly. See how people behave and then see how people speak. Are they speaking flowers but growing weeds? Be careful with your mind and the trust that you give to people because your soul will be affected either way. Put weight on what they do, not just what they say. Don't give into false prophets because their words weave an enticing web, stand firm in your discernment. We commune with royalty, not serpents.

Prompt: Who is someone who you consistently allow to speak into your life that does not practice what they preach? Who is someone you could rely on instead?

August 31

1 Peter 3:8–9

We live in a comparison culture where the goal is to be better than our peers or at least appear that way. We live in a society where we each have been given a microphone, and we are convinced that everyone needs to hear what we have to say. We live our lives from day to day, creating friendships with our thumbs. Scrolling, liking, and posting while eagerly waiting to see what response comes. How many friends do you have? And I don't mean "followers," I mean real people that are actually present and caring. Our souls desperately need relational repairing. We were created for relationships so that we could build relationships, but we have conformed to the world's standard of distance. Social distancing was happening *long* before the pandemic. We think friendship is posting a picture of a moment we spent with someone because it validates our public image. We have allowed our thoughts to be confined by a character limit. We are called to be like-minded and sympathetic people who walk this world according to God's plan. But how can we hold onto each other when we prioritize the iPhone in our hands? How can we pour out our hearts in empathy towards another by clicking a little red heart on a picture? How can we move past the social media norm onto a relationship that's bigger? The truth is we must prioritize God and then live like He has called us to live. We must forget how to "like" and remember how to give. If social media satisfies your relational needs, then ask God for a renewed heart for people and the ability to be a proper friend. It's time that we reconnect with reality and stop living life trend to trend.

Prompt: What value do you find in social media? What would happen if social media disappeared tomorrow?

_____

_____

_____

_____

_____

_____

_____

_____

_____

SEPTEMBER

September 1

Isaiah 58

We must not just follow the commands of God; we must follow His commands for the right reasons. Sometimes we expect daily change when, in reality, God is creating a new season. We fast for twenty-four hours from food, but on that day, we consume twelve hours of television. We ask God to lead the way, and then we make all of our own decisions. It's not always about the act; it's also about the action. You can fast all you want, but you will never see a benefit from it if you are filling yourself with distractions. The same goes for prayer; you can get down on your knees, but if you are thinking about your to-do list, then the prayers are void. It's not because God does not like your effort; it's because God wants His commands to be enjoyed. A half-hearted attempt at fasting is equivalent to physical starvation. It's supposed to lead to an encounter of abundance, not a time of distracted depravation. We must approach the commands of God with willingness and a focused mind. We must be willing to follow God and leave everything else behind. We must participate in acts of servant hood out of willingness, not just because we "should." He wants His commands to be comprehended, not misunderstood. So whether it be fasting, praying, or serving, we must do it for the right reasons. It can't be something we "do;" it must be something we believe in. The mindset must shift from not eating bread to the bread of life we have been given. Fasting is not a twenty-four-hour ritual; it is a way of life we should be living.

Prompt: When are you most focused? When are you most distracted? How can you cultivate an environment (mental or physical) for focus?

_____

_____

_____

_____

_____

_____

_____

_____

_____

_____

_____

September 2

Jeremiah 30:18–21

Our God is the God of restoration; He is so faithful to put things back together. He not only puts pieces back in their place, but He makes the puzzle even better. We hear it said a lot in Christian verbiage that He would turn ashes into beauty. And I can believe it all day long for you, but it's harder to believe for me. Because when things are upside down in my life, I tend to get swept up in the chaos of it all. It's hard for me to believe that I would ever stand on my feet again when life is constantly making me fall. I'm fully disclosure; I am here right now...I am in the midst of a fall, and I am desperate for God's intervention. I am ready to see beauty come from those ashes that I mentioned. But my faith is strong, and my patience is present, so I believe in the work that God is doing. Even if I do not see that He is moving. I know in a year, a month, or even a day, my scattered puzzle will be aligned into a perfect picture. I trust in the promises of God in the Scripture. So I hang onto hope, and I pray that you do, too, when life is in a state of utter chaos. You might feel out of place but trust that you are *never* lost. He will piece it all back together in a way that is far more beautiful than you could have ever planned. Don't believe in the lie of the enemy that you are alone...when the truth is you are in the palm of the Most High's hand.

Prompt: If your life were a puzzle, what picture would the puzzle be? And how many pieces would it be?

_____

_____

_____

_____

_____

_____

_____

_____

_____

_____

_____

_____

September 3

Matthew 5:3–12

The beatitudes are so beautifully stated but so opposing to our human nature. Where the world shows us destruction, God shows us favor. "Blessed are the poor in spirit, for theirs is the kingdom of heaven." You can be broken and empty-handed, and God will still give you more than expected. "Blessed are those who mourn, for they will be comforted." You can trust that God will wipe your tears away and be there for you when no one else is. "Blessed are the meek, for they will inherit the earth." Instead of proving yourself, trust in your inherent value and worth. "Blessed are those who hunger and thirst for righteousness, for they will be filled." Live like God is your sustenance, and His promises to you will be fulfilled. "Blessed are the merciful, for they will be shown mercy." Trust that causing other people harm will not make you stop hurting. "Blessed are the pure in heart, for they will see God." Focus on everything that He is, not all that you are not. "Blessed are the peacemakers, for they will be called children of God." Replicate God's patience, and do not fall prey to what the world is doing. "Blessed are those who are persecuted because of righteousness, for theirs is the kingdom of heaven." Do not let the world's "noes" stop you from saying God's "yeses." Do not fall prey to the "shoulds" of this world; stand firm in the promises of the great I am. Satan is all about what "could" or "should" happen if you act out in righteousness, but God's vocabulary is what "will" and "can."

Prompt: What beatitude stands out to you most? Why?

_____

_____

_____

_____

_____

_____

_____

_____

_____

_____

_____

_____

SEPTEMBER 4

Jeremiah 12:5

God can do anything and everything, but it's our responsibility to take action too. After all, life is how we live, not what has been done to us. Our raw spots in faithfulness should be taken seriously, not disregarded, in an attempt to seem righteous. We must use the wisdom that He supplied us. For instance, if your raw spot is alcohol, it's probably best that you avoid testifying in bars. If your raw spot is gambling, you should probably avoid casinos and stay where you are. If your raw spot is rage, you should be careful not to purposefully put yourself in an environment of a trigger. And if it's self-obsession, it's probably best to have fewer mirrors. God can give you the strength to overcome anything, but the question is, will you allow Him to help you? Our raw spots tend to be something we actually like to do. And we use "His strength" as an excuse when, in reality, it is our own selfish desire for sin. So instead of avoiding the raw spot, we explain and defend. I don't know about you, but my raw spots are still too raw to be exposed to any more abrasion, and I want them to heal and be callous. I want to act out of purpose, not habits. I want to receive God's strength while also using the wisdom that He has so graciously given to me. I do not want to be my own worst enemy. Do not jump up in weight class when you have not won a match in this class yet. Do not be so caught up in confidence that you ignore a threat.

Prompt: What is a "raw spot" or weakness for you? It could be something like alcohol, porn, or even something like online shopping. What has a grip on you that you would do better to avoid? How could you take steps to avoid this?

_____

_____

_____

_____

_____

_____

_____

_____

_____

_____

_____

SEPTEMBER 5

Ezekiel 12:15–16

Have you ever really thought about the fact that where you were born and raised had a purpose? Our environments matter much more than just what is on the surface. God could have placed you anywhere, and He chose to place you where you have been and where you currently are. You are not an outsider; you are one of the parts. And maybe it's not where you will be for the long term, but trust right now that you are there for a reason, even if it is just for a very short or specific season. How can you impact your surroundings today and amplify the noise in your environment? How can you get on board with the truth of your reality instead of fighting it? If you showed up each day like you were on a mission, how would that look in your life and in your community? How would your impact change if you shifted from selfish pursuits to pursuits of unity? Look back on your childhood and teenage years and where you were born and raised. Think about how the environment around you left the path paved. Don't even for a second think that your life has been an accident because God has sent you every place for a reason...even here. You have not been randomly forgotten; you have been placed with purpose and care. So live like it...don't let life and the people around you pass you by. You are here right now for a reason. Just take a moment and ask God, "Why?"

Prompt: Take a moment and write down all of the places you have lived throughout your life. It might be a ton, and it might be one. Write down at least one specific attribute or blessing that came from living in each place.

_____

_____

_____

_____

_____

_____

_____

_____

_____

_____

_____

_____

September 6

Proverbs 21:6

What good is having success if it is not righteous success? Why pursue fleeting accomplishment if it is not God's best? We are all guilty of pursuing personal ambitions instead of the ambitions of God. We have all ignored God's guidance for the pursuit of society's applaud. Where did that lead you? Because I can tell you exactly where it led me. It led me right into bondage and away from being free. It led me into the chaotic waters of society's approval and away from the safety of Jesus' boat. Instead of walking on the waves, I was struggling to stay afloat. That is because a life spent seeking anything other than Christ will lead to a broken heart and a void spirit. You will see wholeness but never be able to draw near it. Personal pursuits will never fill up the God-sized hole that is in your heart. And He isn't here to tear down your dreams; He is here to put all of the brokenness back together that has been torn apart. If you want to achieve your dreams, stop pursuing them, and pursue God instead—just trust me. With God, you will find more than you could ever want or need. Success without Him is fleeting because it's not really success at all. The path of your own creation is nothing compared to the path in which you have been called. Do not chase after society or personal promotion on the basis of fame. You will find much more success if you boast in Christ's name.

Prompt: What title or goal are you currently pursuing? Have you asked God if this is His plan? How would achieving this title or goal bring you closer to God?

_____
_____
_____
_____
_____
_____
_____
_____
_____
_____
_____
_____
_____

September 7

Ecclesiastes 10:18

Being "lazy" is often a way to describe relaxation, but in the Bible, it is clearly regarded as a sin. It is a posture of the heart and mind, not just the place where productivity ends. It feels to me like we have split laziness up into two distinct categories: "self-care" and "being careless." We have created the barometer for judging as well as the test. I love being busy; idleness is uncomfortable for me. I am hyper-aware of laziness, and I do not ever want it to become my identity. But we all have laziness in our life, and it's time that we name it and claim it. If it is untamed, it's time that we tame it. Ask God to show you where you are acting out of a posture of laziness and really stop to listen. It might have less to do with your actions and more to do with your decisions. Maybe you are hardworking but choose to get drunk after work instead of taking a long bath. Maybe laziness isn't about what you do (or don't do)...maybe it's about what you have. Our smart phones have made us all a little bit more lazy, and they have influenced every other aspect of our life. Just because something is the social norm does not mean that it's right. How can we be better and be people of integrity and purpose? How can we shift it from an efficiency mindset to a mindset of service? I do not want laziness to creep in and steal any part of my virtue or identity. I pray that God sees a hard worker when He sees me.

Prompt: Where has laziness crept into your life? What actions could you take to become less lazy in that area of life?

_____

_____

_____

_____

_____

_____

_____

_____

_____

_____

_____

_____

September 8

1 Samuel 3

Do not wait on earthly confirmation when you have been called by the Lord's voice. Too often, we depend on others' stamp of approval, and we mistake a command for a choice. You do not have to gain permission from your peers to follow God's command. If you wait for their opinion, you might just miss what God has planned. We are easily influenced by our peers and tend to follow popular opinions. But at the end of the day, aren't we under God's dominion? If we are called by the voice of God, then why do we wait for confirmation from our peers? Shouldn't God be the most important voice that we hear? We should not avoid reasonable advice, but we should not allow an earthly voice to drown out the advice from the Almighty. The chance that someone else's plan is better than God's is 100 percent unlikely. So often, our prayers are "Here I am, use me, Lord," followed immediately by, "If You want me to do this, can You just give me a sign?" The amount of moments we spend waiting on confirmation is truly wasted time. If you hear God's voice clearly, then why wait and ask Him if it was really His plan? God has never once accidentally given a command. He wants us to be dependent solely on Him, without the need for outside advice. He wants us to understand that He is the only one that provides. He provides the plan, purpose, command, supplies, and outcome. He speaks a word into your soul, and He intends for it to be done. He does not want your secondhand commitment; He wants your trust and your first step. He will provide you with His best if you trust Him with your right now and your what's next.

Prompt: When was the last time you made a decision completely on your own? How did it feel to make that decision, and how did others respond? What makes you second-guess yourself?

_____

_____

_____

_____

_____

_____

_____

_____

_____

_____

September 9

Psalm 49:20

What if you had all of the money in the world, but everything was free? There would not be any need or value for that money. Can you imagine having millions of dollars and walking up to buy your dream car and being told that you could have it? Honestly, the thought of wealth having no value is hard to imagine. And I do not think we will ever live in a time on Earth where money is not valued. I think it will always be what we earn and what we use. But God operates outside of the realm of monetary wealth, and He cares more about the wealth of our hearts. He sees how money has torn us all apart. Because the greatest detriment of having money is not having the wealth alongside it to know how to spend it properly. Sometimes physical wealth leads to spiritual poverty. Because you don't need God anymore, you can buy anything that you would ever need. You can become less eager to pray and less easy to please. You can spend money on foolish ambitions and lose your character in the process. Money cannot buy peace, but soon enough, it becomes a peace-seeking contest. Remember, everything that you have is the Lord's, and it has been given to you on loan. On Earth, we rent...we do not own. Are you handling His gifts with wisdom, or are you spending without asking His advice first? Wealth is having the money; wisdom is knowing when to open the purse.

Prompt: If you won the lottery, what would be the first five things that you bought? Do you think that your life would be inherently better in the long term?

_____

_____

_____

_____

_____

_____

_____

_____

_____

_____

_____

_____

_____

_____

September 10

Job 36:13

Resentment will rot you from the inside out if it is left undealt with. There is no room for resentment and contentment to co-exist; they simply do not fit. So if you are holding onto resentment, it's time to let it go. Because right now, it is like torrential rain on your soul's garden, and nothing will grow. I am guilty of harboring resentment; as a matter of fact, I am harboring some in my heart right now. It is as if I want my world to be calm, but this one resentment is making my heart *so* loud. But you know what could take it all away and make everything better in an instant? If I asked for help instead of being stubborn and resistant. God wants to take it all away from me, and I promise that He wants to take it all away from you too. He wants you to see the full picture, and so He desires to get rid of anything that is obstructing your view. And resentment is a *big* obstruction; it's like the elephant in the room—even others feel it. It's hungry for joy and attention, and it's parasitic, so it steals it. If you have any resentment in your heart, I am asking you to join me in crying out to God for help. It's time to stop "dealing" with it and just make sure that it is "dealt" with. Resentment will ruin your heart and soul, and it will deprive you of relationships and contentment. It's time that we admit and release our resentment.

Prompt: Who or what are you harboring resentment towards right now? Are you ready to let it go? Ask God to intervene and take it away, then...give it up.

_____
_____
_____
_____
_____
_____
_____
_____
_____
_____
_____
_____
_____
_____

SEPTEMBER 11

Proverbs 21:7–8

On this day twenty years ago, the unfathomable happened. It was worse than anything we could have expected and more terrifying than we could ever have imagined. We watched as evil shattered buildings, a city, and a nation's sense of safety. Not only was our national security breached, but personal security was also doubted greatly. Hearts broke over the tragic loss of friends, family, coworkers, and life as we knew it. We never thought that we could have all that we had and still lose it. Evil reared its ugly teeth that day, and it's been present in our world since. Some 9-11-2001, we all began to see life through a different lens. Similar things could be said about your personal life when tragedy hits. You become much more aware of what evil is. God does not want us fixated on evil, but He does want us focused on Him. And when you are walking in the light, it becomes a lot more evident when any amount of darkness creeps in. Evil can seem suffocating, but it has no right to steal your breath. It might think that it takes all, but there is always more left. We remember the tragedy of the towers, but it left behind a unified city bound in love and humanity. The truth is—evil is organized, but love happens organically. It took years for them to put together a plan of terror but seconds to react in unity, love, and support. Evil may start them, but love wins wars.

Prompt: What bad thing has happened in your life that goodness overflowed out of? In other words, where have you seen beauty come from ashes?

_____
_____
_____
_____
_____
_____
_____
_____
_____
_____
_____
_____
_____

September 12

Ecclesiastes 3:1–8

It is really easy to talk about the perfection of God's timing, but it is really hard to find peace in the waiting. It seems that one percent of our life is spent experiencing while the other ninety-nine percent is spent anticipating. It seems to be less about a lack of patience and more about a lack of control. We seem to find ourselves needing to know—when, how, and what will unfold. We surrender our hearts to the Lord, but just not our calendar. We ask God to take the wheel of our life, and then we refuse to be the passenger. If you find yourself struggling with God's timing, He understands your affliction, but He does not want you to stay there. He does not keep us waiting to cause pain; He does it because He cares. We become so fixated on the future that we forsake the gift of the present. We are so eager for the test that we fail to learn the lesson. Just as there is a time for action and a time for rest, there is also a time for every other activity. Just as bad things happen, so will the good, and they will balance out in perfect symmetry. We must understand that we will have a full range of experiences without having the fullness of understanding. We must trade the attitude of control to follow in the direction that God is commanding. No bad moment will ruin a lifetime, and no good moment will last a lifetime. No matter how beautiful of a plan you have created, it will always pale in comparison to God's design. So do not question the timing of God or even try to speed up the ticking clock to get to the "good stuff." God has given you a portion for each day that is more than enough.

Prompt: What exciting thing are you looking forward to or anticipating right now? Is that anticipation causing you to be less present?

_____

_____

_____

_____

_____

_____

_____

_____

_____

_____

_____

September 13

Zechariah 10:2

We are all creations of the creator; therefore, we all were made to sit at the feet of our king. If you refuse to sit at the feet of God, you are still sitting at the feet of someone or something. Because we were created with a "God-sized" hole in our hearts and a desire to be obedient to our ruler. And if it's not God that we choose, there will always be another pursuer. Maybe you think it's God because you call yourself a Christian and go to church every Sunday. But do you ask for other people's opinions more than you listen to what God has to say? Maybe you have placed your spouse or your child in the position that is rightfully the king's. Or maybe even your phone has taken that role. Or some other unliving thing. It is so easy to begin worshipping idols; it happens without even realizing it. Because we live in a fallen world, it is what often happens when we go on autopilot. When we stop making God our priority, it is so easy for other things to immediately fill His place. Because without Him, we are empty, and we do not function well with empty space. So be careful who you are bowing before and where your praise is going. We were made to be owned, but who is doing the owning? Who or what has claimed your heart? Ask God to show you if it's not Him. This is not a one-time process, unfortunately.... We must do the same thing again and again.

Prompt: Who or what has a claim to your heart? Have you given them or it more space than God?

_____
_____
_____
_____
_____
_____
_____
_____
_____
_____
_____
_____
_____

September 14

Isaiah 44:1–5

I do not know when we got so bad at asking for help, but our independence has become an epidemic. I think we all have reached our capacity and our limits. I do not know if it is a cultural thing or a deep seeded grip of pride that has us all in such a self-reliant mindset. We have associated the word "help" with debt. But help is a natural byproduct of community and a genuine way to instill connection. It's a display of service, gratitude, and affection. But "doing it all ourselves" has taken over, and we have lost the ability to voice our needs, so we all walk around weighted down. We are too prideful or scared to lay out tough exteriors aside and make a sound. If we won't ask another human for help, how can we expect to run to God with our needs? Let's act like we trust Him, not just say that we believe. What is the worst thing that could happen if you ask for help? They say no? Would that really be the lowest of the lows? I am terrible at asking for help; I fear burdening other people. But by me masking my needs, I lack being real. We are really needy, and guess what? That is how we were made to be. We were not created to have our own kingdoms; we were created to be reliant on the king. Start today, ask one person for help in an area that you would normally handle all by yourself. I guarantee you will feel better, and they will feel more connected to you if you ask for help.

Prompt: What is an area of life that you could use help in but have been too stubborn to ask? Who could you ask to help you, and how do you think they would react? If you are doubtful, think of how you react when someone comes to you and asks for help.

_____

_____

_____

_____

_____

_____

_____

_____

_____

_____

_____

_____

September 15

Psalm 52

It is difficult to live in this world and not place judgment upon others. It takes constant reminding to understand the extent of what God's grace covers. It's easy to point out others' faults as a way of magnifying our awareness of unrighteous actions. But it is not our job to condemn; it is our job to show compassion. I can assure you that God sees, hears, and knows everything that happens. He doesn't need us to point a finger and expel accusations. God has the ability to make decisions, surprisingly enough, without the help of our evaluations. He does not need our help judging others; we need His help not to judge. We must be quick to cast mercy instead of habitually holding a grudge. Instead of looking at someone's sin with content, it should absolutely break our hearts. Instead of condemning them with judgment, we should help them get a fresh start. What good will bringing a list of sinners do when you are ignoring the sin within yourself? What benefit does calling out someone's unhealthy behaviors have on your health? We do not have the capacity to handle the judgment of others while also living life to our full potential. That is because each of our individual walks with God was created to be confidential. Not confidential in the means of being hidden, but instead of being protected. If we spend all of our time rummaging through others' business, our own souls will be neglected. Trust that God has everything under control. He sent you as a servant, not a commander. We are made to serve and save, not prosecute and slander.

Prompt: Who is someone you find yourself judging often? Why or what do they do that you feel garners judgment? How could you shift your mindset in a positive, more merciful direction?

_____

_____

_____

_____

_____

_____

_____

_____

_____

_____

_____

SEPTEMBER *16*

Luke 6:46–49

Christianity is grammatically listed as a noun, but it is often treated as an adjective. Because what was made to be an identity has simply become an additive. It has become a description and has been ignored as a demonstration. It has become a beautiful house without any form of foundation. This is because Christianity is not a noun or an adjective; it is actually a verb. It is learning to put action to the Holy Word. It's not just believing in the truth of God; it's walking in His commands. It's not the discussion of His promises; it's making His promises your plans. It's way easier to say that we are a Christian than it actually is to be one. But our job is not to commentate the race; our job is to run. Without action, our beliefs are just titles on our résumé. They become a piece of who we are because it's a description that we choose to say. But if you did not have a name tag, would people still know that you were a Christian? Not because of what you describe, but because of your decisions? Is your faith an adjective, a noun, or a verb? Is your faith a walk or just a descriptive word? Do you have a foundation that can withstand movement? Is it something that you are *and* something that you are doing? We must be willing to take action and not just be voices. Our faith must be a combination of our characterization as well as our choices. If we are true vessels, then anything that is poured in from God will be received in abundance and will lead to overflow. His great command did not say to "be;" it said to "go." The title means nothing if the experience is absent. It cannot be a part of who you are if it is not put into action.

Prompt: What are ways that you "do" faith? What are ways you want to start "doing" faith? How can you hold yourself accountable?

_____

_____

_____

_____

_____

_____

_____

_____

_____

_____

SEPTEMBER *17*

Proverbs 28:10

As humans, we are responsible for our own actions, but as children of God, we are also responsible for the accountability of others' actions. What that means is that when others fall from God, we should intervene and alleviate their distractions. Others may fall into sin on their own behalf, but we must never be the stumbling block for their bad behavior. We must be sure that our encounters never point people in the opposite direction of our Savior. For instance, you may be able to drink alcohol in moderation, but what if you are unknowingly around a recovering addict? And now your personal preferences have caused a brother or sister to slip? It's not a matter of "not drinking alcohol;" it's a matter of being aware. We must be willing to give up creature comforts if it will allow us to show greater care. What if we know where all of the obstacles are and how to avoid them, but someone else falls trying to keep up with us? I think we have a greater responsibility than just helping them up and brushing off the dust. I believe that when you surrender your heart to God, you are accepting the responsibility of being the sheepdog among sheep. Which means that we must protect, keep watch, and lead. We are the eyes, ears, and body of the shepherd while He is physically away from the pasture. We must be eager to defend, comfort, and gather. Sheepdogs do not lead sheep into the trap of the enemy; they always herd them into pastures of greater richness. As Christians, when we put something into action, we are inadvertently giving it our permission. So take control of your own actions because you will *always* have a witness. Do not cause others to stumble because of your thoughtless decisions.

Prompt: What actions have you made lately that have caused you or another person to stumble in their faith?

_____

_____

_____

_____

_____

_____

_____

_____

_____

_____

_____

September 18

Proverbs 12:19

We are taught to tell the truth from a young age, but somewhere along the way, lies are given a stamp of approval. Because in some situations that seem like an out-of-control fire, the truth seems like it would be more fuel. So we created the term "white lie" to somehow mitigate the severity of not telling the truth. If a lie is a weed, a white lie is its root. But so often, we tell white lies to protect ourselves or others from the harsh reality of now. We think that editing the script will help somehow. And in some situations, it might...a white lie might actually de-escalate a situation. But removing the habit from your heart will take excavation. We are not strong enough to pick up sins and use them as tools in our tool belts. Once we start, it's hard to stop. When you have the choice between lying and being honest, just convince yourself that you will always get caught. Because that is the truth, it might not be by others, but God will always catch you when you lie. If we never walk down the path of dishonesty, then we will never have to explain or deny. No matter what the situation might be... tell the truth; do not open the door to allowing lies to sneak in and suffocate your spirit. And if you are in the midst of a lie, find courage and clear it. We are children of God; let's represent Him with honesty. We cannot live out of habit; we must live consciously.

Prompt: What lie have you told recently or are in the midst of telling? Why was or is the truth worse?

September 19

Ephesians 4:29–32

We all have a weapon that can be used for destruction if we do not keep the safety on, and that is our mouth. We each have the responsibility to determine what kind of ammunition is allowed. Just as a gunman is responsible for their fired shots, so are we for our words. It does not matter if you meant it or not; it matters that it was heard. If someone has been shot, we do not ask them why they got in the way of the moving bullet; we find the one who pulled the trigger. Blaming the victim in this situation would not be something that we even consider. We cannot become defensive when our mouths cause destruction and blame it on the recipient's response. We must become more attuned to the way in which our words come across. We are called to show love and compassion to one another—not attack and discourage with words of aggression. Just because we have the ability to cause destruction does not give us permission to use the weapon. Once a bullet is fired, we cannot control the extent of its harm, and it becomes an uncontrollable instrument. Before you know it, your careless pull of the trigger might just lead you to imprisonment. So instead of firing shots because you have a weapon, holster the weapon and unload all of the ammunition. No destruction will ensue if there is no bullet in the ignition. We are called to build one another up, but all that unwholesome talk does is tear one another down. Let's learn to listen with empathy instead of instinctively firing another round. When you get to heaven, are you going to show God the people you saved or the bullet holes you left behind? We were created to be kind humans; that's why we are called humankind.

Prompt: What do you wish you could go back and do/say differently? What would you have done or said instead?

_____
_____
_____
_____
_____
_____
_____
_____
_____
_____

September 20

Proverbs 3:5–6

Our world is consistently inconsistent, which makes predictability impossible. You can guess how something may turn out, but even your best guess may be improbable. It's funny to think that it's even impossible to completely trust ourselves. Because half of the time, even we do things that are bad for our own health. That is one of the many reasons that trusting God has infinite benefits in our life, even in the mundane details of the day-to-day. Consistency and truth hang on every word that He has to say. That is why it is so important that we do not lean on our own understanding but submit to God and trust His wisdom. One hundred percent of the time, God has a perfect operating system. It can be difficult for us to give up control, but why would we want to control when we can follow the unmistakable leader? Don't you trust the creator way more than you trust the creature? The beauty of this submissive life is that blessings will fill the void that control once inhabited. Your peace will rest on the steadfast creator, who is simultaneously the same and infinitely multi-faceted. If we give God our everything, we will receive *much* more than everything in return. He does not just want us to blindly follow; His desire is that He would teach and we would learn. So why lean on your own understanding when you can lean on the certainty of God's plan? Why spend life trying to control the uncontrollable when you can rest in the palm of God's hand? I promise that God's plan is greater than the feeling of control that you attain from being independent. But God cannot help a hurting heart that refuses commitment.

Prompt: What are some habits you want to give up? What would be the outcome of giving those up? What would be the outcome of *not* giving those up?

_____

_____

_____

_____

_____

_____

_____

_____

_____

_____

September 21

Matthew 22:1–14

It's important to realize that we are not marching toward our funeral; we are actually marching toward our wedding. We must fully embrace the direction that we are heading. The end of our life is not bound to a cemetery; it's found walking down the isle of eternity. We do not die with finality; we are born again with certainty. Our bodies may be missed on Earth, but they are welcomed home by the arms of our groom. How glorious is it to know that our life does not end in a tomb? Instead of resting in peace, we will rest in His presence. Why would we want to cling to Earth when we were made for heaven? If you are a Christian, then there is no last breath, only the last breath that you take on this earth. Similarly to how your mother's delivery of you was only your physical birth. Your body experiences certain processes, but our soul has a completely different operating system. We are aligned with eternity's operations even though we regularly practice Earth's traditions. It's okay to participate in ceremonies of remembrance, and God fully understands our process of grief. But do not allow these traditions to override your belief. The day we die on this earth is just the first day of our eternal life. We may leave behind our family, but we also become a wife. So do not dread the day of passing on from this life; look forward to what happens next. We are not even close to experiencing God's best! A funeral is for the living, not for the one that has passed on. Your soul is finally home, although your earthly life is gone. A wedding day means anticipation and preparation, so let's begin to live like a bride. We are not one day closer to the grace; we are one day closer to where we were meant to reside.

Prompt: What have you learned from the death of a loved one?

_____

_____

_____

_____

_____

_____

_____

_____

_____

_____

September 22

Isaiah 14:24–27

"Thy will be done," we mutter those words often, but do we actually allow them to hold weight? It's not just a phrase used for fun; it describes our fate. For some reason, it's used more around the context of loss or disappointment. We feel hopeless because our plans have become disjointed. So we state "thy will be done" as a reluctant surrender drenched in the sorrows of hopelessness. When we can't have what's ours, we open our hands to what's His. This is where we have it backward...we should desire His will be done and not our own. Not because we dismiss our desires but because we just trust that our desires are known. His will includes goodness, joy, and unmatched blessings. It just might come in a package that is different than what we were expecting. It's not scary to surrender when you believe fully in His love for you. It's beautiful to realize that He has a plan for everything that you do. The truth is—His will *will* be done; you can either get on board or drag your feet. Life is much more enjoyable when you trust and believe. God is all-loving, all-knowing, and all-powerful; you do not exceed His limitations. Hope is birthed out of the absence of hesitations.

Prompt: Do you tend to talk to God more in times of distress or joy? Why?

_____

_____

_____

_____

_____

_____

_____

_____

_____

_____

_____

_____

_____

_____

September 23

Matthew 6:16–18

We do not sacrifice for a spotlight; we sacrifice for surrender. If you are only willing to sacrifice when other people know about it, then I would say that you are less devoted and more of a pretender. We have to remember that our faith is personal, and we do not need other people's approval to establish our alliance. In other words...we do not need to be celebrated for our compliance. In this verse, we are specifically taught about this through the lens of fasting. Would you still do it if other people were not applauding or asking? Would you go a day without food if you could not tell anyone about your sacrifice? The answer to that question will provide you with true devotion in your life. Because if we are really making sacrifices unto the Lord, then we should be able to keep that between us and Him. Our intimate walks with God for not need to involve "them." Not because others ruin our intimacy but because we are so quick to turn a sacrifice into a show. If we have the opportunity of an audience, we are going to let them know. Pride can ruin an act of obedience in a split second. Surrender fades away when good intentions are threatened. Do you love God enough to sacrifice behind closed doors? Are you still willing to surrender even if you have no outside support?

Prompt: Would you rather be the best in the world at something but no one knew about it, or be mediocre at something, and you could share it with the world? Why?

_____

_____

_____

_____

_____

_____

_____

_____

_____

_____

_____

_____

_____

September 24

Psalm 127:1-2

If the Lord is not involved in your plan, it will fail to succeed. You might get what you want, but you will not get what you need. We are quick to make our plans according to our desires and standards and then ask the Lord to bless them. But if they are our brain's plan and not God's, then they will always be less than. Jesus is our firm foundation, and if we do not build on Him, our house will collapse. We build like a brick house with no mortar—which seems good but is actually full of gaps. If we continue to construct without His guidance, we will eventually be left with piles of pieces we chose over God. You won't be basking in independence; you will be trying to form something out of flaws. If our desires do not align with God's, then it's best to forfeit them immediately. Would you really choose your expectations over something that God calls "abundant and exceedingly"? If you build on God's foundation and allow Him to choose every brick, you will live in safety and pleasure. To state it plainly...whatever you can do best...God can do better. Surrender your plan unto the Lord, and do not miss out on perfection because of independent stubbornness. Our life is so much more fruitful when we allow God to govern us.

Prompt: In what ways are you stubborn? How is this behavior getting in the way of blessings?

_____

_____

_____

_____

_____

_____

_____

_____

_____

_____

_____

_____

_____

September 25

1 Timothy 6:2–5

Preaching is not a profession; it's a piece of God's ministry. We have turned gift-ings into careers and church into an industry. Even Jesus was more than just a teacher; He was also a carpenter. I think we have become expectant on God to give us harvest when He is expecting us to be harvesters. Our view of church is not biblical; it's a production of our modern world that often in-volves more entertainment than instruction. Church was never a one-man show; it was a gathering of love, prayer, and discussion. This is not meant to place blame on the modern church; it's meant as a gentle rebuke. I am not condemning the established church; I am just offering an honest biblical view. We are commanded against using godliness as a means to financial gain, yet we have created thou-sands of career Christians. Church is supposed to be an intimate gathering of learning and discuss-ing, not a congregation where one person speaks and everyone listens. Pastors are important in the kingdom of God, but they are *not* the foundation of the church. They are not the mouthpiece of God's authority; they are gifted to help us learn. If Jesus was walking the earth today, I think He would be in the nursery room, not on the stage. I just think we need to be careful with making a career based on our faith. We are too prone to idolatry to allow only one person to stand above the altar. God has given us many teachers, but He is the one and only Father.

Prompt: Think about pastors you have had in the past or your current pastor. In what ways did/do they use their authority well? In what ways did/do they abuse it?

_____

_____

_____

_____

_____

_____

_____

_____

_____

_____

_____

_____

September 26

2 Corinthians 3:1–6

When you think of yourself, do you think of a person who has great confidence? More times than not, do you feel sure or self-conscious? If I had to guess, I would say that the answer to that question is mostly the latter option. We tend to think of ourselves with disdain and exude boldness with caution. I think it has to do with humility, but somewhere it gets tangled along the way. Instead of thinking of ourselves less, we think less of ourselves every day. God does not get glory from that—He does not delight in our self-loathing. We run so far from praise that we actually do the opposite of gloating. But here is the truth, you are good because of the one who created you and the one who lives inside of you. Not because of what you look like or what you do. You have immeasurable value because of the portion that God has given you to use with your time on this earth. You have not earned it; it was yours from birth. So if we walk around cowering with timidity, we will miss out on our true calling and purpose. It's not an authority of power; it's an authority of service. Walk with boldness in who you are and in who God created you to be. If you are following the right leader, it's impossible not to be confident in where He will lead. Live a life of confidence, not because of your abilities or achievements, but because of His. It's not confidence in what might be; it's in what is.

Prompt: In what ways are you confusing being "selfless" with thinking "less of yourself"? What things do you do or say that you portray as humility that are actually self-harm?

_____

_____

_____

_____

_____

_____

_____

_____

_____

_____

_____

_____

_____

SEPTEMBER 27

Luke 17:11–19

Praying is not hard to do when you need something, but what about the moments when your needs have been met? Are you quick to praise Him after the breakthroughs, or do you tend to forget? God is faithful to answer our prayers, and it delights Him to have His children receive blessings. But forgetting to praise Him on the mountaintop is like forgetting to love after your wedding. God is not a 1-800-Help line that you call to fix your negative situation. Prayer is not a "to-do" list of desires; it's a two-way conversation. Should you talk to God in moments of despair and ask Him for help? Yes! But include God in your mountaintop if you are going to include Him in your mess. He deserves our praise in the season of highs, the season of lows, and the season of the mundane. Because no matter what season we are walking in, His love stays the same. He is no greater when He allows a miracle to take place than when He grants you a period of waiting. He is no more loving when He is giving you exactly what you want than when He is taking you through a time that is frustrating. We must be just as grateful in our praise during the breakthroughs as we are during the brokenness. We must be dependent on Him in our social abundance and in our loneliness. We must love Him the same when He grants us our desires and when He puts us on a path that we least desire. No matter the outside conditions, we cannot allow them to disturb our fire. He is a steadfast God of love and mercy, so let's show Him consistent love and praise in return. Our never-ending praise is what He always deserves.

Prompt: Are you in a "valley" or on a "mountaintop" in life right now? How is God showing up in this season?

_____

_____

_____

_____

_____

_____

_____

_____

_____

_____

September 28

Matthew 18:1–5

There is a difference between being "childish" and "childlike," and it all comes down to maturity. One is hungry for attention, and the other is hungry for security. I think that we often behave like children, not out of innocence but out of desperation. What was meant to be a beautiful posture of the heart becomes a limitation. Jesus stated that children are the greatest in the kingdom of heaven. And I believe that there is a lot to learn from that lesson. I think we can all agree that their hearts are pure, and they are blessings untouched by the world's darkness. They are eager to learn, full of love, and harmless. That is what God wants us to replicate...not their maturity level but their worldview. He wants you to get back to what He instilled in you. Because think about it...when we were born, we were straight from the hands of the creator. And every moment since we arrived has been a battle between society and our Savior. I want to get back to the childlike version of myself—the unique stuff that made me, me. I want to see the world through the lens that God wants me to see. I want wonder back, innocence, and a simple way of living. I want to take back all of those parts of me that are missing. I want to open my eyes every morning with energy, joy, and vigor for the day that awaits me. When we assume the posture of "adult," we become the leader and stop following God's lead. Reclaim that inner child that God created so uniquely. Let's get back to a childlike posture and allow God to lead us completely.

Prompt: What do you miss most about being a child? What is one thing that you can incorporate into your life from childhood?

_____

_____

_____

_____

_____

_____

_____

_____

_____

_____

_____

September 29

Amos 7:7–9

How often do you do what you think is right vs. doing what the Lord has deemed righteous? It's important that we evaluate what we let guide us. In this chapter of Amos, God sets a plumb line among His people as a measuring barometer. Because the truth is—our life should look different from the lost if we are followers. That is why it is important that we measure ourselves against the standards of God and not the standards of society. If we do not establish our boundaries, we may fall into compliance. This way of living requires more patience and obedience, but it is absolutely worth it. Instead of living with unpredictability, you live with purpose. How often throughout the day are you comparing your choices to God's commands? Do your "yeses" and "noes" align with God's plan? If there was a visible plumb line in your life, would you be aligned closely or way out of balance? It's important that we review our behaviors before they become habits. Righteous living is our call, but too often, we get caught up in the speed of society to recognize our decisions. We need to be certain that we are living out God's standards and not our own visions. So...slow down, discuss life with God, and walk behind Him instead of in front. Consult the builder before you construct.

Prompt: How often do you ask if the decisions that you are making please God? Do you include Him in your decision-making, or only after the decision has been made?

_____

_____

_____

_____

_____

_____

_____

_____

_____

_____

_____

_____

_____

September 30

Matthew 12:33–37

The words that we outwardly speak are the inner meditations of our hearts. The period at the end of your sentence had a place to start. If goodness pours out, that means that there is goodness lying present within your Spirit. You might think that you know your own heart, but it can surprise you when you actually hear it. We judge our own character based on our intentions and claim righteousness based on our actions. But we are biased and blinded by the truth that has happened. Our brain is opinionated and easily conformed, but our hearts are steadfast and true. Our heart reveals what actually is, not what we might do. So when we open our mouths, our heart speaks openly regarding its genuine focus and meditation. Think of your voice as being the subtitles of your heart's narration. Today, we have more opportunities to share our voices than we ever have before in history. Not many thoughts or opinions are left up to mystery. So we have a world full of loud and exposed hearts, all beating at opposing rhythms. All clinging to their superior opinions. Voices radiating the sound of conflicting beats of meditation. Words radiating maliciousness because of hearts rooted in hatred. Every word that we speak, we will have to answer to and explain in heaven. A transformed heart starts with cleaning up your reflection. What is your heart focused on today? If you do not know, just open your mouth and speak. You are either focused on your faith or focused on unbelief. Our responsibility is not to polish our vocabulary; it's to meditate on God's glory. If we give Him our entirety, He will narrate our story.

Prompt: Who's voice brings your comfort? What about their voice makes you feel so comfortable?

_____
_____
_____
_____
_____
_____
_____
_____
_____
_____

OCTOBER

OCTOBER 1

2 Samuel 5:6–10

We serve a limitless God, so any limits that are placed on your life are not final. We are quick to succumb to the limitations of our given title. When we are told that "this is the way something is done," we do not question the protocol. But what would have happened if David had listened to everyone telling him that he was too small? On our own, we are confined to the limits of our environment, our body, and our mind. With God, we are able to break past the barriers that our world has designed, not because of our ability but because of God's will and God's strength. The same God is living inside of us that rose up from the grave. If we are following the call of God, then no limitations will persist. If we fill our minds with belief, then no doubt will exist. If we say "yes" to God, then we must say "no" to the regulations of our environment. God can use anyone; He does not need people with pre-qualified requirements. If you are facing a battle that is too big for you to fight, allow God to fight in your place. If you are wearily putting one step forward but losing momentum, allow God to carry you through the race. Do not allow the world to dictate your purpose based on your ability. Allow the vision of God to help you approach situations differently. We are not to be like this world, so why do we confine ourselves to the world's likeness? We were made for the infinitely impossible, not the world's "finest." Do not accept limits on your life that are created by the world; follow God and expect the impossible. The world simply cannot stop a God who is unstoppable.

Prompt: What areas of your life do you wish you could be more confident in?

_____
_____
_____
_____
_____
_____
_____
_____
_____
_____
_____
_____

OCTOBER 2

1 Peter 4:16–19

Suffering is not enjoyable, but it always produces exceptional growth and strength. It's the willingness to toe the line even though you know what it is going to take. Following Christ is the single greatest privilege that there is in this life that we get to live. But it also can be the greatest reason for judgment because this world is combative. If we do not endure the suffering for the sake of God's name, what does that look like to the lost? Why would they ever be inclined to surrender if we are not even willing to pay a small cost? We should count it all as joy, even the painful slander and suffering. The world's disdain towards us just reveals that we are drenched in the Lord's covering. Jesus, the Messiah, God in the flesh, was despised, mocked, and tortured. They accused Him of everything bad even though He left everything healed and restored. Why does this world hate Jesus so much even though He came to save the world for eternity? Because Satan rules the world, and he hates God with fervency. Satan hates healing, restoration, hope, joy, and peace. The minute you open your mouth about the promises of God, he will do anything he can to make that talk cease. The closer you get to God, the closer you become to being the bull's eye on Satan's target. But do not dare allow him to stop, but God has started! We were sent for one purpose: to do the work of God and bring the lost souls back to the arms of the Father. The suffering that you endure in the process will only make you stronger. God is always worth the trials, so persevere for the one who died for you. It might be tough, but eternity in heaven will outweigh any suffering that you go through.

Prompt: What has been the greatest moment of physical suffering that you have ever endured? What feelings were present in your body? Have you ever had emotional or spiritual suffering that has come close to that feeling?

_____

_____

_____

_____

_____

_____

_____

_____

_____

_____

October 3

Proverbs 21:21

We live in a process/outcome society where our choices directly impact our fate. You are defined by your successes and defined by your mistakes. If you do "A," it will always result in outcome "B." Our society loves having multiple doors with individual keys. Now it's true that if we act in a sinful manner, we will reap what we sow. But it is also true that there is not one proper way for a plant to grow. Some trees grow straight up, while others twist and turn with a dramatic disposition. Each one categorized as a unique special edition. A garden may be watered every day and exposed to sunlight at the same rate, but one plant may grow a bit taller. But a harvest is a harvest; why does it matter if one stem is smaller? All of our walks with God will look different, so do not compare your branches to the branches of others. God does not intend to bless you in the same way; He has another blessing that He wants you to discover. If you pursue God's righteousness, you will find life, honor, and prosperity. But do not be upset when you cannot walk through someone else's door with your unique key. God's world is a process/outcome entity that has one process with an infinite variety of outcomes. Our games will all look different, but our battles have all been won. So do not compare your plant to another; just be grateful for your portion of the harvest. In the end, why does it really matter if your branch is not the largest? A blessing from God is always the perfect portion for our current situation. So surrender to God's process abs avoid adding unnecessary complications.

Prompt: How does who you are comparing yourself to translate to a deeper longing?

_____

_____

_____

_____

_____

_____

_____

_____

_____

_____

_____

_____

OCTOBER 4

Luke 12:47–48

I do not often picture God as my boss, but in some context, I think it's fitting. It reminds me that I am below the throne on which He is sitting. He has given me a job, benefits, and a promised eternal retirement. I am honored to be a part of His work environment. But just like a boss expects hard work, God expects responsibility. We are working for the kingdom, not for industry. To whom much is given, much is required, and as Christians, we have been given the most! That is why we cannot disregard or avoid our posts. We must spread the good news of the gospel, pray for the sick, and hand out love endlessly. At the top of our résumés, it should read "employee of ministry." Too often, we mistake our life's purpose for our earthly interests. Sometimes we become so entangled in our work that we cannot tell the difference. As believers, we must claim the work of Christ as our number one priority and actually do the work. And we do it because God loves us so much, not because His love needs to be earned. That's the purpose of our lives and the beautiful task we have been given. It's the reason you were created and the reason you are still living. Take pride in your purpose and be grateful for your responsibility. Let's "wow" God with our gratitude, faith, and productivity.

Prompt: If you were the boss of a company, what would you look for in employees that you hired? How can those attributes translate to your own work in the kingdom of God?

_____

_____

_____

_____

_____

_____

_____

_____

_____

_____

_____

_____

OCTOBER 5

1 Timothy 4:1–10

Exercise is just a part of my everyday life, and I find it absolutely necessary for me to be my best self. It's important for my physical, mental, and spiritual health. I make it a top priority, and every person in my life knows that it is important to me. Without it, I truly do not know what kind of person I would be. Think about some aspect of your day that requires discipline and prioritization. What is one thing that is never an option but an obligation? I am sure for some, exercise will be it, and for others, it might be reading or spending time outside. What is your "thing," and what is your "why"? God instills these passions in us for a reason, but we also need to prioritize Him as a passion. Because if we are not intentional, our priorities actually become distractions. Training my body is important to me, but only if it adds to my faith—not if it takes away. And that is how we must examine every part of our day. We must wake up with priorities that culminate into a day of testimony. If we do not include God in our lives, then we cannot be surprised when we are lost and lonely. And we can't be shocked when those around us are, too, because we haven't led the way. God needs to be at the top of our priority list every single day. What is important to us will get done, so we must examine our heart's desires. We get to decide what we do each day—we are our own schedule designers.

Prompt: What are things that you *must* do in your day for it to feel complete? Examples include exercise, drinking coffee, talking to a loved one, etc. Why does this thing(s) captivate your soul so much?

_____

_____

_____

_____

_____

_____

_____

_____

_____

_____

_____

_____

OCTOBER 6

2 Timothy 2:25–26

It is so important that we understand that we are representatives of the kingdom of heaven. The way we behave and treat other people sends a message. Our great commission in life is to make disciples out of the lost and broken people. So, how we treat them is a really big deal. Christians know how to interact with other Christians, but what about people who do not believe? A lot of the time, we act like they are in some rival team. When in reality, they are not our opponents; they are actually not even playing the game. We also forget that, at one point, we were the same. If we refuse to hang out with unbelievers, then we are refusing to serve God. It's easy to point out the flaws of others, but do not forget that you are flawed. Do not avoid people that believe differently; Jesus never did. Instead of up and running, stop and sit. Sit with the unbelievers and represent the love of your Father in heaven. You do not have to preach; let your actions be the message. What good does arguing do? Especially with those that do not know Jesus. I can promise that your argument will not be something that they, all of a sudden, believe in. Choose conversation over conflict and love over legality. We must meet everyone with open arms and intentionality.

Prompt: Who do you interact with on a regular basis who shares differing beliefs from you? If you have people—how does the way they think influence your life? If you cannot think of any—who are some people you could start interacting with?

_____

_____

_____

_____

_____

_____

_____

_____

_____

_____

_____

_____

OCTOBER 7

Luke 23:13–25

When you hear the words "peer pressure," what do you think of? For me, I think of not necessarily wanting to but feeling like I have to do stuff. In high school, this mostly revolves around alcohol, drugs, sex, and general rebellious behavior. Not giving in to peer pressure can save you from a lot of danger. But it's not just a "teenage" problem; we are susceptible to it at every age. The peer pressure story is always the same; we just might be on a different page. Look at Pontius Pilate, he wanted to let Jesus go, but the crowd shouted, "Give us Barabbas." So instead of acting out of intelligence, he acted out of habit. He gave orders to release Barabbas and crucify the Son of God. Because, at the moment, he cared less about his beliefs and more about the applause. We shame Pilate for his weak morals, but we fall into peer pressure all the same. There are things in our life that we should be firm with that we actually end up willing to change. What are those things for you? How are you giving in to peer pressure? And how could you stop? What are things that you should 100 percent be doing and things that you 100 percent should not? Whatever the answers are—hold firm and stay true to the commitments you have made to yourself. Don't let the story of peer pressure be the story that you tell.

Prompt: Do you do certain things because of peer pressure? What things? How often? What would happen if you did not?

_____

_____

_____

_____

_____

_____

_____

_____

_____

_____

_____

_____

_____

OCTOBER 8

Proverbs 2:9–11

There are times in life when God's rules and commands can seem overly strict and unfair. The world will make you second-guess if certain rules should even be there. And the world will also manipulate our minds into thinking that certain commands hold more weight than others do. The world will convince you that the final judgment call should be made by you. And it's an easy trap to fall into when the pull of sin is so enticing and strong. But something will never be right when it is wrong. And by God's grace, He is patient with us, even when we fall on sin's side. He loves us all the same when we are surrendered or engulfed with pride. It's not God loving us that we must worry about; it's our mind that we must be concerned about. Faith tends to spiral when we open up our minds to doubt. God's words are true, and His commands are ever-lasting; they will never change. He does not have to give reasons why or explain. We just have to trust that He has our best interest in mind, even when it seems like it's unfair. A lot of times, "no" is the greatest expression of care. Don't give into the world's lies and miss out on the blessings that flow from obedience. Be grateful that He isn't lenient. We need parameters, and He has given us free will to make our own choices and commitments. If we commit to the world, we will never find fulfillment.

Prompt: Think of a time that you had to comply with a policy or rule that you did not agree with. How did it feel to have to submit to the rules? How often do you find yourself in positions like this?

_____

_____

_____

_____

_____

_____

_____

_____

_____

_____

_____

_____

_____

OCTOBER 9

Psalm 46:5–6

When things get tough, where does your mind go? I battle depression, so I tend to go into really low lows. Where the world around me feels void, and all of the vibrancy vanishes. It's an emotional and physical emptiness that is difficult to manage. And when I try to look to the world to help, it actually gets much worse; the only thing that helps is Jesus. It's in those lows that I truly realize how much I need Him. It can be hard to go to Him in prayer, so I always start by turning on worship and listening to someone else praise. And I just keep listening until my heart is one and the same. For me, depression is like nap time for my body, mind, and soul. Except I did not choose to fall asleep, and I have no control. But worship is like an alarm clock for my soul, and once it awakens, my mind and body begin to stir too. It's in those moments that I realize it's from within that I am renewed. Because the Spirit lives within me, and God calls that Spirit, "the Helper." I can count on the Spirit to help make everything better. But I have to want the help, and for me, the cry for help is pushing play on a song of praise. How kind is God to come help when I don't even have the strength to say His name? He is within me, and He is within you—call on Him, or at least send up your personal flare. You won't be waiting on rescue for long; He is already there.

Prompt: When you get in a "low," what helps? What makes it worse? Who can you talk to when you are in these "low" moments?

_____

_____

_____

_____

_____

_____

_____

_____

_____

_____

_____

_____

_____

October 10

Luke 8:40–48

In times of despair and desperation, we often begin to pray for a touch from God. We know that with one touch of His presence, He could heal every part of our lives that is broken and flawed. But have you ever thought that maybe it's *you* that should be reaching for the touch instead of receiving the contact? Maybe God has been reaching for you, but you have constantly been taking steps back. Do not blame God for being absent when maybe it's you that has the lack of action. Maybe it's your unjust cynicism and not God's lack of compassion. Jesus did not stop in the middle of the crowded road to heal the sick woman; she reached out and touched His hem. She knew that the healing did not come from a show-stopping spectacle; it came from belief within. We do not have to pray for a touch from God; His presence surrounds us constantly. We do not have to prove our desperation by praying more despondently. We simply must be willing to reach out and touch His garment. God has given you access to unending nourishment, but if you refuse to eat, then do not blame Him when you are starving. He has, and is, and will do anything for His children to be happy, whole, and dependent on His glory. But if you do not give Him the pen and open your page, how will He write your story? A touch from God is not the miracle; the true miracle is when we touch Him. When we take action and put our hope in a process that we could never comprehend. Do not expect your breakthrough to come if you continue to build walls that He must breakthrough. The touch is not up to God; He is waiting for you.

Prompt: What walls might you be putting up that are preventing other people in or your emotions out?

_____

_____

_____

_____

_____

_____

_____

_____

_____

_____

October 11

Matthew 6:25–27

Why is worry our default response to situations that are out of our control? It's almost as if, if we cannot predict the outcome, we begin to punish our souls. I want you to think about this for a moment: when has worrying ever solved the problems of your position? Has worry ever proved to be the cure for the condition? Now, let me ask you this: do you trust that God's plan for you is always good and full of purpose? Do you believe that He is always working on something much deeper than what we see on the surface? It's not our job to begin worrying about the ending when the first act curtain has just opened. Sometimes we must learn to be comfortable with the uncomfortable instead of trying to fix all of the pieces that are broken. God never promised us "easy," and He never promised that we would be able to control and predict the outcomes. But what He did promise is that all of our battles have been won. The antidote to worry is not relaxation; it's trust. It's acclimating your body to the reality of having to walk into the unknown and having to adjust. Having faith is not defined by sitting on a pew; it looks more like standing at the edge of the Red Sea. Knowing that, naturally, every door is closed, but remaining rooted in the fact that God has the key. Worry is not the cure for uncontrollable situations; it's actually the cause. Because no situations are out of control when they are in God's arms. Worry is not our natural reaction to stress; it's our natural reaction to being away from God's certainty. It's the absence of faith, not the response to adversity. Do not allow worry to suffocate your faith; run closer to God when worry begins to draw near. God's plan is beautiful and good; you have absolutely nothing to fear.

Prompt: Would you consider yourself a "worrier"? What things do you do to cope with the feeling of "worry"?

_____

_____

_____

_____

_____

_____

_____

_____

_____

_____

OCTOBER 12

Psalm 30:4–5

Emotions are fleeting. Even if it does not feel like that at the moment, they will pass. Even the deepest emotions won't last. So if we put our confidence in our emotions, we will lose sight of the beauty of consistency. We will either live in extreme joy or in extreme misery. But a life with God allows a constant sense of regulation which keeps emotions in check. It's not a life of constantly feeling "the worst" or "the best." And isn't that so nice to know that God will regulate your emotions so that you do not have to? You get to control them; they do not get to control you. I tend to fall into "black or white" thinking—I am not great with the grey area. So life often feels like bliss or hysteria. And it's frustrating, honestly, because I allow my emotions to control my life's movement. When, in reality, God can and should be the one doing it. And if I allowed Him to do it, I would see that His steadfast love and consistency are much more inviting than my roller coaster of emotions. I don't want to follow my path—I want to go where He is going. I don't want my emotions to drive anymore; I want God to drive, and they can ride in the back seat. I no longer want any part of myself to take the lead. God is steady, and it's a beautiful blessing that He is. Praise God that we do not have to be controlled by what's ours; we can be controlled by what's His.

Prompt: Do you find it easy to share your emotions with other people? Why or why not? Who is someone you share/or could share with?

_____

_____

_____

_____

_____

_____

_____

_____

_____

_____

_____

_____

_____

October 13

Deuteronomy 33:13–15

Praying for someone is a common occurrence in Christianity, but when was the last time that you spoke a blessing over someone? Praying can call forth heaven to address a current issue, but speaking a blessing over another can dictate who they become. Our words alone cannot dictate situations, but our words, paired with God's will, can enable the miraculous. Do you really think that your spoken well wishes have happened by accident? God loves when we speak blessings over our lives and the lives of others. He loves when we have a heart for heaven and words that attach to His wonders. One of the greatest miracles we can ever experience is the miracle of joining our voice to heaven. To be an ambassador for His will by declaring a blessing. True love can be shown in a multitude of ways, but one of the most forgotten is words of spiritual affirmation and words of abundance. Praying it's a meditation of your heart, but blessings are the expressions of spiritual substance. A prayer is asking God for healing; a blessing as declaring health over a family for generations. The prayer is asking God to protect our country a blessing is stating that no harm will come to our nation. Blessings are not greater than prayers, and prayers are not greater than blessings. One is just to find your dependence on God and the others sharing with God what you are expecting. Let's be quick to pray for people but let's also be eager to speak abundance over them with blessings. Let's turn meditations into prayers and our dreams into words that we are professing.

Prompt: When was the last time you prayed not just *for* someone but *with* someone? How did that feel? Could you find a way to include prayer with people on a routine basis?

_____

_____

_____

_____

_____

_____

_____

_____

_____

_____

_____

OCTOBER 14

Leviticus 26:2–4

We are all eager to do what we have been called to do, but what about what we have been commanded? We must not expectantly eat the fruit of harvest without acknowledging the process of the seed that was planted. We are willing to love each day in the Lord's plan, but what about knowingly following His set guidelines? Have you done the research, or are you dependent on Him to continually define? We often ask the Lord to speak while ignoring words that He has already spoken. We wait patiently for a situation to be fixed while, all along, He has provided us with the tools and instruction to fix what is broken. If you are desperate for the next step, maybe look back and see the pattern of your past prints. Examine your life in relation to the Bible's content. If you have been feeling overwhelmed and stressed, have you also been observing the Sabbath? We cannot blame God for the situation if we have refused to make His commands our habits. Has your marriage been unstable lately? Well, have you been approaching your relationship following the biblical plan? Has the wife been acting in accordance with Scripture, and has the husband been leading like a faithful man? Instead of desperately seeking a fresh word from God, begin to activate the words that He has already said. Stop blaming Him for destruction if you are ignoring the words in red. God loves to speak to us and pour out fresh new wine. But He also expects us to drink His old wine that withstands the test of time. If we adhere to the commands of God, most of the unnecessary distractions will disappear. If we know what we know and do what He said, the devil will not be able to tell us what he wants us to hear.

Prompt: In what ways do you feel like your life is out of alignment with Scripture?

_____

_____

_____

_____

_____

_____

_____

_____

_____

_____

_____

_____

October 15

Ecclesiastes 10:20

We have been warned from a young age to be careful with the words that we allow to escape our lips. You know the old saying we were told about words, stones, and sticks? But what about the words that we think never escape our heads? We forget that they still have power even if they were never said. Sometimes they even have more power over our lives because we ruminate without an outlet. We think, and think, and think, but *never* talk about it. Those are the words that stain our souls because they settle without action. Lack of dialogue can still cause incredible distraction. God knows the thoughts in your mind just as He knows the words that you speak out loud. Whether they are kept in your quiet mind or spoken to a crowd. Words and thoughts hold weight, and negative ones weigh more. These thought processes and patterns are not something to be ignored. We must take our minds captive and repent for all destructive thoughts. *All* of them, not just when we open our mouths and get caught. Because they more our thoughts align with the Lord, the more our words will too. Think, don't judge...speak, don't spew. God delights in our righteous words, but He also delights in our mind's devotion. Thoughts still take action even if they do not have outward motion.

Prompt: What words have you never spoken out loud but kept in your heart that would be hurtful to another person (or yourself) if they were spoken out loud? You do not have to write them out—instead, ask God to rewrite them into something positive. Write those words out. Let those become the truth.

_____

_____

_____

_____

_____

_____

_____

_____

_____

_____

_____

_____

OCTOBER 16

1 Chronicles 16:32–33

Our voices are an instrument of worship, but so are the silent movements of nature. It's hard to envision the reality that every single part of creation is worshipping our Savior, from the waves crashing on the sandy shore to the leaves falling off of the trees. Nature is in a constant state of bowing on its knees. That is why we are so overcome with peace when we surround ourselves with the bareness of nature. It's the reason our bodies ease, and there are shifts in our behavior. It's the innate draw that we feel for the untouched articles of our world that remain unchanged by society. We attribute the draw to escaping stress, but I believe it's our souls' desire to worship silently. It's important to calibrate our hearts by admiring the basic reality of our surroundings. You can approach a mountain with an expectation of silence but find a cry to heaven that is resounding. The birds of the earth do not sing hymns, but they do praise God with every intricate whistle and tone. That is because their praise is not taught; their praise is innately known. Just as the trees reach up to heaven and the flowers bloom with open arms of surrender, we, too, are naturally made to praise God's splendor. God loves when we verbalize His praise, but real praise is found within the heart. Our default setting is to worship, and it has been from the start. If your heart has been yearning for a greater connection with God, surround yourself with nature and watch the unending praise of creation. There is a reason that when God wanted to deeply connect with one of His children, He made going into the wilderness an obligation.

Prompt: Where in nature do you feel closest to God? What would you want to see if you could see anything out of your window every morning?

_____

_____

_____

_____

_____

_____

_____

_____

_____

_____

October 17

Jeremiah 6:13

We all fall short of the expectation of righteousness, but do you remind yourself of this daily? That our ability to be perfect is impossible, and our commitments, at best, are shakey. We are all broken people serving a God of absolute immaculate perfection. That is why it is critical that we must look to Him and not our peers for guidance and correction. It's not bad to look up to someone and admire the way that they approach life or handle certain circumstances. But we need to be careful not to focus so intently on others for our navigation of self-advancement. We place labels on people and deem some more virtuous than others, therefore, worthy of our attention and imitation. But in the process of admiring another, we simply forfeit our dedication. It's not inherently bad to look up to another, but just make sure that your gaze is not locked and that it can go higher. You can admire the virtuous nature of peers as long as God is your number one desire. This is less about God being your main focus and more about focusing less on the portrayed virtue of another. Why strive to imitate a peer when you may not like the truth that you discover? We are all broken, we all sin, and we fall short of God's glory. God's righteousness and mercy are the only common threads in our weaving stories. Do not idolize others and place expectations on them that are impossible to achieve. You surrendered idolatry when you spoke the words "I believe." God wants you to depend on Him for everything and look to Him for self-growth. Do not look for goals on Instagram; look for them on the pages that He wrote.

Prompt: Who are your role models? What parts of them do you admire? What parts of them have you adopted? Why?

_____

_____

_____

_____

_____

_____

_____

_____

_____

_____

October 18

Proverbs 22:24–25

There is a difference between encountering and associating, and oftentimes, we fall into the latter. We choose to fill our time with people, and the people that we choose matter. It's easy to blame your association with others on being inclusive but do not forget that you can always exclude yourself. It's better to avoid association and receive questioning than it is to risk your emotional, mental, and spiritual health. Of course, it's right to approach others and show kindness to everyone that you connect with. But do not allow the magnitude of the connection to cause a spiritual drift. Encountering others is expected, and recognizing their importance is respectful. But many of us focus so intently on making others feel comfort that we personally become neglectful. God encourages us to give a hand up, a hand out, and to lay hands on others for healing. But a handshake or a handhold is not spiritual; it's sealing. We must be careful who we associate with, not because of others but because of our hearts' devotion. We must first commit to following God before we give in to following our emotions. This is not a call to destroy relationships; it's a call to recognize distance. It's a call to be more respectful of your heart, not live a life of social resistance. Encountering leaves room for impact; association established expectations and regulations. You can still be caring and cooperative without allowing their behavior to impact your spiritual relation. Do not avoid contact or touch, but regulate your commitments and connections. Putting up a guard for your spirit is necessary for your protection.

Prompt: What boundaries have you set recently with people in your life? What boundaries do you need to set? What is stopping you from setting those boundaries?

_____

_____

_____

_____

_____

_____

_____

_____

_____

_____

OCTOBER 19

2 Timothy 4:6–8

As an endurance athlete, I can say that there is no feeling of disappointment quite like finishing a race knowing I could have given more. It's like leaving a cup half empty, knowing that there was more to be poured. The finish line floods feelings of vacancy and regret. When the race is over but you realize that your body is not done yet. This is the same as spiritual endurance and can be translated to our walk with Jesus. Are we willing to give our all to the one who frees us? I do not want to finish this life with more energy reserved at the end. I do not want to cross the finish line and have it *not* feel like a win. I do not want to get to heaven and recount all of the moments in life that I could have given more. I do not want there to be an ounce of energy left stored. I want to collapse across the finish line, knowing that my body and spirit did everything they could in the race. I want to be proud of my performance when I see God face-to-face. But in order to achieve that level of personal fatigue, we must be willing to work hard without thought of preservation. Not as a means of self-sacrificing but as an expression of gratitude for our salvation. Why would we not give our all for the God who has given us everything and more? I do not want to get to heaven with anything remaining; I want to just absolutely pour.

Prompt: How do you know when you are giving something your all? In what areas of life are you giving your all? In what areas of life do you feel that you could give more effort?

_____

_____

_____

_____

_____

_____

_____

_____

_____

_____

_____

_____

OCTOBER 20

Philippians 1:15–18

It is not our responsibility to uncover people's motives. What encourages people into action is their business. We are so eager to find fault among others that we have ignored others' personal limits. For example, if a person is willing to pray in public for another, why does it matter if they are doing it for attention? It's true that they may be solely doing it for a pat on the back but isn't God still receiving the recognition? Is it right for a church to make millions every year and have chandeliers in the sanctuary? No.... Probably not. But the lives that have been saved because of that church are not fake because salvation cannot be bought. We could spend our lives determining whether or not a person or institution's motives are genuine, but why does that information matter to us? Too often, because of our judgment, we look upon the gospel being preached with disgust. I am not here to burst your bubble, but your ways are not always superior. That is why under no circumstances can we look upon others' interpretations of the Bible as inferior. Do we have to agree? No, but if Jesus is our commonality, then remember we are on the same team. Why would the lost ever want to be found if all they see is us pitting against each other with aggressive schemes? Our job is not to judge or uncover the reason behind the action. Our job is to encourage one another and highlight the name of God by dismissing distractions. What if we focused on what we have in common instead of what makes us different? At the end of the day, the cause of Christ is the only thing that is significant.

Prompt: What is your biggest pet peeve? Why does this bother you so much? How is your way of seeing it superior?

_____

_____

_____

_____

_____

_____

_____

_____

_____

_____

_____

OCTOBER 21

1 Timothy 2:1–6

In the midst of what seems to be an ever-increasing divide in our country, we need unity with heaven more than ever. Hatred is rampant, slander is the norm, and there is more injustice than we could ever measure. When the world seems bleak, it is easy to succumb to one side of the division. But we must remember that we will have to answer to any and all of our decisions. Instead of getting swept up in the storm of the chaotic currency, we should be on our knees and rooted to our foundation. Instead of picking sides and ridiculing the opposition, we should be praying for the leaders of our nation. What good does your judgmental opinion do if it leads others down a tunnel of hatred? One moment spent slandering a human's beliefs is a moment of sharing the gospel that is wasted. How can we expect the lost to want to run to our loving Father if they see us overflowing with judgment and hate? At the end of the day, what has more value to you: improving the growth of the kingdom or making America great? I understand that our country is important, but is it more important than valuing a human being? We have to set the example that you can be patriotic without being demeaning. Division is of the devil, so do not give into his schemes. The blood of Jesus covers us all, no matter which side we lean. Instead of scrolling through media outlets, thumb through the pages of God's Word and speak truth over our leaders. Our world needs more intercession and a lot fewer opinionated speakers. Pray, do not protest; intercede, do not insult. Our nation is desperate for unity. We must be willing to protect and pray for all members of our differing community.

Prompt: Are you extremely opinionated when it comes to political beliefs? If so, why? If not, why? How do you think your stance is beneficial to your health?

_____

_____

_____

_____

_____

_____

_____

_____

_____

_____

OCTOBER 22

Ecclesiastes 9:11

Not everything in life happens how it "should," I think we can all agree that is true. It's comprehensible and even expected until it happens to you. Think about any moment in your life when you concluded that something "was not fair." Maybe you worked for a reward, but there was no reward there. Or maybe an illness overtook the body of you or someone that you love without any discernible reason. It's hard to place blame when there seems to be no meaning. And it often results in mistrust or, at the very least, a sense of skepticism. It is hard to take your next step when every step feels out of rhythm. Here is the truth...our broken world is not fair, and it does not ebb and flow in predictable ways. It's not like the changing of the tides or the time of the day. And it's absolutely unnerving and, by all means, discouraging. You will starve if you look to the world for your nourishing. That is why we must look to Jesus for our true North and stand rooted in His firm foundation. That way, we can walk with faith instead of cowering in frustration. With Jesus, we do not have to have things figured out; we can trust that He does. Our hope is not found in what is or was; it's in what becomes. Fairness cannot live in a broken world; the two go together like oil and water. It's not our job to label chapters in our story...we have to trust the writing of the author.

Prompt: How do you advocate for injustice? What "unfairness" in the world are you most passionate about?

_____

_____

_____

_____

_____

_____

_____

_____

_____

_____

_____

_____

OCTOBER 23

Luke 19:1–10

You cannot out-give God; that is why you must give with a cheerful heart. Giving is not something that you do; it's part of who you are. The moment that we turn giving into duty is the moment that we lose the grace behind the gift. It cannot be viewed as a job; it just has to be part of the way that we live. I love the story of Zacchaeus because Jesus noticed him. He pointed him out and demanded to have lunch with him. This story would not be as significant if Zacchaeus was the town priest, but he was the tax collector. And he immediately began to explain all of the ways that he would change to be better. But Jesus did not confirm dinner reservations after Zacchaeus gave all of his possessions away—He asked to eat with him before. Jesus wants you to give, but He wants your heart more. Giving is a product of loving God, not the action required to love God. It's better to be genuine than it is to be a fraud. If you are giving to please God, but your heart is full of resentment, do you really think that God is pleased? We each have to determine the line between genuine giving and greed. God loves you right now just the same if tomorrow you gave all of your possessions away to the poor. No action that you do could ever make God love you any less or any more.

Prompt: What is the greatest gift you have ever given? In what ways do you give on a routine basis? (This does not have to be monetary; it could be your time, your attention, your words, etc.)

_____

_____

_____

_____

_____

_____

_____

_____

_____

_____

_____

_____

_____

OCTOBER 24

Psalm 73:21–28

It's beneficial to recognize our weaknesses, but we should not give them glory. They have value, but they are not our whole story. Our weaknesses magnify the strength of God because He meets us where we fall short. But you are not a "loser;" He is just Lord. Our weaknesses reveal a lot about our personal battles, and they tend to stir up conviction. The tend to offer insight into our innermost affliction. So although we should not glorify them, we also should not discard them. We do not want to be acquainted, but we do want to be aware of sin. We want to despise our sin but use it as a barometer for spiritual growth. Weakness can seem devastating, but with God, it just reveals hope. God can and will turn your weakness into strength, but it requires recognition and effort. You see, it's not about all of the ways that you are bad; it's all of the opportunities to be better. God has no interest in leaving you where you are as long as you have no interest in staying. Conviction is not there to encourage complaining. It's there to magnify the weaknesses in your life so that you may lean on God for the strength to change. God is not in the business of leaving people the same. Don't avoid your weaknesses; own up to them and boast in God's strength. The conviction is the initial step of an opportunity to obey.

Prompt: What do you think others would consider is your greatest weakness? Would you agree? How could this be turned into a strength?

_____

_____

_____

_____

_____

_____

_____

_____

_____

_____

_____

_____

_____

_____

OCTOBER 25

1 Peter 5:6–7

Fishing is a game of patience, and I am not a very patient person. That is one of the lessons that I may spend a lifetime learning. So up until this point in my life, I have not spent a lot of time fishing, but when I do, one part is my favorite. I love the bit of action before waiting for the casting; I savor it. I love picking a spot on the water and trying to get as close as possible to it. I like seeing where it lands and knowing that I threw it. I like the sound it makes as the line spoils out of the reel with reckless abandon. I like the ripples it makes when it's found its place and finally landed. How the quick movement turns into complete stillness as it rests upon the water. And you know what? We can learn a lot from that bobber. We are instructed to cast all of our anxiety on Him because He cares for us. And we know from fishing that the casting part requires letting go and trusting. What if we took anxiety and mentally visualized casting it away, like in fishing? If instead of reeling and taking it all back, we did some casting and sitting? We tossed our anxiety out like a hard cast and let it land upon the waters of God's control. We let it go with our minds and then trust Him with our souls. Pull it back and let it go; it's time to watch it fly and settle outside of our hearts and minds. Let's truly let it go and see where it arrives.

Prompt: What is something in your life that you are scared to give up control over? What would happen if you did?

_____

_____

_____

_____

_____

_____

_____

_____

_____

_____

_____

_____

_____

OCTOBER 26

Ecclesiastes 7:8–10

One of the most enjoyable topics of conversation is discussing times from the past and stopping to reminisce. It's tempting to become so overwhelmed with the past and the old things that you miss. It's even easier to miss the old times when the future seems bleak. So we search for past moments to invoke some sense of relief. How often do you say: "I wish I could go back to the good old days." Maybe you lived in a different place or could act in a different way. Maybe your responsibilities were smaller, and the world seemed like a better place. Or maybe you simply want to go back to the times when you had fewer wrinkles on your face. The past may hold special memories and special people, but do not write off God's intention for what is ahead. That would be like being okay with never speaking again and just living in a repetition of everything you have said. If you often reflect on the past, how often do you also say: "I did not know how good I had it back then." That is because, at the moment, life was still difficult and more complicated than we could comprehend. God gives us what He knows we can handle in every season, and each of them has trials and joys. Each moment of our life has been established, and we have simply been deployed. Was the past good? Yes, absolutely! Will the future be good too? Yes, of course! Not because of any outside circumstances but because God is the source. You can reminisce all you want but do not wish for an old season when God is graciously allowing you to walk into a new season. Life would not be easier if it was twenty years ago; life will keep improving because of God. He is the *only* reason.

Prompt: What season of life do you wish you could go back to and relive? Why? What part of the current season of your life do you like the most?

_____

_____

_____

_____

_____

_____

_____

_____

_____

_____

OCTOBER 27

Luke 22:17–23

It's typical to pray before meals, but have you ever really thought about why? I have always thought that it was weird that we thank God for the food that we buy. Now, don't get me wrong, I get that God is the ultimate provider of everything that we have. But I guess the prayer just feels like more of a ritual that is done repetitively and fast. What if, instead of treating it like a habit, we truly treated it as communion? What if instead of thanking Him for our groceries, we truly remembered His persecution? Just like the Last Supper, where Jesus broke the bread and poured out the wine. What if we habitually remember this before we dine? I guess on a macro level, I just want my prayers to have belief behind them instead of just air. I don't want to speak words of gratitude just because others are there. If I am going to pray before a meal, I want it to be a prayer of gratitude for something even greater than my groceries. I don't want to be in a room of people and still feel lonely. I want my words to mean something, and I want to constantly be reminded of His merciful sacrifice. And more importantly...I don't want to forget about it after I take my first bite. I want my communion with God to be an ongoing process and to use my meals as the physical manifestation. Praying out of pure remembrance and gratitude, not obligation.

Prompt: Do you view prayer as an obligation or a desire? Why?

_____
_____
_____
_____
_____
_____
_____
_____
_____
_____
_____
_____

OCTOBER 28

Job 32:6–9

Do not refuse a message just because it comes from an unlikely messenger. Always keep in mind that God's ways might seem a little different and irregular. Do not place stipulations on the voice of God because God can speak through anyone. God does not require a qualified twelve-step process to get His desired outcome. Wisdom of the world might be found in the number of years that you live, but spiritual wisdom operates differently. It has everything to do with your spiritual maturity, so you could be eighty-two years old but still in the stages of spiritual infancy. It's hard to tell on the outside the wisdom that lies within a person; that is why we must listen with discerning ears. You will know in your spirit if it is something that God wants you to hear. But too often, we ignore someone's voice because they have lived fewer years on Earth than we have. We silence the opinions of the youth because how could they possibly have anything to add? What if that child has been a devout follower since taking their first breath, and you are new to the faith? Would you have the humility to listen to what they have to say? God can, and will use anyone, so we must open our ears to His voice. Our spirit of discernment will be able to separate the pieces of wisdom from the noise. Personally, God has spoken to me multiple times this year through the voice of my four-year-old nephew. The messenger's appearance has nothing to do with whether or not the message is true. Allow others to speak into your life without judgment or choice. Open your ears to hear the magnificence of God's voice.

Prompt: Have you ever received a piece of advice from an unlikely messenger? Who was it, and what was the piece of advice?

_____

_____

_____

_____

_____

_____

_____

_____

_____

_____

_____

_____

OCTOBER 29

Proverbs 12:22

Truth seems to be more elusive and less common than ever before. It's sad, but you never know what ulterior motive that someone has in store. We have been trained to become cynics, always expecting the worst in others. Expecting lies but being pleasantly surprised when the truth is what we discover. Just look at our world today...it is almost impossible to trust immediately. The default setting seems to be lying about what is being discussed. It's heartbreaking to think that our world has fallen into such a state of deceit. It's hard to be hopeful in an arena of defeat. But just because the world acts a certain way does not mean that we must conform to its conduct. Just because the world is sinking into quicksand does not mean that we have to be stuck. In the days of lies and deception, we must be the stark contrast of truth. Practice what you preach by telling the whole truth. Own up to your mistakes, claim responsibility for your actions, and communicate with transparency. Act righteously and speak with sincerity. Do not cower to the expectations of this world. Rise about the bar that has been set by society. Do not allow words to escape your mouth unless they are true and true entirely. What good does a profession do if all of your other words are full of falsities? How could someone ever trust the authenticity of your Savior if you lie about other guarantees? It is better to go against popular opinion if it means that your opinion is honest. It is better to be real and unpopular than fake and flawless.

Prompt: Who do you trust with your whole heart? Who do you think trusts you with their whole heart?

_____

_____

_____

_____

_____

_____

_____

_____

_____

_____

_____

_____

OCTOBER 30

Romans 7:4-6

The law of God comes before the law of man, but do we always uphold that truth? Our rebellious flesh often boycotts a law until we have seen the proof. The law of man is based on a code of morals deemed upright by society. We are taught to obey the laws of the land and follow along quietly. But what happens when man's perfect laws oppose the commands of our creator? Are you more likely to bow to the worldly ways or the will of your Savior? As a citizen of this country, I have promised to live in accordance with our governing authorities. But it is important that I routinely check-in to be sure that my citizenship is not leading my spirit into conformity. When we surrendered our lives to Christ, we died to the ways of this world and claimed citizenship of heaven. It's okay for constitutional laws made by man to be questioned. Does that mean that we can disobey the law? No, it means that we can question its absolution. We must first uphold the ways of the Bible and, secondly, the laws of the Constitution. Do not allow the government to become your God; commit to God and, in turn, respect your authorities. We can still be good citizens while recognizing that God has seniority. We are in a divisive time in our country but keep in mind that no matter who becomes president, God is still God. That is why we follow the laws of our Father and do not worship man-made authorities who are flawed. We are people, living among people, and our ways will always fall short of moral perfection and spiritual standards. It's okay to follow the rules of the land as long as you recognize that they are not the answer.

Prompt: What authority figure do you respect but do not personally know? Why have they earned your respect?

_____

_____

_____

_____

_____

_____

_____

_____

_____

_____

OCTOBER 31

Luke 24:36–44

I think we have all heard the saying, "So as I say, not as I do," and it usually pertains to instructions for behavior. Most of us can speak the truth all day and still fall into habits of sin later. We know what is right, but our flesh often takes over our righteous thoughts. We know the directions, but somehow we still end up lost. It's important to know the Word of God, but knowing it isn't enough. If the knowledge does not transcend into behavior, it's just your capability to recite stuff. Even in Scripture, we see this happen. Jesus had told the disciples that He would live again after being crucified. Then when it actually happened, they were absolutely terrified. It's easy for me to ridicule the disciples for their lack of faith, but I do the same thing every day. I see the path that God has instructed me to walk on, I point people towards it, and still, sometimes, I walk the other way. God's instruction and His example must become our reality—it can't just be words we have memorized. They have to be part of our existence, not just advertised. We have to speak about the resurrection and then live like we actually believe it. Let's not just speak truth for others; let's actually mean it. Let's be people that can lead others with our speech and our actions. The Word of God is alive; it's not just captions.

Prompt: What is something that you preach but do not necessarily practice? Why? How would practicing this thing influence your life in a positive way?

_____

_____

_____

_____

_____

_____

_____

_____

_____

_____

_____

_____

_____

NOVEMBER

November 1

1 Timothy 6:11–12

It's hard to keep moving forward when you feel emotionally, physically, and mentally depleted. It's hard to believe that you are a conqueror when you feel overwhelmingly defeated. It's draining to wake up each day with your chin up when your head feels so heavy. It's hard to stay steadfast when you feel ridiculously unsteady. If this is you today, then I am here to tell you that God is proud of your willingness to fight. It's not about reaching a level of perfection; it's about facing each day with all of your might. God does not need you to be the greatest person on the planet; He needs you to be the greatest version of yourself. He needs you to be willing to take action and do what He has called you to do. That does not always look like being the one preaching from the rooftops; sometimes, it looks like crawling out of bed. It's okay not to be 1,000 percent full of joy and a little full of dread. If the battle that lies ahead of you today is trying to find a genuine glimmer of hope, fight for that with all of your strength! We must be willing to give our all because He gave all that He gave. Do not compare your position with others because God has given you a different portion. It's not about making more than you are able to; it's about using your good fortune. He did not ask us to be perfect; He asked us to persevere and pursue righteousness, godliness, gentleness, love, endurance, and faith. Day after day, we must be willing to give all that it takes. Give your best effort to God, and He will bless you in return. He is not impressed when we know it all; He is pleased when we are willing to learn.

Prompt: What has been draining you lately? How could you possibly find a solution to this?

_____

_____

_____

_____

_____

_____

_____

_____

_____

_____

_____

November 2

1 Thessalonians 5:8–11

How often do you think a compliment in your head, but you never actually say it out loud? It's amazing what beautiful things can live in our heads and never come out of our mouths. And I am not just talking about "liking" someone's outfit; I am talking about recognizing others' gifts. Noticing the little things that they do that others miss. Like people who are good listeners and always leave space for others to speak. Or helpers who go above and beyond to supply others' needs. Or what about people who are patient and slow to anger even in situations where they have the right to be angry? People who are still kind even when they could be cranky. What about the tired mom who is raising two kids and running on minimal sleep? How do you think it would make her feel if you spoke encouragement in a life full of critique? It can be the simplest of words, but they can have a lifetime of impact. When you see something good—say it—don't hold back. God made us for community, and one of the reasons why is so we would encourage each other to keep going. It'd be a shame to think something good about someone without their knowing. Be intentional today. Encourage at least one person from who you see goodness pouring out. It's just another way in which we can show Jesus' love.

Prompt: What is something you have been thinking of telling someone but have not told them? Why are you keeping this to yourself?

_____

_____

_____

_____

_____

_____

_____

_____

_____

_____

_____

_____

_____

_____

November 3

Romans 7:7–12

We would not know good if it wasn't for bad, and we would not know bad if it wasn't for good. It is not something that we think about; it is more or less just understood. But laws are put in place because they have been broken, and rules are established because things went haywire without them. Righteousness would be much harder to spot without sin. That is why, as Christians, we are called to follow God's commands and obey the laws of this earth. Remember, we came to serve, not be served. It is not our job to question leadership or earthly processes; our job is to pursue righteousness and avoid sin. The minute that questioning becomes our default, we let doubt win. It does not matter if laws are "holy" or not; it is deeper than superficial agreement. It's a posture of the heart to not get caught up in riots and rallying for impeachment. It's a stance of peace in the midst of chaos. It's not complacency; it's confidence. Not in who our lawmakers are but in who God is. And God instructed us not to go against the laws of the land, and He is my master, so I will do what He says, even if it feels wrong to my flesh. Our flesh is prideful, and we always have to check our filter for price and ego. It's not about our opinions; it's about walking where we are told to go. And if your body is opposing this message (like mine is)—check if it's your flesh or your spirit. My spirit knows it's right even though my flesh does not want to hear it.

Prompt: Are you quick or slow to anger? What really triggers your anger, and why? How might this anger be causing harm to you or others?

_____
_____
_____
_____
_____
_____
_____
_____
_____
_____
_____
_____

November 4

Isaiah 33:2-3

We often speak about God's new morning mercies in the context of His love for us, but do we actually think about what it means? It's amazing how it can be something we never truly think about but still firmly believe. On my "best days," I am intentional with Jesus and aware of His love for me because I seek Him in the morning. I don't have to wonder why I am full; I see Him pouring. But other days, I am short-sighted and honestly too self-centered to see His mercies being poured out on me. Walking around to open doors and egotistically thinking that I had they key. But it's always God...always, and He greets us with new mercies every single morning; we just have to see it. We must seek Him in the morning and not just "say it" but "mean it." If we all spent ten minutes of our morning opening our Bible, praying, or praising—His mercies would be evident. But it takes us focusing on what is real, not just on what it relevant. Feelings will ebb and flow, but Jesus will remain consistent in our life, so don't grow complacent—be grateful. Let's not be fair-weather; let's be faithful. Let's relish in His consistency and not forget that He is moving. He is so good at production that we often forget that He is the one producing. Be intentional, be aware, and start every day with a few moments of focus and gratitude. Then watch how you see His involvement in everything where you once only saw solitude.

Prompt: How do you spend the first ten minutes of your day? Is that productive for your mental, physical, and spiritual health? If yes, what could you do to make this even better, and if not, what could you do instead?

_____

_____

_____

_____

_____

_____

_____

_____

_____

_____

_____

_____

November 5

Hebrews 13:9–10

Reading our Bible is not just for gaining knowledge; it's also for reorienting. It provides us insight and reflection on what we are called to worship and what we are actually worshipping. The world makes us all busy, and if we do not carefully examine our routines, we may fall into unrighteous habits. Things that might fill our schedule and elevate our social status. If you do not ground yourself in Scripture, you can be tossed in the waves of the mainstream. Going places you were never called to go and staying places you are called to leave. If your only means of reflection is the world, then you will most certainly prioritize unnecessary practices. We are a sum of our surrounding averages. We know that we must live in this world and interact with society, so we must balance the scales. If this world is a set of steep stairs, the Bible is our handrail. It grounds us, it protects us, and it reminds us that we are prone to stumbling. It's there to inform our steps, not just there for moments when we are struggling. Because it's so easy to look at the ways of the world and then begin to model the world's behavior. But we are not made in the image of the world; we are made in the image of our Savior.

Prompt: Where and what makes you focus? How do you regain focus when you have lost it? How could you use the same tools or places to refocus your spiritual life?

November 6

Job 5:17–18

Punishment is not always bad. Punishment is often initiated because of affection. We may view it as a dead end, but to God, it may be the first step in the right direction. I do not know when this started, but discipline is now viewed as an exploitation of independence. If we are told what we can and cannot do, we are distraught because of the impartation of limits. Instead of listening to constructive criticism, we cry about being told to change our behavior. We blame others for constructing our freedom when all that they were doing was helping us avoid danger. We run away from God's discipline because it feels so harsh and limiting. So, as a result, we chose slavery to the world instead of God's freedom which we find "crippling." How many tough seasons have you walked through in your life that you can look back now on and see that they could have been much worse? How many disappointments should have lasted a chapter but only lasted a verse? That is because God uses discipline to reset our hearts and reorder our steps. He knows that He can get our attention when He is all that we have left. Be grateful for His discipline and the hard times that He puts you through because He is saving you from experiences that are even more difficult. So do not curse Him for the momentary disappointment. Praise Him for the coming result. If you are receiving discipline from God, it's because He is setting you on the path of your greatest potential. Discipline is not stunting your growth; it's actually 100 percent essential.

Prompt: Think back to childhood; what were disciplines that your parents imparted to you that did not make sense at the time but make sense now? What disciplines might God be imparting on you now that are beneficial (even if they don't feel like it)?

_____

_____

_____

_____

_____

_____

_____

_____

_____

_____

November 7

Romans 10:1–4

Can you imagine what our world would be like if the energy used for hatred was used for love? If we spent half of the time arguing the things of this world and more time praising our God above? Being zealous is a beautiful attribute, but only if the zeal is rooted in spiritual foundations. But more times than not, people's zeal is rooted in degradation. How can we have such passion for earthly things but no energy for our creator? We are satisfied with being chased by God, but in all other avenues of life, we are the chaser. I am zealous for God, but I am also guilty of being zealous for this world and things that I find exciting. But when I allow my passions to pursue aspects of this earth, my attention is divided. It's not about ignoring your passions of this lifetime; it's about including God in the process. If God cannot be included in your zeal, then that zeal needs to stop making progress. God wants us to live our life with passion and fullness, but in order to do that, He must be included. Find zeal in what you have been commanded, not in what you have been constituted. If God cannot be found in your passion, then that is your red flag to step away. We cannot live our life with split personalities. God has to be included in every part of our day. Be zealous for God, exude passion for life, and establish energy in eternal occasions. Represent the glory of God, not just some man-made organization.

Prompt: Name the top five things that you are most passionate about. How can you see God's involvement in these things?

_____

_____

_____

_____

_____

_____

_____

_____

_____

_____

_____

_____

November 8

2 Chronicles 6:28–31

It's not if hard times come or if people will treat you wrong, but rather when. This has nothing to do with optimism or pessimism and everything to do with sin. It would be ideal if we never had to experience pain on Earth, but Earth is not ideal. So instead of living in waiting for impossible expectations, let's learn how to live in what is real. In times of trial, we must learn to depend on God and trust Him for the right outcome, even if the now looks dreadful. God is good, whether life is good or it is stressful. And when it comes to people, try to realize that hurt people hurt people. Harsh words will not kill you, but unforgiveness is lethal. Instead of awaiting offense, we must seek out forgiveness. And instead of explaining our sins, let's just seek out repentance. It's impossible to move on with unmet expectations; that is why we must only have an expectation of mercy. Our judgments do not change the fact that other people are worthy. They are worthy of love, forgiveness, and opportunities to try again. Not because you feel like it but because God died for your sin. Forgiveness is a choice, and hope is too. It has nothing to do with what you want and everything to do with Christ living in you. So choose hope, choose mercy, and watch as God's peace drenches your life. We get to live in abundant blessings because of His sacrifice.

Prompt: What expectations are you holding onto that might be unfair or unreasonable? Why are you folding onto these things, and how could you change them to be more attainable?

_____

_____

_____

_____

_____

_____

_____

_____

_____

_____

_____

_____

_____

November 9

Matthew 23:8–12

Superiority is on a rampage in our world today. There seems to be a power struggle everywhere on display. Think about it—your turn on the TV, and it's one news station against the other. People getting "canceled" and feuding is on the front of every magazine cover. Counties are at war with one another, and some are at war with themselves. It's tied up in the stubbornness of being right but being too prideful to ask for help. Winning used to be about games, but not everything in life is attached to winning. If it's not God's victory, then it is sinning. Because His is the kingdom, the power, and the glory—He is above, we are all below. We are all given the honor of being a part of His show. So when you see society battling for superiority, remind yourself that it is a battle for pointless power. It's about as real as that argument you won in your head while taking a shower. What good does it produce? None. What bad comes from it? A lot. It overrides your faith and overtakes your thoughts. If they are a person on Earth, regardless of their title or social media following, then they are a child of the king. God sees no ranking of authority; He just sees His offspring. The ranking we have created is only a distraction to relation. Superiority does not lead to power; it leads to spiritual devastation.

Prompt: What makes you feel superior? What makes you feel inferior? Examine your answers and why you might feel this way.

_____

_____

_____

_____

_____

_____

_____

_____

_____

_____

_____

_____

_____

November 10

2 Corinthians 6:14–18

We are called to be in community with everyone, but we must be careful of who we allow to speak wisdom into us. Everyone is deserving of our love, but not everyone is deserving of our trust. This goes deeper than just societal roles...this is more about spirituality. It's about choosing our influence with intentionality. The Bible uses the term "yoke" often in reference to connecting yourself with another person. Relationships bind with blessings and burdens. When you commit to another person, you are tying yourself to them. The yoke is the bond of sanctity and sin. And this isn't just about sexual relationships; it's also about friendships and family members. It's about anyone who knocks on your heart that you allow to enter. I once heard that we become a combination of the eight people that we hang around the most. So it really is important who you are keeping close to. This doesn't just mean limiting your interactions; it means limiting your influence. Make sure you are aware of how others affect your movement. We are called to love others like Jesus and allow others' love to make us more like Jesus. We must be free with our love but careful with who we allow to teach us. We have to find a balance between loving and protecting because we are broken humans, after all. Let's not allow letting someone have influence over our life; that shouldn't be our downfall.

Prompt: We have made "influencer" a job title—but in what ways are you an "influencer"? Who do you influence, and how do you see that influence affecting others or your environment? Are you proud of the influence that you are having?

_____

_____

_____

_____

_____

_____

_____

_____

_____

_____

_____

November 11

2 Peter 3:11–13

If we are truly living for Christ, then shouldn't He be at the center of our life? We tend to get so entangled in the here and now that we forget about the sacrifice. We are quick to say phrases like: "God is in control" and "I am blessed and highly favored." But yet, we are more dependent on ourselves than we are on our Savior. The truth is that one day this earth will be destroyed, and all that will remain is heaven and hell. And that day could be tomorrow...only God can tell. All of the "stuff" we are wrapped up in on Earth will fade away, but our relationship with Christ will remain. So instead of waiting for Christ's return, why don't we go ahead and make a change? Let's look at our priority list and see where God is currently placed. If He is not at the top, what things or people are in His place? Because the truth is—the more time you give God, the more productive you will be in work and your relationships. Doing things on our own doesn't make us more efficient; it's actually just dangerous. What would your life be like if all of the "stuff" in it was removed? Do not get so cluttered that you forget to give God room.

Prompt: What are you dependent on? It could be people, substances, routines, etc. Examine your responses and evaluate how these are benefitting or impairing you.

_____

_____

_____

_____

_____

_____

_____

_____

_____

_____

_____

_____

_____

November 12

1 Thessalonians 5:12–15

It is easy to get so carried away with the happenings of your life that you lose touch with others. It's normal to pour so much of your energy into your own world that you lose sight of what God wants you to discover. We are to put God first before all, but by doing this, others will inevitably come next. We were purposed to live like Christ, and that means giving others our best. It's important to intentionally spend time with God alone, but do not avoid community in the process. Without creating a community with other people, the kingdom will stop making progress. We must be people who are so excited to run after God that we cannot help but recruit others to do the same. The less we involve ourselves in ourselves, the more souls we can gain. This world has created such large divides that it has scared us into self-isolation. But the Holy Spirit that lives within will not conform to the world's adaptation. We must be the unusual ones that go out of our way to welcome others in. We must care less about popularity and more about alleviating the world from sin. Do not become so consumed with your life that you lose touch with building the kingdom of heaven. We were not created to be alone; we were created to be a blessing. So remember "joy" —Jesus, others, yourself, your focus should be in tune with that order. Don't live for yourself; live out your purpose of being a servant and a supporter.

Prompt: Who is your biggest supporter? Who are you the biggest supporter of? How does others' support impact your life in a positive way, and how does your support of others have a positive impact?

November 13

Proverbs 10:31–32

Have you realized that, lately, everyone has a platform, and on that platform stands their opinions? We have been afforded the freedom to think, establish, and make our own decisions. But what good is an opinion if it's based on feelings and not off of actual facts? That is like claiming territory over an area without first looking at a map. Is it right for you? Okay, no one can argue with your own personal point of view. But the problem with our freedom of personal beliefs is that we have convinced ourselves that our thoughts are always true. Christians are not called to have opinions, we are called to have wisdom, and only one of those is factual. Why spend time building a personal platform of thoughts when you could revel in the wisdom of the supernatural? We are so proud of the personal freedoms that we have been constitutionally assigned that we have freed ourselves right into bondage. We have become boastful and untrue to the point of being completely dishonest. If you want to use your platform for good, speak of the kingdom, not of the nation. Speak scriptures that are righteous instead of feelings of anger or words of degradation. Do not become so chained to your freedoms that you actually become captive. We are called to be humble and steadfast, not irritable and reactive.

Prompt: If you knew your reactions in stressful situations were being videotaped, how would you change the way that you reacted?

_____

_____

_____

_____

_____

_____

_____

_____

_____

_____

_____

_____

_____

_____

November 14

Proverbs 24:13–14

Have you ever tasted honey straight out of the honeycomb? It may be one of the most delightful treats I have ever known. Or what about a cold glass of lemonade on a hot summer day? Doesn't it seem to melt all of the discomforts away? Or what about a warm bowl of soup after being absolutely freezing? Is it not one of the best feelings, if not one of the most pleasing? That is because it's the opposite of whatever the current environment is, so it brings shock and pleasure. Having warmth when you are cold, cold when you are warm, and a touch of nature's sweetness makes everything better. The same goes for wisdom; it is sweet, comforting, and unquestionably refreshing. But wisdom is not a given; it is a blessing. So if God has given you the honey, you must allow other people to have a taste. Sharing comforting and refreshing gifts will never be a waste. Wisdom is not of this world, so it will always alter the environment. It's ours to share because it's a gift of entitlement. We should be the people handing out lemonade to the thirsty and soup to the cold and hungry. And our words should be comforting and sweet like a spoonful of honey.

Prompt: What is the most comforting thing to you? I will tell you mine—it's a crackling fire and a hot cup of coffee. Now you share yours. Describe it in detail. Why does this make you feel such a sense of comfort?

_____

_____

_____

_____

_____

_____

_____

_____

_____

_____

_____

_____

November 15

Matthew 10:1–8

Jesus often "sent out" the disciples to do work or heal on His behalf. They were told many times to walk on a different path. Not because He did not want their company but because He wanted their confidence to grow in the ministry. If they wanted to be "with" Him, they would have to see His presence a little bit differently. And although we aren't walking with Jesus physically, we must see our life through the same lens as the disciples. We have to connect our modern-day to the Bible. And to me, this connects with not needing "spiritual milk" anymore and instead needing "spiritual meat." Instead of instant sustenance from being fed, we have to learn how to use our teeth. We have to learn to walk our own path and "go" out and spread the good news and heal. It's time for us to walk by faith instead of walking based on feel. Because Jesus needed the twelve disciples to work and multiply His reach. If they had perpetually been the students, they would have never learned to teach. We don't become the master, but it is time for us to become active servants, not just observers. We are not called to watch; we are called to be the workers. Let's ask God to be "sent out," and then let's actually go. I know that we have free will, but let's no longer say "no." It's time we take hand in the game and not just sit back and watch from the sidelines. No more waiting and watching...it's time.

Prompt: What part of life are you sitting on the sidelines in? How could you take hand in the game?

_____

_____

_____

_____

_____

_____

_____

_____

_____

_____

_____

_____

_____

NOVEMBER 16

Proverbs 16:1–3

It is important that we wait for confirmation from the Lord before we take any steps. Because if we are not careful, we can think we are pursuing His path when really we are pursuing our best. It's easy to get caught up in planning the future and forget that God has already planned it out perfectly. Would you rather trust your imagination or God's certainty? Because the truth is that God's plan for our life is perfect, and our plan for our life is an assumption. God's is based on all-knowing power and love, and ours is based on nothing. Our way seems perfect to us, but that is only because we have put on blinders of personal desire. We have no way of knowing what will actually transpire. But God does, and that is just one of the reasons to trust His plan over your own. I would rather not trust the plans of uncertainty that I have and instead trust the *known*. Our plans are usually really good at producing short-term pleasure for ourselves, but they fail to last, and they fail to include others' best interests. But God's include everyone's best because they are perfect and deliberate. So we must check our direction and be certain that we are aligned with God's compass and not our own. Or else we will be wandering blindly into the unknown.

Prompt: What are you waiting on the Lord to confirm right now in your life? What does confirmation from Him look like? How will you take steps of action if you receive confirmation from Him?

_____

_____

_____

_____

_____

_____

_____

_____

_____

_____

_____

_____

_____

November 17

Hebrews 8:13

When God says something is made new, He means it. When He promises you a clean slate, He actually cleans it. He so kindly gave us the new covenant as the replacement of the old, not an addition. But I feel that we often hold onto the "old ways" as Christians. For instance, we work, and we work to try and redeem ourselves from sin, but it is not necessary. God is merciful, not discretionary. So we cannot hold onto pieces of the old covenant; we have to completely move on from it and step fully into the new. It's not disrespectful to ignore the old rules; even God says that the old rules are no longer true. But what it does require us to do is *know* the promises of the new covenant. It's hard to believe in His mercy if you are only knowledgeable about His judgment. God doesn't want us holding onto the old; that is why He created the new. In the same way that you hate when people blame your current self for the "old you." It seems outdated because it is...so let's honor God by moving forward with Him. He has offered us freedom; stop putting yourself in prison. Let's not move backward; let's continue to make relentless forward progress. The old has been thrown away because He knows the new is what's best.

Prompt: What part of the "past you" have you not forgiven yet? Why can you not forgive yourself for that thing? Ask God to help free you from this sense of self-imprisonment.

_____

_____

_____

_____

_____

_____

_____

_____

_____

_____

_____

_____

_____

_____

November 18

Ecclesiastes 5:10-11

Satisfaction is not the solution; the only solution is surrender. The more we acquire, the more it actually hinders. Wealth might produce comfort on Earth, but that comfort will soon come to pass. Because in the eyes of yesterday's abundance, today's abundance must surpass. The logical thought is that the greater the wealth you have, the happier you will be. But if you decide to allow wealth to dictate your joy, you will always be one paycheck away from acquiring all that you need. The more you receive, the greater you will need to receive next time. Because the desire for abundance increases in a linear progressing line. So if you live for the next deposit of riches, how will you ever live for God? Do not lose the gift of salvation because you are seeking wealth's applause. The things of this world will pass away, so where will your joy be found when it all disappears? Would you be able to find contentment in the scarcity, or would you be overwhelmed with fear? You do not have to run away from wealth if you are a Christian, but you certainly must not make it your number one priority. Do not surrender your soul to wealth's authority. Do not chase the next promotion; chase the eternal peace of God. Heaven is confirmed; wealth is just a fraud.

Prompt: What things bring you the most satisfaction in this world? What would life be like if you did not have these things? What things are you seeking that will bring you satisfaction, and how would your life look differently if you had these things?

_____

_____

_____

_____

_____

_____

_____

_____

_____

_____

_____

_____

November 19

Jeremiah 31:31–34

I think sometimes I take for granted the blessings of the new covenant because I never personally experienced the old. It's a life I never lived, just a story I have been told. But if you read something enough times, it becomes less of a novel and more of a narrative. That is why reading the Old Testament is imperative. Not only does it tell the whole story, but it brings to light the blessings of our current circumstances. It's the story of God's power, His love, and His plans. It's a gift to read the book of Jeremiah and realize that God already had my life in mind. Every person was created and appointed for a specific time. And ours happens to be now, under the law of the new covenant and surrounded by each other. God chose to send us in the time of salvation, not the time that we would have had to suffer. It's hard not to take things for granted when it is all you have ever known. Just like your comfortable bed in your cozy home. But sometimes, after a long day, you pull the covers up and sink into your bed with appreciation. Let's do the same thing with the new covenant/old covenant realization. It's a gift we have been blessed with, so the least we can do is acknowledge it. It's our reality as well as the Holy Script.

Prompt: If you could live in any time period, which would you choose and why? What do you like about the period of time that you live in, and what do you wish was different?

November 20

Isaiah 44:22–23

It's easy to get caught up in the idea that our lives are routine and mundane. It can be difficult to find significance in the sunrise when all of the sunrises are the same. There are 86,400 seconds in a day, and I can guarantee that they are used differently today than they were the day before. But it takes recognition of the knowing to realize that there is more. On an hour-to-hour basis, your week might look constant and unexciting. But to label today as "already lived" is to ignore the gift that God is providing. Yes, there was another sunrise this morning, but guess what? God painted the sky with a never before seen shade of blue! You might just miss the once-in-a-lifetime snapshot of this world because you are used to the view. There is nothing wrong with routine, but do not convince yourself that you are living the same day over and over in repetition. If you approach each second with curiosity, it will be much easier to give God recognition. Today might be Friday, but it's only *this* Friday *once* in eternity! Do not succumb to passive progression; live life purposefully! Purpose does not equal more; sometimes, it just means slowing down and celebrating the seemingly mundane. To-morrow will only be like today if we approach it the same. God woke you up today for a reason, and it was not to live yesterday again. He has called us to live a life of intentionality and celebrate the second that we are in.

Prompt: What parts of your routine do you love the most? What parts of your routine do you dislike the most? What things would you like to incorporate into your daily routine?

_____
_____
_____
_____
_____
_____
_____
_____
_____
_____
_____

November 21

Psalm 138:6–8

Our God is not seasonal, and He is not a fair-weather Father. Your problems do not impact His desire to help you prosper. His love for you reaches past the depths and into the tragedy of our humanness. He does not just protect us; He also pursues us. He sent us to live on Earth, but He never leaves our side. Regardless of our circumstances, He is with us all of the time. Think back to a season of trial in your life, and remember the exhaustion. When your back was against a wall, and you were left with no other options. What got you out of that season? What broke the cycle of endless struggle? What gave you triumph instead of trouble? The answer is God, even if it came in the form of a person, place, or opportunity. God can use miracles, and He can use community. He pulls us out of the wreckage of life like a first responder and stabilizes our spirit. If God wants something to be more clear in your life, I promise that He will clear it. In case no other words caught your attention, please let this next sentence sink in. He heals your life from within. Only God can provide peace in the storms and confidence in the chaos. He will put you back on track no matter how far you have been lost. God loves you enough to step down from His throne and pull you up from the lowly places. He wants us to follow, but if we don't, He chases.

Prompt: Think back to a season of struggle. What pulled you out of it? How can you look back and see God's hand in it?

_____
_____
_____
_____
_____
_____
_____
_____
_____
_____
_____
_____
_____
_____

November 22

Luke 2:41–52

People should be able to find you when they themselves get close to Jesus; let me explain. Like a husband and wife, they should be one and the same. When Jesus disappeared at the Passover festival, His parents eventually found Him at the temple. Then He explained that, of course, He would be at His Father's house, like the decision was simple. And I do not mean that we should always be found inside a church building because the church is no longer just a building. Where will you be found in the chaos and the milling? Because we now have the temple built inside of us, which means we have access to commune with Him at all times. When people search for your heart, where and what will they find? I want to be found with Jesus, no matter what is happening in my life or the lives of those around me. When people look my way, I want it to be Jesus that they see. And vice versa, when people see Jesus, I want to be associated with Him like a relative or a spouse. No matter what is going on, I want to be found in my Father's house. The world does not get to occupy any more of my time and space; it's all about Him as my first priority. I want communion, not conformity.

Prompt: In what ways do you resemble Jesus? In what ways do you resemble the world?

_____

_____

_____

_____

_____

_____

_____

_____

_____

_____

_____

_____

_____

_____

November 23

Hebrews 10:32–37

Becoming a Christian is the best decision that you will make in life, but it is met with suffering. It can seem odd that by accepting Christ, you actually will experience greater struggle. That is why Paul writes about perseverance so many times throughout Scripture. He wanted to give us the full view of the realistic picture. Because the truth is—why would Satan make your life difficult if you are obeying his commands? You see, the only time that he gets upset is when we refuse to follow his plans. And then what happens is he begins to panic when we commit our life to God. So he creates chaos and tries to instill doubt and heaps of guilt to make us feel flawed. But the beautiful truth is that it's not doom and gloom living in this reality with Jesus. Because even though life is tough, we have hope in what we believe in. Our eternity in heaven far outweighs any and all trouble that we will face in this lifetime. Satan's destruction is nothing compared to God's design. So we must persevere, not by our own strength, but by the strength of our Father. Instead of viewing it as a burden, let's view it as an honor. God does not want us to suffer, but He knows that it is part of our humanity. It is a massive part of Christianity.

Prompt: How do you tell the difference between God testing you and Satan tempting you?

_____

_____

_____

_____

_____

_____

_____

_____

_____

_____

_____

_____

_____

November 24

Psalm 84:10–12

I love the anticipation of a coming event, and I enjoy relishing in the moments just before it happens. I love envisioning the way that something will play out and then having it play out in ways far greater than I have imagined. I love the days leading up to a big trip, where you are packing and planning for your long-awaited vacation. Knowing that joy will be actualized when you finally reach your destination. I know that you know the feeling too, think about the day before you leave for the beach. Life seems a little lighter, knowing that tranquility is within reach. As Christians, the earth is our day before, and heaven is our much-anticipated paradise. Every day on Earth is simply preparation for eternal life. You can be certain that everything that you experience on Earth will be far exceeded when you arrive in heaven's embrace. We will finally experience relaxation as we are removed from the world's rat race. Even if we are a doorkeeper in the house of God, we will experience more joy than any moment of Earth's bliss. There will not be one single thing on Earth that we long for or miss. I do not know about you, but that makes me so giddy and excited for my final destination. I cannot wait for the day that He calls me home, but until then, I will live in preparation. I will ready myself and try to envision the joy and peace that awaits me when my life ends and I walk into what I have only imagined. But until that day, I will keep loving every moment I am given until that actually happens.

Prompt: What are you looking forward to most? Why does this thing excite you, and how are you preparing for it?

_____

_____

_____

_____

_____

_____

_____

_____

_____

_____

_____

November 25

Job 12:7–10

If you are struggling to believe that there is a God, allow the earth to inform you of His existence. We are the only species on Earth that has any doubt or resistance. The birds sing every morning as the sun appears over the horizon. The plants extend towards heaven as the new day brightens. The wind goes where God sends it in an act of humble obedience. When God commands a wave to form, its formation is immediate. The fish of the sea swim in the expanse, knowing that their creator is more expansive. As they swim amongst the currents as the water dances. Creation knows it has a creator, but somehow, we fail to acknowledge God's creativity. We view the most complex creation through the lens of simplicity. What benefit is found from doubting that God is the creator? What power is received by refusing to acknowledge that Jesus is your Savior? Why would you choose to live a life blind to the fact that there is a purpose for everything? Our hope is resurrected. Why is it something that you want to keep burying? I urge you to get among creation and ground yourself in the reality of God's power. It's on display every second, minute, and hour. Why would you not want to see the creator when you gaze out at creation? It provides endless proof, hope, and inspiration.

Prompt: What parts of nature do you see God the most in? What about it resembles God? How often do you get to experience this?

_____

_____

_____

_____

_____

_____

_____

_____

_____

_____

_____

_____

_____

November 26

Mark 5:40–43

It's easy to get frustrated and sad by the happenings of the world, especially things that are out of your control. It's amazing how fast removing the sense of control wreaks havoc on our souls. I think about this in relation to timing and how some things happen unexpectedly or, even worse, slowly. It can feel chaotic, hopeless, or even lonely. And in moments like that, it's when you have to realize that God is 100 percent in control and not you. Trust in His control, and do not allow yourself to be consumed. God does not operate under the laws of this world; He is willing and able to do anything that He deems appropriate. Our standard is not society; it's the Holy Spirit. And when we can truly believe that with every ounce of our soul, we will feel a true sense of peace. What would happen if you changed your death grip to a release? Instead of being anxious about your circumstances, how can you give it all to Him instead? Let's be people who live with our souls, not with our heads. Because God can and will perform miracles in our life, but we just have to trust that He will. It's not our puzzle to figure out; it's His promise to fulfill. Let Him have control. He will not fight you for the position. Allow Him to participate in your life, not just supply supervision.

Prompt: What is making you anxious right now? How are you coping with that anxiety? What would it feel like if God took this away?

_____

_____

_____

_____

_____

_____

_____

_____

_____

_____

_____

_____

November 27

Proverbs 11:18–21

It's better to do things the right way with the potential to fail than it is to do things the wrong way and take shortcuts. Giving it your best effort is always enough. To me, a clear example of this is performance-enhancing drugs in sports like cycling or baseball. People become the greatest of all time, but they did it all wrong. Maybe they achieve the status of greatest in their sport, but it's just them cheating. The title "greatest of all time" suddenly loses its meaning. Because they altered themselves in a way that is cowardly and deceitful. So all of the work becomes null and void when you reach your end goal. That is why we must work with patience and pursue our goals in life with righteous morals. Let's chase after our goals like people, not performers. Pursue everything in life with morality in the driver's seat, leave ego in the rearview mirror. You don't have to be an expert; it's okay to be a humble beginner. God will bless your pursuits that are cemented in righteous motives, but He will not bless ego or deceit. An unrighteous win is actually a big defeat. Let's be people who do things the right way, not the quick and easy way. God's opinion of us is eternal, but other people's admiration and opinions fade.

Prompt: What part of your personality do you wish was different? What is stopping you from changing that part of you?

_____

_____

_____

_____

_____

_____

_____

_____

_____

_____

_____

_____

_____

November 28

Matthew 21:12–17

Be careful what you say and do in the name of Jesus, do not associate Him with bad intentions. People might begin to associate Him with unrighteous occurrences even though every piece of Him is missing. As bad as this is, this is true for many churches around the world that claim God as the center. When, in reality, they are not obedient or seeking righteousness, they are greedy pretenders. And then God's name gets associated with them, and people who don't know God only come to know that false version. When, in reality, they never met God, just a broken person. But the same is true in our day-to-day life when we claim God to be the cause of the reasoning behind certain actions. When the truth is...He had no say in how/what/or why it happened. It was a choice of free will or a consequence of that choice. It was not His declaration; it was your inner voice. And yet we blame God and then wonder why our view of Him is negative. It's not fair to blame Him for the story when we did the writing and the editing. God is holy; He is not meant to be brought down from His throne and entangled in our deception. Other people's relationships with God can be greatly influenced by their perception. Let's make sure that we are being accurate representatives of God and not falsely associating Him. When it comes to our actions looking like God, let's try to be more of a synonym than an antonym.

Prompt: What behaviors are you associating with God that could potentially be harmful to the way others view Christ? *Remember, you are a representative of Him, so everything you do is associated with Him.*

_____

_____

_____

_____

_____

_____

_____

_____

_____

_____

November 29

Job 34:21–23

It's so easy for us to dismiss God's presence when we are entangled in devious behavior. We know that when we really need God, He is there to be our Savior. But His presence does not turn off and on depending upon your plan of action. God is with you and sees your behavior no matter what you allow to happen. It is so easy to welcome His Spirit when we are acting in a way that should gain His approval. Just as easy as it is for us to sin and mindfully allow His removal. But God is always with us, always present; He never leaves our side. No matter how well you think you have done it, there is nothing that you can hide. So instead of ignoring His presence or avoiding His unending love, why don't you just embrace it? Instead of trying to outrun His presence, why don't you face it? Instead of spending energy avoiding His commands, why not just do what He has intended? Why spend your life cowering in conviction when you can willingly walk the path that God has recommended? There is no place that you can hide. Is that comforting to you or scary? The answer is dependent upon whether God is your friend or adversary. Don't you want to be friends with the God that you will spend eternity worshipping? His omnipresence is meant to be encouraging.

Prompt: What are things that you do in private that you would never want other people to know about or see? How does it feel to know that God sees those things?

_____

_____

_____

_____

_____

_____

_____

_____

_____

_____

_____

_____

November 30

Hosea 6:1–3

It's important to understand that God only tears down to build back up better, take a minute and think about what that means. We are quick to question and blame God when our life is splitting at the seams. How could a God of love knowingly wreck my perfectly planned-out strategy? Maybe because He is giving you a blessing instead of allowing you to experience a tragedy. In the moments of the wreckage, it is hard to understand that the ashes are God's blueprint. Where we see an unfixable pile of destruction, He sees a mere dent. Sometimes we must be torn to pieces in order to be woven back together stronger and more pliable. Our resiliency is established because our God is so reliable. It is easy to look back in hindsight and see all of the ways that God has worked tragedy for triumph. It is nice to look back on the trials that you have faced knowing that they made you tough. But what about the hard "right now?" What about the breaking that has yet to come? Do you have the faith to trust what He is doing and has yet to do, based on what He has done? Will you praise Him in the breaking, in the crushing, and in the rebuilding? Can you thank Him for the end result in the midst of the beginning? God's intention is always good, and sometimes, it must get worse before it gets better. Sometimes you might need to fall apart before He can piece you back together.

Prompt: What hard thing are you facing right now? How might good come out of this?

_____

_____

_____

_____

_____

_____

_____

_____

_____

_____

_____

_____

_____

DECEMBER

DECEMBER 1

Psalm 100

It's one thing to celebrate Thanksgiving; it's another to live a lifestyle of gratitude. One is a day marked on a calendar, and one is an attitude. It's easy to stop for one day and thank God for the blessings that He has given you. But the true nature of gratitude is being grateful even in the difficult situations that you are walking through. Are you grateful for your job, even when the last place you want to be right now is at your desk? Are you grateful for your children, even when they refuse to listen and leave you stressed? Are you grateful for the food on your plate, even when it's not what you wanted to eat? Are you grateful for the clothes on your back and the shoes on your feet? The easy answer is— "Yes!" but the true answer is— "No, not always." The truth is that sometimes I am so self-concerned I forget to stop and give God praise. And you know what? God forgives me, but I refuse to keep letting myself slide. I want to live a life of gratitude and suffocate my tendency for pride. I want to truly live each moment with thanksgiving in my heart, not because of the holiday but because of my Savior. I want His goodness to be evident in my life and my behavior. Am I grateful for every second of the day? Not yet, but I am going to start by being grateful for each hour. Selfishness will lose its spark if you stop giving it the power. Thanksgiving is not one day; it's 365 x eternity. It's impossible not to be grateful when you know that God is working every second together perfectly.

Prompt: What is something enjoyable that you get to experience every day that you have come to take for granted?

_____

_____

_____

_____

_____

_____

_____

_____

_____

_____

_____

December 2

Matthew 25:31–46

It's common sense to do good when you are in the spotlight, but what about all of the shadow moments of your day? Where no one is around to praise you for what you do or what you say? It's easy to serve others when it is organized, but what about when it is spontaneous? Are you still willing to serve others even when it's not met with praise and lasting radiance? Society has formulated "serving" into a charity that we partake in from time to time, either physically or monetarily. But service is a posture of the heart, not a once-a-year donation to charity. There is nothing wrong with giving to organizations, as long as that is not the extent of your willingness to serve. Because God plainly states that based on the way we serve others is the key to eternity that we will earn. It's not about giving to get or serving for safety; it's about a lifestyle of service that is instinctual. It's a gift of being born again; it's not even an act that is teachable. It's a life of service because that is the only option, not because of rewards but because of responsibility. It's an attitude, not an activity. We were created to serve, not sent to serve on occasion. Service is a gift we receive along with our salvation. Is service a part of your heart or just a day on your calendar of discomfort? Are people in need really people to you, or are they just numbers?

Prompt: In what ways do you physically serve? In what ways could you start serving?

_____

_____

_____

_____

_____

_____

_____

_____

_____

_____

_____

_____

_____

December 3

Colossians 3:12–14

People are hard. Personalities clash, feelings entangle, and pride is always involved. Our relationships with other people are always going to be like a puzzle that must be solved. This is not a statement of annoyance or arrogance; it's just a statement of truth. Our mood changes, interest shifts, and passion projects provide the proof. On a macro view, we might seem unchanging, but tiny changes happen from day to day to change our personality. Too often, we approach other people with an expectation of finality. We expect other people to always be there, and when they are not, we blame their lack of allegiance. But people change and then change again, like a tree from season to season. You do not expect a tree to provide you shade in the winter; all of its leaves are gone, and you need the warmth of the sun. So if you are looking for trees of shade amongst other people's seasons of winter, you will find none. We are to bear with one another and uphold each other with respect, kindness, patience, humility, and compassion. But we also must remember that this world is full of distractions. Show mercy to others by lowering your expectations of their prescribed involvement. Do not expect people to solve your problems; only your Savior can do the solving. Be gentle with others and treat them well, but do not become discouraged when they fail to meet your expectations. Our God is unchanging, but people will have and are allowed to have fluctuations.

Prompt: Where have you seen the most growth in yourself over this last year? In what ways do you look different? In what areas do you wish to see change?

_____

_____

_____

_____

_____

_____

_____

_____

_____

_____

_____

_____

December 4

Acts 20:24

What if you could wake up with no set routine or things to do? What would you choose to keep in your life, and what would you lose? If you could live the perfect day, what would influence how you spend your time? Maybe a person or an activity would influence your design. But what about if your only aim for the day was to live for God and grow closer to Him every moment? What if He was the full composition, not just a component? What would change about your life and your routines, and how would your day-to-day look different? How can we turn God from an observer into a participant? The truth is that He doesn't have to do anything differently; we just have to prioritize His influence. He cannot just be who we praise; He has to be a part of all that we are doing. What can you change about your life today that would make your life center more around Him? How can He turn into your beginning and your end? Throw off everything else and allow your mind to contemplate a life with just you and God—how would that look? If Paul's encouragement was actual instruction instead of just words in a book. What is one thing that you could implement or give up today to align yourself more closely with your creator's interests? What would remain the same, and what would be different?

Prompt: What does your ideal day look like? Where would you be, what would you eat, who would you interact with, what would you do?

_____

_____

_____

_____

_____

_____

_____

_____

_____

_____

_____

_____

_____

December 5

1 Corinthians 12:12–26

It is way easier to spot differences in other people than it is to spot similarities. We tend to cover up connections by focusing on disparities. Case and point—denominations, the differences between each range in diversity. Some believe things are wrong, and some believe things are righteous with certainty. We are masters at creating a list of cons, but what about the pros? Aren't we all similar in nature when our core is being exposed? What if we focused on our similarities instead of getting hung up on our differences? Why does it matter where you are from or what you look like when we are all heaven's citizens? You do not remove your foot because it's different from your hand; you know it has a different strength and purpose. Why do we focus on the specific way a foot may move instead of praising God that it is working? We all make up the body of Christ. Our differences combine and weave into a seamless operation. It is important that we stop focusing on the paint color or brick type and start focusing on the foundation. It's hard to comprehend others' opinions, but guess what...we were all made in God's image. We have a limited understanding of a God that has no limits. Take off the glasses of magnifying others' diversity, and focus on the unchanging core of love and humanity. Denominations have nothing to do with the wholeness of Christianity.

Prompt: Are you comfortable being in places where everyone around you seems to think differently than you? Why or why not?

_____

_____

_____

_____

_____

_____

_____

_____

_____

_____

_____

_____

December 6

Luke 7:1–10

We pray with faith for God to move, but do we have enough faith to know that God will move without prayer? Do we trust that God is present even when we forget to acknowledge that He is there? Do we have enough faith to trust His will, or do we pray for our will and His blessing? Is your time with God an intimate time of connection, or is it simply you just confessing? I like to think of myself as a person of deep faith, but I still feel compelled to tell God the appropriate plan of action. The spirit of conviction is engulfing my heart with this question: if you do not pray for your desires, would God still be good enough to make them happen? Now do not get me wrong, prayer is *vital*, but I am just wondering if my personal prayers fall short in faith. If I am praying for His will or praying to complain. Do I trust that God has it, even when I do not tell Him what "it" is? Are my prayers conversations or just some kind of "to-do" list? Do you trust that God would heal you, even if you did not ask Him to? The trust is you may have unknowingly had terminal cancer in your body, and God healed you without you even knowing what you were going through. God wants us to pray, but we ultimately need to have the faith to know that His will is good and it will come to pass. I want to have faith big enough to fully trust that He will grant me a good and fulfilling life even if I never ask.

Prompt: What does prayer look like for you? What kinds of things do you pray for or pray about?

_____

_____

_____

_____

_____

_____

_____

_____

_____

_____

_____

_____

_____

December 7

Zechariah 10:1-2

The Lord is faithful to provide you with everything that you need, but we sometimes confuse our needs and our wants. We conclude that God cannot be loving because He has provided less than our ideal results. But our results sometimes are based on unrighteous motives, and to gain them would actually mean loss. God freely gives us all that we need, so we need to be wary of things that come at a cost. The Lord will send rainstorms when there is a drought and food when there is a famine. He will provide you with everything that you need while you are on this side of heaven. But if you compare your provisions to your desires, you might see that there are differences. He is the God of abundance, not a genie that grants your wishes. If you feel slighted by God, examine your life and compare it to His commands. If your life is out of control, have you been attempting to control it with your hands? God is always going to give you exactly what you need. The truth is that most of the time, we do not even know what that is. We will find contentment when we give Him our desires, and all that we desire is being His. Do not live in a drought begging for a drink when God could give you a downpour. I promise that whatever you want in this life, God will give you so much more. He is the provider, but it's up to us to surrender to His will. We are an empty vessel that only Jesus can fill.

Prompt: If you could have three wishes granted immediately, what would they be? Do you trust God with those desires too? Why or why not?

_____
_____
_____
_____
_____
_____
_____
_____
_____
_____
_____
_____

December 8

Ecclesiastes 3:9–15

I know that we view kingdom work as prosperous, but what about all of the other work that you do daily? Have you ever thought about the fact that even your job can impact the kingdom greatly? Maybe not directly, but indirectly it can have a great impact. It's actually really cool to see how our world and the kingdom interact. Let's say, for instance, that you're a lawyer—God cares greatly about the people that you represent. Or if you're a doctor—He is using you to help people mend. What about if you're a teacher? He is allowing you to shape the next generation. And if you're a recruiter—He is allowing you to make connections. A farmer is providing sustenance, and a counselor is providing care. An engineer envisions, and a social worker provides welfare. I could keep going on and on about each and every job, but the main point is that on a macro level, your job has kingdom value. If you are having s hard time finding what it is—ask God to reveal it to you. I think if we could all find deeper meaning in our jobs outside of just making money and getting work done. We would see that there is deeper value to our work where we previously saw none. You have an opportunity to make kingdom impact today, no matter what line of work that you do. You just have to be willing to let God use you.

Prompt: What do you do (or want to do) for a living? How can/could you impact the kingdom of God through that line of work?

_____

_____

_____

_____

_____

_____

_____

_____

_____

_____

_____

_____

December 9

Romans 8:9–11

It can be hard to believe that we are not only beings of flesh when the flesh feels so real. As Christians, we know that we have a spiritual side, but it's only something that you feel. The world can get so distracting and demanding that we lose the reality of our being. Instead of beings of faith, we become fixated on only what we are seeing. This might seem like an "out of reach" thought, but it's something that we must focus on every day. What will we bring to the forefront, and what will we allow to fade away? It might seem cheesy, but putting on your spiritual glasses can give more meaning to seemingly annoying situations. Because we might realize that it satisfies His plan, although it does not meet our expectations. In the flesh, we might see a traffic jam, but in the Spirit, we might see a twenty-minute opportunity to be alone with the Lord. In the flesh, we might be injured, but in the Spirit, it is just an opportunity to be restored. In the flesh, a relationship may have ended, but in the Spirit, you can see God leading you into a new season. The flesh will convince you that everything is by chance; the Spirit gives everything reason. We have a choice each day to put on the lens of faith or the lens of flesh. To live in the chaos of the now or gain insight into what is next.

Prompt: What is a problem that you are facing right now in your life that could possibly have a "spiritual silver lining"? What do you think the beauty could be from the ashes?

_____

_____

_____

_____

_____

_____

_____

_____

_____

_____

_____

_____

_____

DECEMBER 10

Zephaniah 3:9–13

"**If it cannot be said** in front of little ears, then it should not be said by big mouths." I read that quote the other day, and it has given me a lot to think about. If you really stop and think about it, none of us mature enough to reach the point where degrading words are acceptable. Because it has nothing to do with getting older or reaching some new level. God calls us to be pure in spirit, and slinging profanities around is not pure. Saying derogatory words does not make you more mature. If anything, it makes you more immature because it proves that you cannot control your tongue. You are choosing to push those words out with the air Christ has given you in your lungs. What does that say about us as adults that we deem it acceptable to speak profanity? We have to remember that what is acceptable in our culture is not always acceptable in Christianity. Our mouths are the tool of testimony; do not corrupt it with ill-informed speech. Why curse when you could teach? Why use your breath for words only some can handle when you could speak words of life? Why would you want to dim your light? God delights in our voice, but it breaks His heart when we speak with a harsh tone or a sharp word. Everything that you speak will be heard. If you would not say it in the presence of a child, why would you say it in the presence of your heavenly Father? You will never mature out of being His son or daughter. Guard your mouth with discipline; do not allow it to lead the way. Whether you believe it or not—we always mean what we say.

Prompt: If your life were a reality TV show, how much of it would need to be censored? Not just profane language but derogatory comments.

_____

_____

_____

_____

_____

_____

_____

_____

_____

_____

_____

DECEMBER 11

Philemon 1:8–9

Just because you have the ability to do something does not mean that you should. Our authority and power must always be used for good. It breaks my heart when I hear that people refuse to follow Jesus because they have been treated poorly by Christians. If people feel anything other than love from us, then we are not following our mission. We have the authority and the truth, but we still must be loving above all else. Because truthful words spoken in a hateful tone never help. I have the authority to preach the gospel, but if I do not love people well, my words fall void. I may be speaking truth, but if I act high and mighty—people will probably just be annoyed. I have the power through Christ Jesus to lay hands on the sick and watch them be healed completely. But that does not mean I make a display about it. Sometimes it needs to happen discretely. Jesus always stood firm, but He met people right where they were. You do not have to be stubborn; just be sure. I am sure that God is real, but I will still love people who don't. I am sure that reading the Bible transforms lives, but I will still love people that won't. I am sure that this world would be a much better place if everyone followed Jesus and kept His commands. In the same way that I am sure that Jesus still loves everyone regardless of where their beliefs land. Yes, we have authority, power, and truth, but it is nothing without love. Don't just speak it; show people that it is what you are made of.

Prompt: Does your personality accurately represent your heart? How is it aligned or misaligned?

_____

_____

_____

_____

_____

_____

_____

_____

_____

_____

December 12

Luke 7:48–49

Sometimes our "need to know" blocks our blessing, or at least our ability to receive it in full. Just like a kid that wants knowledge but dreads going to school. It's okay to be curious, but do not let your curiosity cover up your doubt. It's normal to want to know more as long as you have the patience to wait and find out. If God miraculously answered your prayer today, would you desire to know how? Or could you receive it without question? And what about if He answered it in a way that you were never expecting? We were made to be seekers, always wanting to go one step further than we should. But God's will and His Word do not need to be explained to know that it is good. If your prayer time is full of "whys," how are you questioning the answer? God does not owe us an explanation for not meeting our standards. Even if you question Him out of amazement, like a little kid questions a magician. We can look to God in awe, but instead of rattling off questions, we may be better off just listening. Do not block the fullness of God's blessing by trying to figure out how it happened. Let's teach our hearts to live in gratitude and trust that His ways will always be far greater than we could ever imagine. Live in awe and wonder, but do not allow that amazement to conform to doubt. It is better to trust God and have no knowledge than it is to ignore God and "figure everything out."

Prompt: Is knowledge always a good thing? Why or why not?

_____
_____
_____
_____
_____
_____
_____
_____
_____
_____
_____
_____
_____

DECEMBER 13

2 Peter 2:1–3

It's important that we test the words of others against the Word of God but not with a cynical heart. We must be willing to do the work of studying so that we may tell truth and lies apart. If our faith is built on other people's words, then it will eventually crumble and fade because the word of man and the Word of God are not even remotely close to the same thing. That is the trouble with being taught about a perfect God by an imperfect man. You will learn about the truth based on what they understand. The Bible is a living book which means that it speaks to us all individually. But someone's interpretation of the Word should be regarded as helpful information but not always information that should be taken literally. Because the truth is that men are flawed, and their interpretation might not be the one that God wants you to hear. So as a routine precaution, it's best to check everything that passes through your ear. And you do not have to do it in a hateful way, exclaiming doubt and ridiculing their interpretation. You can quietly do your own reading and studying without an explanation. You can still be an attentive student just do not elevate the status of the teacher to that of God. God is perfect, and people are flawed. Even this writing is my flawed interpretation of what the Lord is speaking to me today. But when you read the same scripture, what do you hear God say?

Prompt: Read the scripture for today. How do you interpret this? What is God telling you?

_____

_____

_____

_____

_____

_____

_____

_____

_____

_____

_____

_____

_____

December 14

Matthew 27:57–61

Have you ever been in a situation where your hope was buried, and your life seemed unreal? You know something has happened, but it's impossible to actually feel. It's like you are numb to reality because you have been handed a reality that you never expected. So instead of feeling hopeful and willing, you feel forsaken and neglected. I can think of many times in my life when my expectations were completely squandered, and I was left sitting in an unfamiliar reality. Like my mind did not quite add up to the physicality. And in those moments, I felt like my life was out of control and would never be right again. But true trust in God starts where our expectations end. Can you imagine giving up your life to be a follower of Jesus and then watching Him be crucified? Can you imagine the grief and hopelessness they must have felt when He actually died? One day they were treated as royalty, and the next, they were mocked and hated. They went from being the definition of delight to absolutely devastated. But guess what—Jesus rose again on the third day. The dark and forgotten tomb is never where He will allow you to stay. It might be three minutes, three hours, three days, or three years, but the stone will be moved! We might be down a few points, but we never actually lose. So if you feel lost, just trust that the grace doesn't last, but sometimes it is necessary for growth. It's better to lose expectations than it is to lose hope.

Prompt: When was the last time you felt utterly hopeless? How did God redeem the situation?

_____

_____

_____

_____

_____

_____

_____

_____

_____

_____

_____

December 15

Psalm 25:1–7

We remember our faults way longer than God does. Once we repent, it is finished. Our mistakes have a way of growing in our minds instead of being diminished. So we remind God of our past just to be sure that He is aware of our mistakes. But He does not need to be reminded of something that He already forgave. We come to God with trepidation and uncertainty, and He always meets us with assurance and acceptance. He does not have to let us live forgiven lives; He lets us. But when we hang onto past sin, we are actively showing our mistrust. We are saying that God could never forgive someone "like us." With statements like that of self-depreciation, we are also deprecating God Himself. When we question our ability to be forgiven, we are actually questioning His help. True trust in God is found in the moments of surrendering one's beliefs of how it "should" work. Doubt will always be present if you think you should only get what you think you deserve. It's an uncomfortable concept to trust that we are forgiven when our minds and the world tells us otherwise. The world is so much more beautiful through the lens of God's merciful eyes. So when you feel the need to remind God of your faults, try to remember that He knows them even better than you do. He knew exactly how your life would go from the moment that He created you. And He still chose to forgive you, and He will never stop choosing forgiveness. Remembering is the antithesis of repentance.

Prompt: How is your past inhibiting your future? It could be thoughts, behaviors, or mistakes. How could these be erased?

_____
_____
_____
_____
_____
_____
_____
_____
_____
_____
_____
_____

DECEMBER 16

Psalm 34:1–3

When life is difficult, it can seem like the least logical option is to praise the Lord. When life is sending you backward, it can feel impossible to look forward. But those moments of difficulty are exactly when our praise meets its purpose. Like a car engine light coming on and taking it in for a service. That is the beauty of praising God; it is the cure for every problem. It may not seem like it, but when God is involved, He solves them. It might seem counterintuitive to praise the Lord when life seems hard, but your praise will never return void. He will provide hope when all other hope has been destroyed. It's easy to read these words and nod your head, but what does this look like in reality? How do you properly weave the wreckage in with your spirituality? Maybe it's listening to worship music on your drive to work or listening to a sermon podcast. Maybe it's opening your Bible every hour and reading one verse really fast. Maybe it's talking to the Lord about your struggles instead of talking to the internet. Maybe it's writing down the thoughts that are overwhelming your head. Whatever it looks like for you—just invite God into your everyday life moments and watch what happens. I would be willing to bet that He provides comfort like you never imagined. He is *so* good, even when our life seems *so* bad. That is why we must praise Him when we are happy and sad.

Prompt: Is God woven throughout your day, or is He more of just a "bookend"? In what ways do you include Him in your daily life, and in what ways would you like to start including Him?

DECEMBER 17

Ephesians 1:3–10

If nobody sees you today or makes you feel loved, please know that God sees you and loves you. He is there during every sleepless night and every heartbreak that you walk through. He did not just create you. He chose you to be created. He looked at the earth and saw that it needed a "you," and when you were born, God celebrated. You are not one of billions; you are one of the one. If you have air in your lungs right now, then God's work has just begun. We downplay our importance by claiming humility when really we are downplaying God's handiwork. It's okay to feel real feelings; that's why God gave you nerves. But my heart is broken for everyone who walks through life feeling lonely, uncertain of their worth and importance. I can hear the silent tears being cried by people seeking any kind of reassurance. I am sorry if the world has made you feel like you are any less than what God has called you to be. I am sorry if your norm is to feel unloved and unseen. Because the truth is, that's a lie; you are recognized by the God of all creation. You have been His favorite "you" from the day of your formation. The same God who breathed Earth into existence thought you needed to exist. You may not fit in with the world, but you check off every box on His list. So if you do not hear it from anyone else today—I love you, but more importantly, God loves you. You are a distinct one-of-one creation with infinite worth and value.

Prompt: What things do you love most about yourself? Why?

_____

_____

_____

_____

_____

_____

_____

_____

_____

_____

_____

_____

_____

December 18

Luke 7:31–35

If your goal is to be good enough for the people around you, you will work yourself to death trying to achieve approval. Our worth is found in Christ alone, but for some reason, we have altered it to be communal. Here is the truth: you will never reach God's standard of perfection, but He does not expect you to be perfect. He loves you because you are you, and you deserve it. But people's expectations seem to be too high for our attainment. The actual will never live up to others' expectations of amazement. Even the people surrounding Jesus found fault in His actions, even though He could do nothing wrong! They applauded Him for standing out and then ridiculed Him because He did not belong. They desperately begged for Him to heal and produce miracles and then accused His abilities. They would welcome Him in with open arms and then chase Him out with hostility. If God in the flesh fell short of society's standard, so will we. That is why we must live for God instead of worrying if the world agrees. Can you imagine if Jesus had cowered to societal expectations? He most likely would have never died on that cross. He knew that living for God was well worth the cost. If you are exhausted from trying to fit in or gain approval from others, just relax and let go. Our life is about servanthood, not putting on a pleasing show. Do not care less about people; just care less about meeting their ever-changing expectations. If your flesh is always feeding others, it will lead to your soul's starvation.

Prompt: Do other people's opinions often dictate your choices? Why or why not? How is this helpful or hurtful?

_____

_____

_____

_____

_____

_____

_____

_____

_____

_____

_____

December 19

Judges 16:14–22

God has entrusted us each with unique and individual gifts, and it would be a shame if we took them for granted. It would be like a flower that withered amongst the sunshine because it refused to bloom where it was planted. Samson was given the gift of strength and wholeness from God with only one condition: that he never cut his hair. But as his gift became stale and the world became enticing, the less he seemed to care. I was convicted while reading his story; what gifts do I take for granted and carelessly give up because I fail to honor and protect them? In what ways have I offered my hair over to shears because my focus on God's giftings has been neglected? Maybe you have also treated God's gifts with negligence and forgotten their importance. Maybe they have become so stagnant because you have allowed them to lie dormant. I urge you, just as I am urging myself, not to look at God's gifts with complacency and become blind like Samson. Do not waste opportunities for miracles because you need more "do-over" chances. Samson lost his hair, lost his strength, and then lost his sight. But you want to know how good our God is? His hair started growing back on the same night. God will never take away your gift for God, but never take for granted the goodness of His gift. Our ignorance of his blessing is an opportunity missed. Protect your gift; use your gift. It is a blessing and a privilege. Do not waste the time of fulfillment having to ask for forgiveness.

Prompt: What things are you good at and or interested in that others around you are not? How might these things point you toward your specific gifts from the Lord?

_____

_____

_____

_____

_____

_____

_____

_____

_____

_____

_____

December 20

2 Corinthians 5:1–5

Physical ailments are oftentimes the instances that make us question God the most. We wonder how He can actually love us when our healing is not anywhere close. When we come down with an illness or face a devastating diagnosis, our praise turns to questions. Because illness is never part of the life that we expect. But just like our broken world, these bodies that we are in are broken too. So there might be some less-than-ideal experiences that we go through. And that does not mean that God loves us any less it just means that His spoken Word about the broken world is truth. Illness, disease, and pandemics are proof. But our hope is not rooted in a lifetime of wellness; our hope is rooted in our eternal healing. It's not about the portion that we receive on Earth; it's the portion that He will one day be revealing. If you or a loved one are fighting an illness, I do not write this with a blatant disregard for human pain and grief. I write this as a reminder to re-center and ground yourself in belief. This body is merely a tent; it is not your forever home. It's not yours in full; it's yours on loan. Find hope in the fact that our bodies await a heavenly transformation just like our souls. We are bits and pieces that will one day be whole.

Prompt: Are you or a loved one dealing with an illness or physical ailment right now? Write out a prayer for healing.

_____

_____

_____

_____

_____

_____

_____

_____

_____

_____

_____

_____

DECEMBER *21*

Luke 24:50–53

Hurt people hurt people—think about that for a minute. They feel the need to commit a crime just because they have been a witness. The hard reality is that we will be hurt by others in this lifetime, but the question is: will we reciprocate? Will we forgive them by treating them with an exchange of mercy, or will their actions trigger our mistakes? It's hard to be hurt, broken, overlooked, and mistreated and still offer a smile in return. Most of our fleshy instincts are to make certain that others have their lessons learned. We are bound to be hurt by others, so the question is not "if" but "when." More often than not, it's our pride that we feel the need to defend. Jesus was betrayed, mocked, beaten, tortured, and crucified, and when He rose from the grave, He immediately blessed His people. Not because His feelings were fake but because His love is so real. It's so easy to treat others the way that they treat others, but that is a cyclical life of hurt and revenge. Getting the hurtful last word does not mean that you win. It's hard to bless others when they curse you, but it's even harder to heal your wounds when you are wounding others. You would be amazed at the amount of ground an act of mercy covers. We will be hurt, but let that hurt stop when it hits our hearts. Let it be the end, not the cyclical start.

Prompt: What actions hurt you the most? How do you usually respond in those moments?

_____
_____
_____
_____
_____
_____
_____
_____
_____
_____
_____
_____
_____
_____

DECEMBER 22

Ecclesiastes 5:4–7

When you hear the word "vow," what comes to mind first? For me, it's the promise made in marriages to love, protect and serve. It's the exchange of the "I dos" before a room of witnesses and people who love you both individually and together. Vows are serious promises; they are not fair weather. But if we separate our view of vows from just weddings and into the context of our beliefs, we will find that we speak them often. Some of our vows are good, but when they are not, it is a problem. Think of the things you say often that "you will never do" or even pieces of this world that you have committed to your identity. God has given us all free will, so when we declare something, God will not intrude on that proximity. What have you spoken out loud and declared with your heart's intent? What promises have you established with your consent? What have you said "I do" to that is keeping you bound in matrimony? The beautiful truth is that you can break off those vows without any required alimony. If you have made a harmful vow—*break it!* Tear up that contract and allow God to intercede. Do not speak something out loud unless it's something you believe *and* are willing to receive. Wedding vows are a beautiful display of commitment, promise, and choice. The contract is signed once you speak them out loud with your voice. Think about what you have said, but more importantly, be careful with what you say. What vows will you unknowingly make today?

Prompt: What are things that you say repeatedly, either out of habit or intention? *Examples: "I will never find love," "I will always be addicted to that."* How might these everyday vows be detrimental to your faith and life?

_____

_____

_____

_____

_____

_____

_____

_____

_____

_____

_____

_____

December 23

Matthew 9:1–8

I might be the only person who needs to hear this today, but—Jesus wants to forgive us. He wants our slate washed clean, and He wants our trust. He wants to heal us from our infirmities and redeem our past mistakes. It's not just His duty; it's His desire to save. Read this portion of Scripture a few times and see what part stands out the most to you because, for me, it was about forgiveness. I know that Jesus loves me, but sometimes I forget that His love is relentless. He reminds me of a big brother in this passage sticking up for His sibling in the face of bullies. Providing healing but also the metaphorical shoulder on which the man could lean. I think I have always thought of my repentance as a courtroom case instead of a celebration. Instead of viewing it as a victory, I viewed it as an obligation. But I want to see life through Jesus' lens, and that lens is all about viewing the good over the bad. It's about finding joy in redemption instead of just being stuck in a shame cycle that tells you that you deserve to be sad. Jesus could have healed this man in a million different ways, but He chose to heal him with forgiveness. He wanted to showcase that you can come back from anything, no matter how far you have crossed the limit. Jesus desires to forgive us, and more than that, He delights in forgiveness too! He is happiest when He has all of you!

Prompt: What do you believe about yourself right now that you *know* God would never say to you?

_____

_____

_____

_____

_____

_____

_____

_____

_____

_____

_____

_____

December 24

Proverbs 27:1–4

Jealousy is like an uncontrollable cancer that spreads throughout our bodies. It will take over each room if we allow it into the lobby. One moment of envy can lead to a lifetime of self-loathing. It can be as big as wanting someone's life or as small as wanting someone's clothing. But the minute that thought enters your mind is the minute that you lose gratitude for your portion. Instead of seeing it through the lens of God's gift, you see it through a lens that has distortions. You see other people's gifts and write a narrative in your head about how you are less than because you do not have the same blessings. Your life suddenly seems less important because it is less impressive. But that is a lie from the enemy, and he delights when we doubt our worth. He loves when we feel like we are in last place and everyone else is in first. He loves when we scroll on social media and transform ourselves to resemble other people. He loves when we compare others' filtered lives to our life that is real. Envy is something we all fall into, but God can help you overcome its trap. Wishing you were someone else or had someone else's things makes God sad. He formed you and placed you on Earth with specific gifts, a specific body, and a unique personality. Do not allow altered media to make you second guess your reality. No matter what, you are exactly where and who God called you to be. Envy will wrap you in chains; contentment will set you free.

Prompt: Who are you most jealous of? Why are you jealous of them? What do you think people envy that you have?

_____

_____

_____

_____

_____

_____

_____

_____

_____

_____

_____

_____

December 25

Luke 2:8–12

Today we celebrate the day that hope entered the world in the form of a baby. The day that the Savior arrived to start saving. I have always been able to visualize Jesus' birth so clearly in my head, like a live-action nativity. This broken world longing for peace, and this baby being the remedy. I can see a newborn baby crying and His parents nervously comforting His distress. I can see Mary being exhausted and enamored with God's faithfulness. I can see Joseph with tears in his eyes, knowing that his faith had been rewarded and he was now the father of a holy king. I can see relief and hope erasing the nine arduous months of suffering. Because that is what Jesus does, and that is what today is all about. It's about celebrating the hope that came into the world and shattered doubt. It's about celebrating because our Savior was born in a manger, not in a house of royalty. Demonstrating that no matter where we are, we should be found joyously. I wish you a Merry Christmas, but really, I wish you so much more. I pray that as you celebrate today, all hope and joy that have been lost are restored. Because no matter what today brings or what tomorrow holds for you—remember that hope can be found because the nativity story is true.

Prompt: If you were one of the wise men, what gift would you bring Jesus?

_____

_____

_____

_____

_____

_____

_____

_____

_____

_____

_____

_____

December 26

Psalm 65:9–13

We might feel like we are in a season of drought, but God will never allow us to run dry. Because the moment that we surrendered our hearts to Him, we tapped into the infinite supply. He blesses us with evening showers, abundant rains, and sometimes just a mist. But your field will never be one that He forgets. I have been through seasons of life where I would have assured you that I was in a drought. But when I look back at those times now, it was not a dry season; I was just drenched with doubt. God was still providing for me because that is what God does—He provides. He is the supplier, and He will never withhold the supplies. He filled the oceans with abundance and cut the land apart with rivers. He will never leave you with less than because He is a giver. So if you feel like your field is experiencing a dry season, ask God why your soil is cracking. Ask God why you feel that way and what is happening. God wants us to live into the abundance that He has portioned for us, but we have to be receptive. When He tells us to expect rain, we cannot put our umbrellas up and deflect it. He would never leave His children parched; He is the fountain of living water that never runs dry. So if you are experiencing a drought, what is blocking you from His supply?

Prompt: What behavior or mindset could be blocking you from receiving God's blessings right now?

_____

_____

_____

_____

_____

_____

_____

_____

_____

_____

_____

DECEMBER 27

Hebrews 13:1–2

What if that person you passed on the sidewalk today was an angel? Would it have changed the way that you treated them? Maybe you would have given them some money or maybe just stopped and greeted them. What if the strangers in the airport were actually all angels on a mission? Would you have behaved any differently with that kind of vision? The truth is, we do not know if strangers are angels sent from heaven or just other human beings. But should that title change the importance of their meaning? Would you treat people differently if you treated them all like angels? Why does someone deserve better treatment just because they have a label? We are commanded to love each other and treat other people in the same way that we want to be treated. I know if I was sitting, shivering on the sidewalk all alone, I would want to be greeted. So if you cannot treat others with decency, then I fear you would also mistreat heavenly guests. So to be safe and certain, we better just give everybody our best. I want to be a person that welcomes all of creation into my home and intentionally cares about their well-being. That open-door attitude has to start with a greeting. So here is my goal for you and for myself—let's love others because they are His, not because of who they are to us. Let us treat others in a manner that is loving, merciful, and just.

Prompt: How would you live your life differently if you knew that every person you met was sent directly from God in that precise moment to interact with you?

_____
_____
_____
_____
_____
_____
_____
_____
_____
_____
_____
_____
_____

December 28

Proverbs 1:8–9

God-fearing parents are a gift and a privilege to have in a world full of self-concerned people. It's a blessing to have disciplined role models in a world that is destructive and deceitful. For those of us who know our parents and have both parents active in our life, we truly must acknowledge what a gift that is. Some people have protected their hearts by convincing themselves that their parents simply do not exist. So if you have loving parents in your life, take a moment to thank God for their presence. And if those loving parents believe in God, stop and thank Him for that blessing. I do not care if you and your parents see eye to eye all of the time; it's an honor to all have your eyes fixed on heaven. You have been gifted with built-in spiritual mentors to guide you toward God and teach you lessons. Just as children are a gift from God to parents, parents are God's gift back to the children. God provides us with a coloring book life and our parents help us color it in. Do not become so used to their presence and love that you take the privilege of your parents for granted. God sent you to reap a harvest on this earth, but parents teach us how and when seeds should be planted. If you do not have present parents, I am sorry they are not here, but God always is. Even the most protective and loving parents will still admit that we are first and foremost His.

Prompt: How have your parents (or parental figures) impacted your life in a positive way?

December 29

Luke 11:42–46

Speaking like a Christian is easy, but living as one is tough. It's easy to talk about having the faith to walk upon the waves, but what happens when the waters are rough? It's easy for me to read scriptures about the Pharisees and roll my eyes at their hypocritical spirituality. But it's convicting to read the Scriptures and realize that parts of their behavior remind me of myself. It's hard to admit it, but it's okay to admit it—we all have a little Pharisee in us. We preach what we know is true, and then we do not always do what we have discussed. I thought my words would be about others this morning and about having an awareness of hypocrisy and false teachings. But I feel this burning in my soul to encourage you to practice what you are preaching. Do not worry about "them" or "they"—worry about your own actions and inactions. Do not become so focused on others' shortcomings that you fail to have positive interactions. What I am hearing the Lord say this morning is: clean up your own heart before blaming other people for their uncleanliness. Do your part before blaming all of the rest. We all have a little bit of Pharisee in us because we are part of a world that teaches self-righteousness. But talk is worthless if you are living a life of spiritual idleness. Allow conviction to enter your heart, and then begin to clean up your spirit from speaking but not doing. I want to choose patience and prayer over a life of pointing and proving.

Prompt: In what ways are you hypocritical? Be honest here. In what ways could you be less hypocritical?

_____

_____

_____

_____

_____

_____

_____

_____

_____

_____

_____

_____

DECEMBER 30

Philemon 1:17–21

Our world lacks hospitality, and as believers, we should be hospitable. And I do not mean in a way in which you make your house presentable. I do not mean the "Southern" kind in which I have been taught is polite, where you are kind and welcoming only because society tells you that it is right. What I mean is the genuine kind of hospitality where welcoming people is an ingrained reaction. It's not something that you force; it's something that naturally happens. Where you welcome people in because you love them and care about their hearts. Your doors are always open because you want people where you are. That is what Paul writes about in almost all of his letters—relationships and hospitality. Doing life alone was never God's plan for our reality. We were created for connection and not just bypassing connection but pure knowing. That type of connection is not formed in sections; it is ongoing. That's what Jesus did, too. He did not just "have" friends; He traveled and lived among them. Knowing people on the outside is nothing like knowing people from within. We have a responsibility to love and welcome everyone, but it can't be forced work. You have to do it because it's truly what you think other people deserve. Our life is so short in the grand scheme of eternity; let's meet and love as many people on Earth as we can. Let's make the here and now look a lot more like heaven.

Prompt: If your life was a house, how would it be decorated? Would it be welcoming or have a fence around it? Let your mind and imagination run wild here.

_____

_____

_____

_____

_____

_____

_____

_____

_____

_____

_____

December 31

Romans 4:1–5

You can work hard for God, but just realize that the work that you do will not earn your salvation. Working hard is not a means to the gates of heaven, and it's not an obligation. It's the by-product of pure faith, not the means to receive it. Because faith is just that—received, you do not have to achieve it. But I think the line can get blurred between faith and works, and we often fall out of balance. We lean on one more heavily instead of making both our habits. And when God says that both are required, it's not to make our life more difficult; it's actually so that we will find peace. If we had to work our way into heaven, the work would never cease. But faith is the ticket, and works are the tasks leading up to the flight. Faith secures our seats, and works make sure we are all organized and nice. Why would you pack a bag if you were not going on a trip somewhere? Why would you prepare for takeoff if you were not actually going to make it into the air? That is the balance of faith and works; it's impossible to do one without the other if you live a life of faith. The work is not to gain salvation; it's what happens when you are saved. So work for the Lord, but only if it is coming from the root of your salvation. We have been promised a room in heaven; working will not earn you a mansion. Faith is the way that God established, so let's be people of great faith! Let's let our lives testify to the fact that we are saved.

Prompt: What do you feel like you have to "do" in order to grow closer to the Lord or in order for Him to love you more? Why do you feel this way?

_____
_____
_____
_____
_____
_____
_____
_____
_____
_____
_____
_____

CONCLUSION

From the bottom of my heart, thank you for going on this year-long journey with me. I pray that it has not only led you closer to the Lord but also encouraged you to know yourself on a deeper level. May the Lord continue to draw you closer to Him and reveal your voice. Your thoughts are worthy to be known, your words are valuable, and your voice has a place in this world. You are allowed to take up space in this world; you are a kid of the king.

With love always,
KATHLEEN COFFEY.

Printed in the USA
CPSIA information can be obtained
at www.ICGtesting.com
JSHW062158101123
51834JS00005B/16